THE SURNAMES HANDBOOK

THE SURNAMES HANDBOOK

A GUIDE TO FAMILY NAME
RESEARCH IN THE 21ST CENTURY

DEBBIE KENNETT

FOREWORD BY DEREK A. PALGRAVE
PRESIDENT OF THE GUILD OF ONE-NAME STUDIES

The
History
Press

To Guy, Tim and Alex

First published 2012

The History Press
The Mill, Brimscombe Port
Stroud, Gloucestershire, GL5 2QG
www.thehistorypress.co.uk

British Library Cataloguing in Publication Data.
A catalogue record for this book is available from the British Library.

ISBN 978 0 7524 6862 4

Typesetting and origination by The History Press
Printed in Great Britain

CONTENTS

FOREWORD

I t is a privilege to have been invited to write this foreword and it gives me great pleasure to be able to introduce readers to this new work. The author has a formal background in European languages which, I suspect, may well have provided her with some unique insights into the meaning and structure of surnames. Furthermore she also spent several years working for a publisher, accumulating the necessary experience required in the production of specialist periodicals. As an editorial manager she was involved in writing, editing, and supervising layout – all in the days prior to the general adoption of word-processing techniques.

From quite an early age she has been fascinated by her own family surname, *Cruwys*, which very few people seemed able to spell or pronounce. I have sympathy with her, as in spite of my surname being easy to spell its pronunciation is remarkably variable. It is, of course, not enough just to be interested in a surname – action is required. This is not usually convenient during the first few decades of one's life when formal education, marriage and children normally take precedence. Nevertheless there comes a time, often a specific event, when the family's history comes into focus.

In Debbie's case it was the death of her father-in-law which brought about a resurgence of interest. Sudden access to a large collection of family photographs prompted her to write around to relatives in order to identify the images of the individuals represented. One of those she contacted had already done some research into her mother-in-law's family, *Woolfenden*, so it seemed appropriate to extend this project. This soon provided the further incentive for her to investigate her own family of *Cruwys*. This eventually developed into a one-name study with the objective of painting a comprehensive picture of the evolution of this surname and its subsequent ramification. Registering that surname with the Guild of One-Name Studies was a natural outcome.

She found the generation of her one-name study a fascinating process embracing a great deal more than the mere drafting of family trees. She realised just how important it was to establish how and where the surname had emerged and that some appreciation of early linguistics needed to be invoked. The paucity of early records and their lack of consistent spelling alerted her to the widespread occurrence of variant spellings as there were no means of standardisation when the largely illiterate bearers migrated from place to place.

Her experience of research in this field, coupled with her earlier years in publishing, made her an ideal candidate to take on a systematic review of the wide range of evidence, which is available to anyone embarking on an enterprise of this nature. This book is a careful distillation of her findings. It is also a valuable guide to the published literature in this field, not only that in book form, but also a great deal of the reference material now available on the internet. Most of the classic texts by known writers in this field are mentioned in context: Guppy's pioneering work on surname distribution receives due credit, as do the more recent surname texts by Reaney, Redmonds, Hanks and Hodges, Hey and Rogers.

She devotes a sizeable portion of her review to pre-1600 resources pointing out that quite a significant number are now accessible as published transcripts. Family historians rarely make use of such data as they omit evidence of genealogical linkages. However for details of distribution and early spelling these are particularly useful. Published versions of subsidy rolls, pipe rolls, hundred rolls, poll taxes, inquisitions post mortem, etc. are often accessible in major libraries and occasionally online. Older texts that are out of copyright can often be accessed in the Internet Archive.

Modern developments relating DNA analysis to specific surnames are also included and the author's detailed explanations about this complex topic are remarkably clear. She provides very useful information relating to several practical studies which have been instituted during the last few years.

The final chapter traces the development of what we now define as one-name studies. It recognises that although there were some nineteenth-century family histories which concentrated on a single surname and its variants, it was not until the mid-twentieth century that endeavours of this type attracted this modern definition. In 1979, the Guild of One-Name Studies was launched to support those who had adopted this distinctive approach. The Guild, which has grown in size and stature, recently recruited its 6,000th member.

Among the Guild's members are several who have either pioneered or utilised some of the research procedures described by the author. She has spent a great deal of her time and effort explaining their value and importance within a one-name study. I believe this handbook, which is a significant contribution to our understanding in this field, deserves not only our admiration and gratitude, but also a place on our bookshelves.

Derek A. Palgrave
President, Guild of One-Name Studies and
Vice-President, Federation of Family History Societies

ACKNOWLEDGEMENTS

This book builds upon the pioneering research of all my predecessors who have written about surnames over the last 400 years and who have each in their different ways contributed to our understanding and knowledge. I have quoted freely from many of these authors as their wise words still resonate today. I am particularly grateful to the late Philip Dance. I never had the pleasure of knowing or corresponding with him, but he effectively laid the foundations for twenty-first-century surname research with his Modern British Surnames website, where he gathered together all the many resources on surnames from many different disciplines. Philip's work is now preserved on the new Surname Studies website (**www.surnamestudies.org.uk**), which is sponsored by the Guild of One-Name Studies and serves as a lasting tribute to his memory. I am indebted to Mike Spathaky who took on the responsibility of transferring Philip's work to its new home, and who now maintains the new website. Without this resource the task of writing this book would have been much more difficult and many obscure sources would have remained undiscovered.

I would like to thank Derek Palgrave for kindly writing the foreword to this book, and for allowing me to reproduce his selective substitution table. Derek also provided particularly helpful comments on my chapters on one-name studies and variants and deviants, and pointed me in the direction of some useful references. James Irvine kindly read the first draft of my manuscript, and provided many helpful and thoughtful comments, as well as providing guidance on sources for Scottish research. Andrew Millard also kindly read the entire manuscript and provided me with some very useful comments and valuable suggestions. Chris Pomery gave me constructive criticism on a number of key chapters.

I am grateful to John and Sheila Rowlands for permission to reproduce a table from *The Surnames of Wales*. Sheila Rowlands also kindly checked and corrected my Welsh sections, and helped with the compilation of the list of Welsh lay subsidy rolls in Appendix C. Oliver Padel kindly shared some of his research with me, pointed me in the direction of some very useful references, and also helped with the compilation of the list of lay subsidy rolls. John Plant and Ralph Taylor both commented on my DNA chapter.

Stephen Archer's *British 19th Century Surname Atlas* CD has been an invaluable resource while writing this book, and I am also grateful to Stephen for permission to use maps generated from his CD as illustrations. I would also like to thank Fiona McElduff, Pablo

Mateos, Angie Wade and Mario Cortina Borja for permission to reproduce their tables of the top twenty surnames in England, Scotland, Wales and Northern Ireland.

Family historians are always generous with their time and advice. Karen Williams went out of her way to help me when I made my first tentative steps into family history research. Chris Gibbins has helped me enormously with my Devon research, and has tracked down many obscure references for me. Elizabeth Glover Howard has been a helpful and friendly correspondent on all matters relating to Devon and heraldry, and has also kindly assisted with various aspects of my research. The late John Overholt provided guidance on the most useful medieval sources for family history research.

I would like to thank all the members of the Guild of One-Name Studies who have generously shared their knowledge in the *Journal of One-Name Studies*, in the Guild's wiki and on the Guild's mailing list. I am very grateful to all the people who have shared their research with me for my Cruse/Cruwys/Cruise one-name study, as well as all my relatives who have helped me to research all the other branches of my family tree. I would also like to thank all the people who have participated in my DNA projects.

I am grateful to Katharine Reeve for suggesting that I write this book, and to The History Press for once again putting their faith in me.

Finally, I would like to thank my family who have endured my preoccupation with surnames for the last year and who have had to put up with the prevailing domestic chaos, especially in the last few months as the deadline loomed ever closer.

DEFINITIONS

Surname and family name

The terms surname and family name are, to all intents and purposes, synonyms. The word surname is derived from the Anglo-Norman word *surnoun* and the Old French word *sornom*, which have their roots in the Medieval Latin words *supernōmen* and *suprānōmen*. The earliest printed reference cited in the *Oxford English Dictionary* (OED) dates from 1325: 'Richard queor de lyoun, That was his sournoun.' The OED has no separate definition for family name, but quotes an early reference from 1699 in its entry for the word family: 'He shewed me the Catalogue of Authors ... alphabetically disposed by Family Names.'[1] In most Western cultures the surname follows the given name, but in some countries, such as China and Hungary, this order is reversed and the surname is listed before the given name. Surname has the sense of a second name that is added to or follows the forename or given name, whereas family name is used in a more generic sense, regardless of the name order used. As the surnames of the British Isles are the primary focus of this book I have used the terms surname and family name interchangeably throughout.

Given name and forename

In today's secular and multicultural society the terms Christian name, baptismal name and font name are no longer appropriate to describe the name or names bestowed on a child by its parents. The term personal name has been used by some English surname writers as a synonym for a Christian name, but personal name usually has a broader meaning and is used to denote all the components of a person's name. I have instead preferred to use the term given name, though the word forename has also sometimes been used where it has been dictated by the meaning.

The British Isles

The terminology used to describe the different regions and countries that comprise the British Isles is the source of much confusion, even to those of us who live here. For the sake of clarity, I have provided definitions below:

- Great Britain is an island in the British Isles that consists of England, Wales and Scotland.
- Ireland is an island in the British Isles that now consists of two countries: Northern Ireland and the Republic of Ireland. The name Ireland has been used throughout this book in its historic sense to define the country that existed prior to partition in 1922.
- The United Kingdom now consists of four constituent countries: England, Wales, Scotland and Northern Ireland, and the modern definition has been used throughout. Note, however, that between 1801 and 1922 the United Kingdom included Great Britain and the whole of Ireland.
- The British Isles is the name given to the group of islands off the north-west coast of Continental Europe that includes the islands of Great Britain, Ireland, and several thousand smaller isles. Although for political reasons the term 'the Isles' is sometimes now preferred, it is not yet accepted usage. The alternative form 'Britain and Ireland' is not appropriate as it excludes the Channel Islands and the Isle of Man, both of which are self-governing Crown Dependencies and are not part of the UK.

INTRODUCTION

In my view, all genealogists should carry out a detailed investigation into the surname which they are researching; they should study its frequency and distribution at different periods, and build up a picture of its spelling history. It should always be looked at in the context of the other surnames and place-names in the community. If that means acquiring new skills, and an involvement in other disciplines, so be it, it is the vested interest of the genealogist which can, in the end, help to solve many of our long-standing surname problems.

George Redmonds, *Surnames and Genealogy: a New Approach* (2002), p.194

E very surname is unique and has its own story to tell. Some surnames have their roots in the Middle Ages with a single man. In contrast, surnames such as Smith, Taylor and Carpenter have multiple founders, for every town or village would have had at least one smith, tailor or carpenter whose descendants eventually adopted their occupation as a hereditary surname. Smith is now the most common surname in the UK and it is a name that is shared by 1.2 per cent of the population. However, while surname rankings are dominated by a few high-frequency surnames, the distribution starts to drop off dramatically outside the top 100 names. Counterintuitively, most people have an unusual name. Consequently, while everyone is likely to have a Smith, Jones or Williams somewhere in their family tree, they will also have many more ancestors with a rich diversity of unusual surnames derived from minor place-names and obscure occupations. These surnames have an astonishingly rich vocabulary and are an important linguistic record, providing evidence of the evolution of the English language through their changing spellings and pronunciations. The online OED has definitions for over 600,000 words, yet there were over 1.5 million different surnames recorded in the 2001 electoral register in the UK alone.[1]

The study of surnames is no longer the preserve of gentleman genealogists and university academics with a special interest in linguistics or philology (the study of the historical development of a language). Geneticists are exploring the relationship between the Y-chromosome and the surname, and geographers are using surnames to study the structure of populations, patterns of migration and levels of cultural diffusion. Most importantly, however, surnames are being studied in their thousands by family historians, many of whom are now beginning to make very significant contributions to the field.

The academic studies are mainly focused on studying the broader picture of surnames, whereas family historians enjoy the luxury of being able to study a single surname in depth. Consequently, family historians can provide unique insights, and there is much scope for collaboration between academic researchers and the family history community.

Surname research is a natural complement to family history research, and there is much to be learnt by studying a single surname in its entirety rather than focusing specifically on one's own ancestral line. There are many different aspects to a surname study. For less common surnames one of the primary aims will be to reconstruct all the family trees of the surname, and for very rare surnames it is sometimes the case that everyone with the surname can be slotted into one big family tree. It can also be an interesting exercise to study the migration patterns of the surname, both within the country of origin and overseas. There can be few surnames that are now confined to a single country, and most names have left their mark in many different countries around the world. The researcher might also be interested in tracing the surname as far back in time as possible, either in an attempt to discover how many of the different branches of the surname are related or in order to find out where the surname originated. The researcher will need to look at the distribution and frequency of the surname over time, and study the variant spellings of the surname to see which ones are connected and how they have evolved. DNA testing is a new tool that can be used to explore different variant spellings and will help to establish which trees are related, even in the absence of a paper trail. A surname study is not just about the bare facts of names and dates. It can be very rewarding to research the lives of the people who bore a certain surname. Every surname will have its own famous bearers who have left their mark in the history books, as well as a few black sheep who have fallen on the wrong side of the law. There can be few surnames that have been unaffected by the First and Second World Wars, and by researching the lives of the men who lost their lives for their country we can ensure that their contribution is properly acknowledged. The history of a single surname can provide a microcosm of the social history of a country.

A surname study often develops by accident rather than by design during the course of a family history research project. Many genealogists find that they develop a special interest in a few particular surnames in their family tree, and decide to study these surnames in more detail. Men will often study their own surname, whereas women will research their maiden name, but equally any ancestral surname could become the subject of a study. Often a surname study is started when the researcher gets stuck and is unable to trace the line back any further. By widening the scope of the research and reconstructing all the trees in a specific locality it is often possible to work out who belongs where by a process of elimination. Breakthroughs occur in the most unexpected places, and sometimes the missing piece for one tree will be found by chance when researching a different tree altogether.

The amount of research to be done on a surname will vary depending on the size of the surname, the amount of time available and the interests of the researcher. A very rare surname can easily be researched by one person working alone. It might well be possible to study the lives of all the bearers of the surname in depth and to fit everyone into one big family tree. With more common surnames the task will be more manageable and more enjoyable if the work can be done on a collaborative basis. It might be possible to join forces with researchers in other countries, with each researcher taking responsibility for researching the surname in their own particular country. The research can also be subdivided at a more local level with different researchers taking responsibility for specific regions or particular lineages. For some surnames a group of researchers get together to form a one-name society. Members pay a small subscription fee to support the running costs of the society and to defray the costs of the research. Societies usually have a website where the research is collated and often publish a regular newsletter or blog.

Computerised databases and the advent of the Internet have transformed the research process in the last few decades, and it is now easier than ever before to study a surname. Much of the information is readily accessible online on a mixture of free and subscription websites with more datasets being added on a regular basis. These websites now include indexes to millions of surnames and also digital images of the original records. Research that once took months or years to complete can now be done in a matter of days or weeks, and often from the comfort of your own home. Mapping tools can be used to generate an instant picture of the distribution of a surname, and statistics on the frequency of a surname can be produced with a few quick searches in online census indexes or other databases. Many out-of-print and out-of-copyright old books that were previously only available in a few large reference libraries have now been digitised and are freely available in the Internet Archive. Computers and new software programs now enable us to store and organise our data more effectively, and allow us to manipulate that data and find connections that might have been missed when everything was done on paper.

Surnames have generated a vast amount of literature in the last 150 years or so, but it is surprising that most of the books on the subject have had a very narrow focus and have only been concerned with the classification of surnames and their etymology: the meaning, origin and earliest form of the surname. Numerous surname dictionaries of varying degrees of quality have been published. Some of the etymologies given are sound, but many more are misleading or inaccurate, and many rarer names do not even merit a mention in a dictionary at all. Only a few books have looked at the distribution and mapping of surnames. Some books, notably the *English Surnames Series*, have investigated surnames within specific English counties, but surnames do not stay within the confines of a single county and this narrow approach does not present a true picture of an individual surname. In contrast, family history books are concerned with researching the direct ancestral line in detail rather than studying a surname as a whole, and I am not aware of any book that provides detailed guidance on how to research all aspects of a surname.

My purpose in writing in this book was, therefore, to fill that gap in the market, and to provide a handbook that looks at all the different components of a surname study and outlines all the key resources to undertake that research in one compact volume. I've attempted to synthesise the findings from all the many disciplines that are now involved in surname research but with a particular focus on the research of family historians whose contribution is so often overlooked by the surname scholars. The first three chapters provide an overview of the history and classification of surnames and look at the difficult subject of identifying variant spellings. Chapters 4 and 5 look at methods for measuring the frequency and distribution of a surname, and websites and software that can be used to generate surname maps. Chapters 6, 7 and 8 review the key resources and datasets that are used in a surname study from the present day back to 1066. The final two chapters discuss the application of DNA testing in surname studies and the specialist art of one-name studies. Finally I have provided a lengthy bibliography and detailed appendices with links to all the essential online and offline tools and resources.

I have confined the scope of the book primarily to surnames from the British Isles, and to research in the British Isles, though I have included background information on surnames in a few other countries, and some resources for investigating surname distribution in the main emigrant-receiving countries. I am conscious that my approach is somewhat Anglo-centric. This is partly the consequence of my own research experience but is also dictated to a certain extent by the availability of records and sources. I have assumed that anyone reading a book of this nature will already be familiar with the basics of family history research. If not, the BBC's family history website (**www.bbc.co.uk/ familyhistory**) provides a good introduction to the subject, and has lots of useful links. Mark Herber's *Ancestral Trails* (2nd edn, 2005) is the genealogist's bible and discusses all the family history sources in detail, though it has not been updated since 2005 and does not include all the many new online developments of the last few years. Other specialist books for research in Ireland, Scotland and Wales are listed in the bibliography.

I have taken it for granted that anyone reading this book will have access to a computer and the Internet, and preferably a fast broadband connection. Data can be stored in word-processing files and in spreadsheets, and some family historians use a relational database such as Access to assemble their family trees. For most researchers it will be more practical to invest in a dedicated family tree program. There is a list of genealogy software programs on Wikipedia at **http://en.wikipedia.org/wiki/Comparison_of_genealogy_software**. Most of these programs allow the user to download a free trial version. Although there is much genealogical information that is now freely available on the Internet, at some point every surname researcher will need to sign up for a subscription or pay-per-view access to one or more of the main genealogy websites such as Ancestry, Findmypast, and ScotlandsPeople (see Appendix A). Many of the records, and particularly the censuses and civil registration indexes, are available on multiple sites, and the choice of provider will very much depend on the additional datasets that are of most relevance to the individual researcher. Some people pay for simultaneous subscriptions to more than one provider, whereas other researchers prefer to alternate their subscriptions until they have extracted all the records they need. New records are being added to these collections on a regular basis but many of the key resources for surname research are not yet available on the Internet. Every family historian should join his or her local library. Most libraries now subscribe to a number of online databases such as *The Times Digital Archive* and the *Oxford English Dictionary*, which can be accessed from home by signing in with your library ticket. Libraries also provide a valuable inter-library loan service, whereby any book, however obscure, can be borrowed on payment of a modest fee. For some records it will be necessary to visit the relevant county record offices, The National Archives or other repositories. If you live within travelling distance of London you will find a variety of useful surname resources in the Society of Genealogists' library. It is also worth joining the relevant local family history societies.

A surname study can be a very rewarding project. It will give you the immense pleasure of being in contact with many different people from around the world, and the research process itself can be an intellectually stimulating and satisfying exercise. A detailed study of a surname provides a unique opportunity for a family history researcher to become the worldwide expert on his or her chosen surname. I hope that this book will inspire you to start your own surname study and will help you on your journey of discovery.

1

THE HISTORY OF SURNAMES

About the yeare of our Lord 1000 ... surnames began to be taken up in France ... But not in England till about the time of the Conquest, or else a very little before, under King Edward the Confessor, who was all Frenchified. And to this time do the Scottish men also refer the antiquity of their surnames ... Yet in England certain it is, that as the better sort, even from the Conquest by little and little took surnames, so they were not settled among the common people fully, until about the time of King Edward the Second ...

William Camden, *Remaines Concerning Britain* ... 1605,
7th impression (1674), pp.135–6

The historian and antiquarian William Camden (1551–1623) wrote his observations on surnames over 400 years ago in a chapter of a book containing an idiosyncratic and entertaining range of essays on various aspects of British history. No evidence has been found that surnames were in use in England before the Conquest, but otherwise Camden's description paints a remarkably accurate picture of the development of surnames in France, England and Scotland, though his politically incorrect vocabulary might cause offence to modern ears. Around the world surnames were adopted in different countries at varying times. The use of surnames dates back for several thousand years in China, and the practice later spread to other Asian countries. The Koreans adopted surnames from the Chinese during the Three Kingdoms period in the first century BC, and the aristocracy in Japan began using family names in the fifth century AD. The Romans were known by both family names and nicknames, but the modern hereditary surnames that are used today in Europe evolved much later. Surnames began to be used in Byzantium in the tenth century AD. Some Irish clan names can also be traced back before the year 1000. However, in most western European countries surnames started to develop from the eleventh century onwards. The fashion began with the nobility and the wealthy landowners, and slowly spread to the rest of society. By the fourteenth century surnames were well established in most parts of Continental Europe and the British Isles, though usage was by no means universal. In Scandinavia, some parts of Wales and in Shetland in Scotland the traditional patronymic naming system persisted until the nineteenth century, and sometimes later. The reasons for the introduction of surnames are not fully understood but appear to be tied up with the need to prove ownership of land and property for inheritance purposes, the introduction of taxes, and the increasing use of written records during the twelfth to fourteenth centuries, all of which required a more precise means of identification than a single unadorned name.

In some places the population was forced to adopt surnames by government decree. In the Philippines, for example, people were required to adopt Spanish-style surnames in 1849, and in Hawaii a surname law was passed in 1857. Although surnames had been used by the noble clans in Japan for as many as fifteen centuries, it was not until 1870 that the rest of the population was permitted to use surnames. Surnames became mandatory for all Japanese people in 1875 when a new civil registration system was introduced. In Turkey surnames were brought in by decree in 1934 as part of the range of reforms introduced by Mustafa Kemal Atatürk. Special laws were enacted in eastern European countries that required all Ashkenazi Jews to assume a surname. The first legislation of this kind was passed in 1787 by the Austrian Emperor Joseph II, and required all Jews to assume a German surname. In some countries surnames are an even more recent innovation. In Mongolia a law requiring the use of surnames was passed in 1997, but it was largely ignored until 2004, when the government introduced a new identity card that necessitated the use of surnames. Now, more than 90 per cent of Mongolia's population have adopted surnames.[1] There are still some societies that have no surnames. Iceland famously uses a patronymic naming system, and all Icelanders are listed by their first name in the telephone directory.[2]

In most Western societies the convention is to use the given name or forename first followed by the family name. In some countries, such as China, Japan, Korea, Vietnam and Hungary, the family name is traditionally placed before the given name.

China

The Chinese are generally regarded as having been the first culture to adopt surnames. The vast majority of surnames in use in China today existed in fully developed form about 2,000 years ago, with many surnames originating during the Zhou Dynasty (1046–256 BC).[3] Historically ninety-seven of the 100 most common surnames today originated during the Spring and Autumn Period (722–476 BC) and the Warring States Period (476–221 BC) when the territory of China was limited to the central plains. The Han people are the largest ethnic group in China and the ethnic minorities that invaded or migrated into central China were assimilated by the Han people, and adopted Han surnames. In the Confucian culture people were discouraged from changing their surname unless there was a special reason to do so, such as to receive a noble surname from an emperor.[4]

China has a population of over 1.3 billion, and is the world's most populous country, but it is notable for its very limited stock of surnames. In the last decade or so Chinese researchers have made a number of attempts to quantify the number of surnames in use in the country and their frequency. A study published in 2006 by Yuan Yida from the Chinese Academy of Sciences collected surname data from almost 300 million people in China. It was found that 87 per cent of the population shared just 129 surnames. A total of just 4,100 surnames were identified in the survey. Li (Lee), the most common surname, was shared by

7.4 per cent of the population, Wang (Wong) accounted for 7.2 per cent of the population and Zhang (Chang) was used by 6.8 per cent.[5, 6] A more recent report, cited in the *New York Times*, lists the top three surnames in a slightly different order: Wang was the most common surname with more than 92 million bearers, followed by Li with 91 million and Zhang with 86 million.[7] The most comprehensive study to date was published in 2012. The researchers studied the surnames of 1.28 billion people in China's National Citizen Identity Information System. The dataset excluded Hong Kong, Macao, and Taiwan. It was found that the population of China shared just 7,327 surnames.[8]

Historically, there were many more surnames in use in China, the vast majority of which have now become extinct. All known Chinese surnames are recorded in the *Great Dictionary of Chinese Surnames*, the latest edition of which is reputed to include more than 23,000 surnames.[9] The classic Chinese text known as the *Hundred Family Surnames*, composed in the early Song Dynasty (960–1279), is a rhyming poem listing the most common surnames in ancient China. The word 'hundred' in Chinese often just means a large number and the title should really be translated as 'The Many Surnames'. The book originally contained 411 surnames but was later expanded to include 504. Ronald Eng Young's Chinese surnames website (**http://freepages.family.rootsweb.ancestry. com/~chinesesurname/index.html**) has lists of the names in the *Hundred Family Surnames* book and their meanings, shown in both numerical and alphabetical order.

In Chinese culture the surname precedes the given name, but Chinese people settling in the West usually adopt the Western convention of placing the surname last. Most Chinese surnames consist of just a single syllable. Orphans in China were traditionally given generic surnames such as Dang (party) and Guo (state), which defined their status. New regulations were due to be introduced in 2012 that would require orphanage officials to choose from the list of the 100 most common Chinese family names.[10]

The Romans

In the West the beginnings of surnames can be seen in the naming system used by the Romans, who adopted a binominal (two-name) system from around the seventh century BC, though its origins remain obscure. Individuals were given a *praenomen* (a forename), which was followed by a hereditary *nomen* or *nomen gentilicium* that indicated the bearer's *gens* (clan) membership. There was only ever a very limited stock of *praenomina*. In the regal and republican period 99 per cent of Roman men shared one of only seventeen *praenomina*. Outside the family it was the custom to address people by the *praenomen* and *nomen* together, and if only one name was used it would be the *nomen* not the *praenomen*. In the late second century BC a third type of name known as a *cognomen* first started to appear. This was a nickname that was specific to an individual but was often hereditary. Evidence suggests that the use of the *cognomen* was pioneered by the elite, who were perhaps keen to differentiate a noble family ancestry. A rigid convention developed and names were bestowed in accordance with family tradition. The *tria nomina* (three-name) system –

praenomen, nomen and *cognomen* – only became commonplace in the first century AD, and by the middle of the third century AD nearly all men possessed the *tria nomina*. A person could also be distinguished by an additional *cognomen* – known as an *agnomen* – which denoted a particular quality or exploit. With such a limited pool of *praenomina* the new individual *cognomina* became the main identifying names. In formal public usage people were now universally known by the *nomen* and *cognomen* used in combination. The *praenomen* was reduced to a standard abbreviation.

By the second century AD the nomenclature became increasingly complicated. Multiple *cognomina* and even *praenomina* began to be adopted by the senatorial aristocracy. The new fashion for *polyonymy*, as it was known, was the result of a new practice of 'testamentary adoption' whereby beneficiaries were required to adopt the testator's name as a condition of accepting an inheritance. This was especially the case if the mother's wealth or noble pedigree was considered to enhance the family's reputation. There was no limit to the number of names that could be adopted, and some people acquired an exceptionally large collection of pedigree names. In AD 212 the emperor Caracalla granted all free subjects Roman citizenship by means of an edict known as the *Constitutio Antoniniana*. A *nomen* was now required of all Roman citizens for official purposes and a limited number of default *nomina*, such as Aurelius and Iulius, were adopted by the new citizens. The *nomen* thus became a mark of citizenship rather than hereditary status for these New Romans. It was then a natural development for the *nomen* to be changed to reflect status and imperial rank. Flavius became established as the *nomen* indicating higher status, and Aurelius was the default *nomen* for those of lesser status. In parallel with these developments, the influence of Christianity also saw the introduction of new *cognomina* of Hebrew and Aramaic origin from the scriptures. With the ubiquity of Aurelius and Flavius, the New Romans used the *cognomen* as a distinguishing name, and the *nomen* also became increasingly less important for the Old Romans. The identifying *cognomen* evolved naturally into a single-name system, and the *nomen* had effectively disappeared by the seventh century AD. In most Western European countries it was not until the High Middle Ages (*c.* 1000–1300) that hereditary surnames once more came into usage.[11]

The Normans

The Normans began to use surnames in the first half of the eleventh century. The early Norman surnames were tied up with the feudal system of heritable tenure, and consequently many were toponymics – surnames derived from place-names and landscape features – though nicknames were also favoured. James Holt, a former Master of Fitzwilliam College, Cambridge, and a professor of medieval history, provides an informative account of Norman surnames, with names and dates backed up with extensive references, in *What's in a Name? Family Nomenclature and the Norman Conquest* (1982):

> In the charters of the Norman dukes and in such original documents that remain from the families themselves, toponymics, indeed any kind of by-name other than the occasional

patronymic, were exceptional before the reign of Duke William. The general impression of the ducal acts is that toponymics and other hereditary names spread and spread fast, only from the 1040s and 1050s. Some names of the more important families can be driven a little earlier. The oldest of them all is the name Tosny (Toeni) which was in use by 1014 and probably earlier; that is the first appearance of a toponymic in any of the ducal acts. Bellême makes its first appearance in 1023–25, Beaumont and Montgomery in 1035–40, Warenne in 1037–53, Mortimer in 1054, Grandmesnil in 1055, Montfort in 1063. These dates have to be based largely on attestations of the ducal acts and other charter material; there is no other reliable evidence.

The fact that the use of hereditary toponymics was not just an accident is evidenced by the appearance of other forms of byname that became hereditary during the same period. Holt cites the examples of Taisson, which first appears in ducal acts in 1025, Giffard in 1035–47, Malet in 1035–66, and Marmion, which appears in 1060. Patronymics were also used by the Normans at this time in the form 'Richard *fitz* Gilbert' but they do not appear to have become hereditary surnames until much later. Holt suggests that the fitz Alans of Oswestry (after 1175) and the fitz Gerolds (1177–78) were the first to make this transition. He concludes that the nomenclature in Normandy was gradually changing in the first half of the eleventh century, and the roots were firmly planted by 1054 when William's victory at the Battle of Mortemer secured his position as the Duke of Normandy and paved the way for the future conquest of England.[12]

William the Conqueror probably had 7,000 men or more under his command at the Battle of Hastings, but research in the 1930s by members of the Society of Genealogists has shown that the names of only nineteen companions can be identified from reliable contemporary sources, one of which is the Bayeux Tapestry. Of these nineteen men, it has been proven that fifteen fought at the Battle of Hastings, and four 'almost certainly' fought at the battle. The nineteen names are as follows (the last four names on the list are those who have only been identified as being present at the battle):

Robert de Beaumont, afterwards Earl of Leicester
Eustace, Count of Boulogne
William of Evreux
Geoffrey of Mortagne, afterwards Count of Perche
William FitzOsbern, afterwards Earl of Hereford
Aimery IV, Vicomte of Thouars
Hugh de Montfort, Lord of Montfort-sur-Risle
Walter Giffard, Lord of Longueville
Ralf de Tosni, Lord of Conches
Hugh de Grandmesnil, Lord of Grandmesnil
William de Warenne, afterwards Earl of Surrey
William Malet
Turstin FitzRou
Engenulf de Laigle

Odo, Bishop of Bayeux, and afterwards Earl of Kent (William the Conqueror's stepbrother)

Geoffrey de Mowbray, Bishop of Coutances

Robert, Count of Mortain, afterwards Earl of Cornwall (William the Conqueror's younger half-brother)

Wadard, a tenant of the Bishop of Bayeux

Vital, a tenant of the Bishop of Bayeux[13]

A probable descent in the male line can be traced to the present day from only one of those names, William Malet, though there are some gaps.[14] A document known as the Battle Abbey Roll exists in various versions and purports to list the names of those who were present at Hastings, but this is not a contemporary document and is not considered to be a reliable source. Many names appear to have been added at a later date. The earliest version of the Battle Abbey Roll, with a list of 551 surnames, is included in a document known as the Auchinleck Manuscript, which was produced in London in the 1330s. This manuscript is now held in the National Library of Scotland, and is one of the library's greatest treasures. A full transcription with a digital facsimile is now available online at **http://auchinleck.nls.uk**. Other versions of the Battle Abbey Roll were published from the sixteenth century onwards, all of which were seemingly unaware of the existence of the earlier manuscript. Many of these volumes can now be easily accessed in the Internet Archive (**http://archive.org**) by searching for 'Battle Abbey Roll'. The Dives Roll, compiled by Leopold Delisle in 1866, is supposedly a list of Companions of the Conqueror but the author cites no sources. In 1931 the French government arranged for a plaque to be put up in the Castle of Falaise in Normandy containing the names of 315 men who supposedly fought at the Battle of Hastings, but this list was again drawn up from late and unreliable sources. A list of names from the Falaise Roll, the Dives Roll and various versions of the Battle Abbey Roll (with the exception of the Auchinleck Manuscript) is provided in *My Ancestors Came with the Conqueror* (Camp, 1990). While it might not be possible to prove that an ancestor came with the Conqueror, these sources might nevertheless provide pointers to the Norman origin of a surname.

Domesday Book, William the Conqueror's detailed survey of his newly acquired lands in England, is discussed in Chapter 8. *The Origins of Some Anglo-Norman Families* (1951, 1999) by Lewis Christopher Loyd is a scholarly work containing extensive background information on 315 Anglo-Norman families and their places of origin in Normandy where known. *The Norman People and their existing Descendants …* (Anonymous, 1874) has an extensive alphabetical listing of about 6,900 Norman names. These were extracted from the London Post Office Directory and compared with the names in a variety of medieval records such as the pipe rolls, the hundred rolls and the curia regis rolls. The book identifies the possible home of each family name in Normandy and provides some valuable early references.

England

The Norman Conquest not only changed the course of British history but also introduced an entirely new system of family nomenclature. The new fashion for surnames caught on first among the great landholding families who took their names either from their estate in Normandy or their new lands in England. By about 1250 the majority of these families had acquired hereditary surnames.[15] As Holt comments: 'The toponymic served home sickness, family tradition, political domination and social snobbery at one and the same time.'[16]

There is less documentary material to inform us about the development of surnames amongst the minor landowners, but the evidence suggests that the majority of landowning families in the south of England, the Midlands and East Anglia had acquired surnames by about 1250, with the process being a little later in the rest of the country and particularly in the north, though there were some exceptions.[17]

It is impossible to say with any certainty when hereditary surnames began to be used by the lower social classes as the records are inadequate. McKinley (1990) suggests that 'Between about 1250 and 1350, many families belonging to various classes acquired surnames' and that in the south of England and East Anglia 'rather more than half the population had surnames by about 1350 … In the north of England, developments occurred about a century later than in the south and Midlands.'[18] The population grew dramatically during the twelfth and thirteenth centuries in this early period of surname formation. The bubonic plague pandemic, popularly known as the Black Death, spread to England in 1348 and within three years had wiped out between one-third and a half of the population. As a consequence, many of the newly formed surnames became extinct. Of the surnames that did survive, some spread to different parts of the country as families moved to new places to take over vacant farms. This movement helps to explain why some locative surnames are no longer very close to their place of origin.[19]

The fourteenth-century lay subsidy rolls and poll taxes (see Chapter 8) provide a fascinating snapshot of the rich stock of names in use in England at that time. It can be seen that large numbers of people had already acquired what appear to be hereditary surnames, though there were still many people, particularly in the north, without any surnames at all or who were merely described in terms of their relationship to their father. However, without the genealogical evidence it is not possible to prove whether the names that appear in these records are actually hereditary surnames or merely bynames (a second identifying name that was unique to the individual and never developed into a hereditary surname). It is thought that most English people had acquired fixed hereditary surnames by the fifteenth century, though there were undoubtedly exceptions, and there were substantial differences between regions. There are surnames that seem to appear for the first time in the Tudor subsidy rolls (see Chapter 8), and it is quite possible that these names had been in use for many years but had simply not been documented in written records. Alternatively, the surnames might have migrated from their place of origin or undergone various changes in spelling and pronunciation, making it difficult to prove continuity, though DNA testing can now sometimes help to bridge such gaps in the records.

Since the Conquest, the diverse surname landscape of England has been enriched by the assimilation of immigrant surnames. Some of these families can be recognised by their distinctive names, whereas others adopted anglicised spellings. The Flemish and the Walloons from the Low Countries (the area consisting of Belgium, the Netherlands, Luxembourg and parts of northern France and Germany) started to arrive in East Anglia in the thirteenth and fourteenth centuries. Many of these early immigrants were weavers and textile workers. By 1440 it was estimated that there were 16,000 'foreigners' in England.[20] Between 1540 and 1600, over 50,000 people from Continental Europe arrived in England and settled mostly in London, Kent and East Anglia. Many of these immigrants, such as the French Huguenots, were forced to leave their home country because of religious persecution.[21] England has had small Jewish communities for several centuries, but the population increased considerably towards the end of the seventeenth century, and by 1800 there were reckoned to be around 20,000–25,000 Jews living in England, mainly in London and the major seaports. However, most of the Jewish people living in Britain today are descended from immigrants from Russian and eastern Europe who arrived between 1880 and 1914.[22] The mass immigration of the twentieth century introduced a rich tapestry of new surnames from all over the world.

Toponymic surnames constitute a sizeable portion of the English surname pool, a feature that had been noted in an old English proverb cited by Richard Verstegan, writing in the seventeenth century:

In foord, in ham, in ley and tun
The most of English surnames run.[23]

But although there are large numbers of toponymic surnames in England they all occur at relatively low frequencies, and only the names Wood and Green appear in the list of the top twenty most common surnames (see Table 4, Chapter 5). Richard McKinley surveyed the surnames found in sixteenth- and seventeenth-century taxation lists in fourteen English counties and calculated the percentages of people bearing each type of surname. Toponymic surnames were subdivided into locative surnames (from place-names) and topographical surnames (from landscape features). Thirty-seven per cent of the individuals in his survey had toponymic surnames, 25 per cent of which were locative and 12 per cent of which were topographical. Patronymic surnames were carried by 28 per cent of the people, occupational surnames by 20 per cent, and nicknames by 8 per cent. The remaining 7 per cent of surnames fell into other categories or were of uncertain origin. Marked regional differences were found. In Lancashire 59 per cent of the population had locative surnames. Shropshire had the highest percentage of people with patronymic surnames, with 42 per cent falling into this category. Suffolk had the lowest concentration of toponymic surnames; 30 per cent of Suffolk surnames were occupational and a further 30 per cent were derived from given names.[24]

For an understanding of English surnames the most authoritative general works are: *A History of British Surnames* (1990) by Richard McKinley; *Family Names and Family History*

(2000) by David Hey; *Surnames and Genealogy: A New Approach* (1997, 2002) by George Redmonds; and *Surnames, DNA, and Family History* (2011) by George Redmonds, David Hey and Turi King. Percy Hide Reaney provides valuable insight into the surnames and bynames of the medieval period in *The Origin of English Surnames* (1967). *Research Your Surname and Your Family Tree* (2010) by Dr Graeme Davis, a university lecturer with a doctorate in philology, was lacking in sources and surprisingly full of errors.[25] *The Oxford Dictionary of English Surnames* (3rd edn, 2005) by P.H. Reaney and R.M. Wilson, and *A Dictionary of Surnames* (1988) by Patrick Hanks and Flavia Hodges are currently the best starting points for surname derivations, though many of the etymologies have now been shown to be incorrect. These works are set to be superseded by the publication of an online surname database from the Family Names in the UK Project in 2015 or 2016 (see Chapter 6).

English surnames are now the subject of numerous DNA projects of varying degrees of maturity. Virtually all the high-frequency English surnames now have associated DNA projects, and there are hundreds of projects for other less common English surnames. Most of these projects are hosted at Family Tree DNA (**www.familytreedna.com**), but there are also a small number at Ancestry DNA (**www.dna.ancestry.com**). There are regional DNA projects for Cornwall, Devon, East Anglia, Hampshire, and Northumberland, all of which are at Family Tree DNA.

Ireland

Ireland was one of the earliest countries to adopt a system of hereditary surnames. A minority of surnames were introduced before the year 1000, but they came into more general usage in the eleventh century. The first Irish surnames were formed by adding the prefix *Mac* (meaning 'son') to the father's given name or Ó (anglicised to O') to the name of a grandfather or another earlier ancestor. The *Mac* and O' prefixes were later used in surnames derived from the occupation of the father, such as *Mac an Bháird*, son of the bard (anglicised as MacWard). *Mac* and O' were also sometimes used to prefix a word denoting a characteristic or trait of the father or grandfather. The O' surnames are now more common in Ireland than the *Mac* and *Mc* surnames. The *Mac* and O' prefixes were often dropped from the early seventeenth century onwards under the influence of English rule, but some were reintroduced in the late nineteenth and early twentieth centuries.

Surname research in Ireland is complicated by the co-existence of the English and Irish (Gaelic) languages, with the two forms of a surname often being used interchangeably, a problem that was noted by Robert Edwin Matheson, the Registrar-General, in 1890:

> The use of entirely different names interchangeably by the same person prevails in Ireland to a much greater extent than is commonly supposed. This is principally owing to the differences in language – many of these being cases of translation of Irish names into English, or *vice versa*, or equivalents, modifications, or corruptions of them. There are, however, other cases which cannot apparently be accounted for in this way.[26]

The majority of surnames in Ireland are of Irish origin. Norman names, such as Courtenay, Cruise, Cusack, Dillon and Warren were introduced in the twelfth century following the Anglo-Norman invasion of Ireland. Many English names were introduced into Ireland in the 1600s with the Plantation of Ulster in the first decade of the seventeenth century and the Cromwellian Settlement of the 1650s. Some English-sounding surnames are in fact anglicised versions of Irish surnames, a consequence of English rule and influence beginning from that time. Scottish surnames can be found in Ireland, and particularly in Ulster, as a result of the Plantation and later religious and economic pressures. It can be difficult, if not impossible, to distinguish between the Gaelic surnames from the Highlands of Scotland and the indigenous Irish surnames. Welsh surnames are especially prevalent in County Wickford and County Wexford. Some surnames are the result of immigration from Continental Europe. French names were introduced by the Huguenots in the seventeenth century. German refugees from the Palatinate of the Rhine settled in Ireland in the eighteenth century. Jewish surnames arrived in Ireland in the nineteenth century.

Edward MacLysaght is the leading writer on Irish surnames. His key works are: *The Surnames of Ireland* (6th edn, 1985), the authoritative dictionary of Irish surnames; *Irish Families: their Names, Arms and Origins* (4th edn, 1985); and *More Irish Families* (2nd edn, 1982). Patrick Woulfe's *Irish Names and Surnames* (1922) is of historical interest, but MacLysaght warns us that many of Woulfe's derivations are guesses and 'quite untenable'. *The Book of Ulster Surnames* (rev. edn, 1997) by Robert Bell has entries for over 500 names found in the province of Ulster.

The Ireland Y-DNA project (**www.familytreedna.com/public/IrelandHeritage**) is a repository for Y-chromosome DNA results from men with Irish ancestry and surnames. The project now has over 4,500 members and is the fourth-largest volunteer-run DNA project in the world. The Ulster Heritage DNA Project (**http://ulsterheritagedna. ulsterheritage.com**) is using genetic testing to explore the surnames, families and clans of Ulster, and now has over 2,300 members. There are also numerous DNA projects for individual Irish surnames, most of which can be found at **www.familytreedna.com**.

Scotland

Scotland is culturally divided into the Highlands and the Lowlands. In the Middle Ages, the Highlanders spoke Gaelic, a Celtic language, and the Lowlanders spoke Scots, a Germanic language with a close relationship to English. These cultural and linguistic divisions are reflected in the development of surnames in Scotland.

As far as can be established from the available sources, the earliest hereditary surnames in Scotland were of English or French origin, and were introduced in the twelfth century during the reign of King David I (1124–53) who was the sixth son of King Malcolm III of Scotland and Margaret of Wessex. David had spent his formative years in England at the court of Henry I, and had married an English countess. He introduced Norman methods of administration to Scotland, including the Norman system of feudal tenure.

During David's reign some families of English and French extraction, who already had hereditary surnames, settled in Scotland, and some became major landholders. The surnames introduced in this period include Balliol, Bruce, Colville, Fraser, Graham, de Hay, Haig, Lindsay, de Quincy, and Somerville.[27] Most landed families had surnames by about 1300, but the adoption of surnames was a gradual process and surnames were not generally adopted in the Scots-speaking regions until at least the sixteenth century.

Surname development has a very different history in the Gaelic-speaking Highlands of Scotland, where the clan system survived until the eighteenth century. Individuals assumed the surname of the clan rather than that of a family. The Registrar-General of Scotland commented on this 'peculiarity' in his sixth annual report:

> It may be mentioned, however, as a striking peculiarity of the inhabitants of Scotland that, both among the Celtic race in the Highlands, and the Lowland races on the Border, it was the custom for all to assume as their surname the name held by the head of the family, either because they were actually his descendants, or because they were his vassals and property. Hence, in the Highlands we have large Clans of the name of Macdonald, Stewart, Campbell, Mackay, Murray, Cameron, etc., and among the inhabitants of the Border Counties the names of Scott, Graham, Kerr, Johnston, Elliott, Armstrong, etc.[28]

But the late Professor Emeritus Gordon Donaldson, HM Historiographer in Scotland, cautions of a fundamental misunderstanding in the way that Scots people speak of their surnames:

> A man says, 'I'm a Robertson', almost as if Robertsons constitute some unique subspecies of humankind. That at once suggests an assumption that every Robertson is related to other bearers of that name. This is preposterous. The very most that a bearer of the name Robertson can deduce from his surname is that in some generation or other in the past he probably had an ancestor called Robert. It is no more than probable, for men changed their surnames because they moved from one part of the country to another, because they changed landlords or employers, perhaps even because they changed their occupation. To believe even that there was necessarily ever an ancestor called Robert is going beyond what the evidence warrants.[29]

After the failure of the 1745 rebellion, Highland names became stable and soon began to spread south into Lowland Scotland and from there into England. However, in some Highland areas, fixed surnames did not become the norm until the eighteenth century, and in parts of the Northern Isles surnames were not adopted until the nineteenth century. Many Irish surnames were introduced to Scotland as a result of Irish immigration in the nineteenth century.

Patronymic names account for a large proportion of the surname stock in Scotland, and around one in eight surnames in Scotland begin with the prefixes *Mc* or *Mac*.[30] In the crofting counties of Scotland the percentage of M names was found to be nearly 40 per cent, and in the Western Isles the figure was as high as 63 per cent.[31]

George Fraser Black's *The Surnames of Scotland: Their Origin, Meaning and History* (1946) is the definitive work on Scottish surnames. David Dorward's compact *Scottish Surnames* (1978) provides information on the derivation and modern distribution of over 1,000 Scottish surnames. The ScotlandsPeople website has a useful article on Scottish surnames and variants. It can be found at **www.scotlandspeople.gov.uk/content/help/index.aspx?560**.

A Scottish Clans DNA project was set up in October 2001 and was one of the very early geographical projects. The project has since been renamed as the Scottish DNA Project (**www.scottishdna.net**), and is now administered by the genealogical studies team at the University of Strathclyde in Glasgow. It currently has over 4,800 project members and is the second-largest volunteer-run DNA project in the world. The project also has a blog that can be found at **http://scottishdna.blogspot.co.uk**. There are numerous mature projects for the various Scottish clans and for individual Scottish surnames, and links to these projects can be found on the Scottish DNA website. The largest surname projects are of Scottish families: both the Clan Fraser and MacDonald projects claim over 1,300 members. There are also large projects for the surnames MacLaren and MacGregor.

Wales

The use of hereditary surnames was a much later development in Wales than in England, Scotland and Ireland. The Welsh traditionally used a patronymic naming system in which individuals were identified by the name of their father, hence David *ap* Thomas was the son of Thomas, and Elizabeth *verch* William was the daughter of William. It was necessary to have proof of one's lineage to provide legal verification of succession, and consequently a Welshmen would know the names of his paternal ancestors dating back for as many as six or seven generations. These names would often be recited in long name sequences such as Dafydd *ap* Gwilym *ap* Howel *ab* Owain. This practice probably gave rise to the proverb 'As long as a Welshman's pedigree'. The adoption of fixed surnames was a gradual process in Wales. Surnames were generally adopted first in the east and south of Wales, in areas that were more prone to English influences. Surnames across the whole of Wales were adopted first by the landed classes and much later by tenants. With the Acts of Union of 1536 and 1543, Wales was obliged to accept the English legal and administrative system, which resulted in some streamlining of the patronymic naming system, and people in Wales began to assume surnames progressively up to the early nineteenth century. The adoption of surnames was reinforced by the use of printed registers for baptisms, marriages and burials from 1813 onwards, which now included a column for 'surname', and by the introduction of the civil registration system in 1837. However, later examples of patronymics can be found in some rural regions. The new Welsh surnames were formed by dropping the *ap* or *ab* and adopting one of the paternal names in the genealogical pedigree. This was usually but not always the father's given name. Hence, David *ap* Thomas became David Thomas. In some areas of Wales, as a result of English influence, the surname was formed by the addition of *-s*, to give rise to surnames such as Griffiths, Richards and Hughes.

As a consequence of the way that surnames were adopted in Wales, the stock of Welsh names is now dominated by patronymic surnames. Descriptive epithets such as *goch* (red-haired) and *llwyd* (grey or brown hair) were often incorporated into the patronymic naming system, and, as a result, surnames derived from personal characteristics – known as adjectival surnames – are the second most numerous class of surname in Wales. *Goch* was anglicised to produce the surname Gough, and *llwyd* became Lloyd. There are very few occupational surnames of Welsh origin and even fewer Welsh surnames derived from place-names.

For Welsh surnames the most authoritative sources are *Welsh Surnames* (1985) by T.J. Morgan and Prys Morgan, and *The Surnames of Wales* (1996) by John and Sheila Rowlands. A second edition of the latter work, which will include the findings from their more recent research, is currently being prepared.

DNA projects can be found for all the common Welsh surnames at Family Tree DNA (**www.familytreedna.com**), and these projects include some of the largest surname projects. There are over 900 people in the Williams DNA project and over 600 members of the Phillips DNA project. There is a geographical project for Wales (**www.familytreedna. com/public/WalesDNA**) that now has over 500 members. There is also a Welsh patronymics DNA project (**www.familytreedna.com/public/WelshPatronymics**) that accepts everyone with a patronymic Welsh surname regardless of origin.

Surnames from elsewhere around the world

It is beyond the scope of this book to provide a survey of surnames around the world, but if you are interested in reading more about this fascinating subject then the best introduction can be found in *The Dictionary of American Family Names* (2003). This massive three-volume work has an extensive section in the first volume – entitled 'Introductions to surnames of particular languages and cultures', which includes thematic essays provided by subject experts. These pages provide a very interesting history and overview of the surnames of all the many different countries and cultures that are represented in the American population. Much of the content can be accessed through the free 'look inside' feature on Amazon.

The UK General Secretariat of Interpol has produced a very useful document entitled 'A Guide to Names and Naming Practices', which can be downloaded from **www. kyc360.com/article/show/64?set=1**. The US Regional Organized Crime Information Center has produced a special research report entitled 'Law Enforcement Guide to International Names', which provides background on naming practices in a number of different cultures. The report can be found at **http://publicintelligence.info/ ROCICInternationalNames.pdf**. Roger Darlington has an interesting page on his website (**www.rogerdarlington.co.uk/useofnames.html**) looking at the varying use of given names and family names in different countries and cultures. The Wikipedia article on family names (**http://en.wikipedia.org/wiki/Family_name**), while currently somewhat lacking in reliable sources, also provides an introduction to the subject and has links to more in-depth articles for specific countries.

2

THE CLASSIFICATION OF SURNAMES

The most striking circumstance presented by the Indexes is the extraordinary number and variety of the surnames of the *English* people. Derived from almost every imaginable object, from the names of places, from trades and employments, from personal peculiarities, from the Christian name of the father, from objects in the Animal and Vegetable kingdoms, from things animate and inanimate; their varied character is as remarkable as their singularity is often striking.

'Sixteenth Annual Report of the Registrar-General of Births, Deaths, and Marriages in England' (Registrar-General's edition), Her Majesty's Stationery Office (1856), p.xvii.

Surnames have traditionally been placed into four principal categories: surnames derived from place-names, occupational surnames, nicknames, and surnames derived from given names. There is, however, no standard classification system, and no agreed nomenclature. A classification system based on the origins of surnames is inevitably subject to constant revision, as new research alters the proposed etymologies, and sometimes places surnames in a completely different category. The divisions are somewhat arbitrary, and there is considerable overlap. Many surnames belong in multiple categories, and there will also be a minority of surnames that defy classification altogether.

William Camden

William Camden (1551–1623), the eminent Elizabethan antiquarian and historian, is best known for his influential book *Britannia*, a geographical and historical county-by-county description of Britain, but it is his sixty-page chapter on surnames in the popular spin-off *Remaines Concerning Britain ...* (1605) that is of particular interest to surname historians. This chapter was the first published account of surnames, and the first ever attempt to categorise them. Camden's observations were remarkably perceptive, and many of his words are still relevant today. Camden described what he called local names, derived from place-names in France, England and Scotland:

The most surnames in number, the most ancient, and of best account, have been local, deduced from places in *Normandy,* and the Countries confining, being either the patrimonial possessions, or native places of such as served the Conqueror, or came in after out of Normandy … From places in *England* and *Scotland* infinite likewise. For every Town, Village, or Hamlet hath afforded names to Families …[1]

He also recognised that many surnames were derived from topographical features, whether man-made, such as bridges, churches and forts; or naturally occurring, such as hills, woods, rivers and greens. He identified names derived from occupations or professions as the next largest category: 'Neither was there any trade, craft, art, profession, or occupation never so mean, but had a name among us commonly ending in *Er*, and men accordingly denominated …' Other categories described by Camden include surnames derived from 'qualities of the mind', physical features, seasons, parts of the body, garments, colours (of 'complexions, garments, or otherwise'), flowers and fruits, fish, birds and Christian names.

Mark Antony Lower

Over 200 years elapsed before any other major attempt was made to categorise surnames. Mark Antony Lower (1813–76), a Sussex schoolmaster and antiquarian, is best known for his *Patronymica Britannica* (1860), which was effectively the first published dictionary of English surnames. Lower had taken an interest in surnames and local history from an early age, publishing articles on surnames in his local paper the *Sussex Express* in 1838, and a pamphlet on English surnames in 1839. *English Surnames*, published in 1842, was a series of thematic essays with the bulk of the content comprising chapters on the many classes of surnames that he had defined. In addition to categories for local surnames, 'occupations and pursuits', 'dignities and offices', and surnames based on Christian names, Lower included categories for surnames derived from: personal and mental qualities; natural objects and signs of houses; social relations and periods of time; virtues and other abstract ideas; foreign names; and changed names. A whole chapter was devoted to 'surnames of contempt; and more oddities in the nomenclature of Englishmen', and another chapter focused on 'A cabinet of oddities', which featured surnames from body parts, measures, money, numbers, diseases, and the weather.[2]

Christopher Legge Lordan

A fascinating and little-known book entitled *Of Certain English Surnames and their Occasional Odd Phases when seen in Groups* was published in 1874 by Christopher Legge Lordan. Lordan seems to have had great fun gleaning surnames from directories and the Registrar-General's indexes and arranging them thematically based purely on their present-day meanings. He recognised that this was essentially a superficial exercise and that many surnames have completely different meanings from their current forms. He noted, however, that: 'Names *may*, nevertheless, be found to possess a secondary interest to unlearned and merely surface observers, if such observers will only look them steadfastly in the face … and note how, when gathered into groups, they make compact and intimate alliances.' As well as the obvious groupings based on occupations, given names, the natural world (animals, birds, fish, trees, vegetables, herbs, etc.), colours, characteristics, seasons, virtues and vices, he included all sorts of other groups such as food, clothing, household objects, musical terms, heavenly bodies, the body and its members, and even a somewhat creative grouping for the ills of life, which included surnames such as Boil, Corns and Piles. There are also lists of names ending in -man, -son, -ing, and -well; names used as adverbs (ending in -ly); and names containing the word love. Although such a classification scheme has no practical value, Lordan's lists will be of great interest to name collectors and trivia lovers.[3]

Charles Wareing Bardsley

The clergyman Charles Wareing Bardsley (1843–98) devoted the greater part of his leisure time to the compilation of a surname dictionary but sadly died without seeing his life's work in print. His widow spent two years deciphering his microscopic handwriting, and *A Dictionary of English and Welsh Surnames with Special American Instances* was finally published in 1901. Bardsley used a simple classification scheme throughout his work, which he first described in 1873 in *Our English Surnames*, his preliminary treatise on the subject. He initially divided surnames into five classes: baptismal or personal names; local surnames; official surnames; occupative surnames; and sobriquet surnames or nicknames. The nicknames category became a catch-all for all the surnames that could not be placed in any of the other categories. He commented: 'I need scarcely add that under one of these five divisions will every surname in all the countries of Europe be found.'[4] Bardsley attempted to place all the entries in his dictionary in one of these five classes, which he found had proved to be 'amply sufficient for the purpose' of identification. He did, however, concede that 'Practically there are only four classes for it is often hard to distinguish between occupation and office'.[5] He also recognised that there were some names that had several different origins and belonged in multiple categories. For example, he classified the surname Bell as a given name (derived from Isabel, Bella or Bell), as a nickname (from the French *le bel* meaning beautiful), and as a local name from a sign name.[6]

Present-day nomenclature

Numerous books of varying quality have been written on surnames since the publication of Bardsley's dictionary, and the practice of classifying surnames by type based on their origins has continued. The four basic categories identified by Bardsley still underpin all the classification schemes used by surname historians today, though some writers have used further subdivisions, and others have defined additional categories. The nomenclature used to describe the categories and subcategories has also varied from one writer to another. *A Dictionary of Surnames* by P.H. Reaney (1880–1968) was first published in 1958, with expanded and revised second and third editions, edited by R.M. Wilson, published in 1976 and 1995 respectively. Reaney, following on from Bardsley's example, defined four classifications of surnames: local surnames, surnames of relationship, surnames of occupation or office, and nicknames. The simple four-category scheme was also followed by Basil Cottle in *The Penguin Dictionary of Surnames*, published in 1967.

The English Surnames Survey, based at Leicester University, published a number of county volumes in the *English Surnames Series*, starting with a volume by George Redmonds on the West Riding of Yorkshire in 1973. Recognising that 'there is no set of terms used in such studies which is generally known to and accepted by all the varied groups of people who for one reason or another are interested in investigation into the development of English surnames', the survey found it necessary to devise their own terminology. They defined six categories: locative surnames (from specific places), topographical surnames (from landscape features), occupational surnames, surnames from personal ('baptismal') names, nicknames, and surnames of relationship (Cousins, Uncle, Bastard, etc.).[7] Richard McKinley, the overall editor of the *English Surnames Series*, published the comprehensive yet highly accessible textbook *A History of British Surnames* in 1990 in which he describes all these categories in detail, and this remains the standard work on the subject, though some of his etymologies will now require revision.

The lexicographers Patrick Hanks and Flavia Hodges took a different approach when they published the *Oxford Dictionary of Surnames* in 1988. This work had a wider remit than earlier dictionaries and also included many surnames of European origin. In the introduction to the dictionary Hanks and Hodges adopted a more detailed classification and described seventeen different categories of surname. The same classification scheme, with some minor amendments, was also used for the monumental three-volume *Dictionary of American Family Names*, for which Patrick Hanks was the editor.

In the last decade, in particular, surnames have attracted the attention of geographers, who have used surnames to map populations and their migration patterns. This research has been led by a team at University College London (UCL), who have published a number of interesting peer-reviewed papers on the subject of surname mapping (see Chapter 4). In their working paper summarising the current state of research, the UCL team tabulated a categorisation of surnames that was adapted from *An Atlas of English Surnames*, a work produced by the English Linguistics Department at the University of Bamberg in Germany (Barker et al., 2007).[8] Interestingly however, they have not used these origin-based categories in their research, but have instead produced a computer program known as OnoMap (**www.onomap.org**), which can be used to classify names based on their cultural, ethnic and linguistic roots. The user is required to enter both a given name and a surname, and the program then provides a classification. The program correctly classifies my name as English, but its rigid structure can give misleading results, for example, it classifies the Scottish name Irving as English because of its -*ing* ending.

In this chapter, for the purposes of discussion, I have used the following four broad categories:

1. Surnames from place-names and topographical features
2. Surnames from given names and relationships
3. Surnames of occupation, status or office
4. Nicknames

Surnames from place-names and topographical features

Surnames derived from places are sometimes called toponymic, local or locational surnames. They can be divided into locative surnames from specific place-names and topographical names from features of the landscape. It is not always possible to distinguish between locative and topographical surnames as many place-names are themselves derived from topographical features. A surname such as Hill, for example, will have multiple origins. Some Hills will take their surname from places known as Hill: there is a Hill in South Gloucestershire and another one in Cornwall, and there are also numerous other places where Hill forms part of the place-name. Other Hills will derive their surname from an ancestor who lived on or by a hill. Reaney and Wilson suggest that the surname is in some cases derived from the given name Hille, 'a pet form of some such name as Hilger or Hillary'.[9]

Locative surnames

Locative surnames are names derived from places. Some are derived from counties, towns, villages and hamlets, but others take their name from specific farmsteads or homesteads. This category also includes descriptive names that characterise the bearer's ethnicity, such as Cornish, Welshman and Fleming. Locative surnames, and particularly those from French place-names, were the first British surnames to become hereditary. They are particularly common in some parts of England, and are especially prevalent in Lancashire and Cornwall. In contrast, locative surnames are much less common in Scotland and Ireland and are insignificant in Wales. Hanks and Hodges (1988) use the phrase 'habitation name' to describe this class of surname. A considerable number of the surnames that were introduced to Britain in the first 200 years after the Conquest were derived from French place-names.

Locative surnames can be very rewarding to research as it is sometimes possible to trace the name back to a specific location or even the actual house or farmstead where the original bearer of the surname resided. Diligent genealogical research is required to trace the variant spellings of a surname back as far as possible (see Chapter 3) and to find the locations of the earliest spellings of the surname. It should then be possible to identify nearby places that are likely to be the origin of the name. It must be remembered that surnames are not derived from the present-day form of the place-name, but the name by which the place was known several hundred years ago at the time when the surname was formed. Fortunately, place-names have been the subject of much scholarly research, and the early forms are usually provided in the published sources.

Place-names are often easy to identify because there are a number of elements that are common to many of them. Endings such as -*brook*, -*ford*, -*hill*, -*land*, -*wood* and -*well* require no explanation. Other frequently occurring elements with less obvious meanings include: -*bury* (manor); -*ceaster*/-*cester*/-*chester* (fortification or earthwork); -*dun*/-*don* (hill or down); -*ham* (homestead, village, manor); and -*tun*/-*ton* (farmstead, village, manor or estate). Place-name elements often have marked regional variations. Places ending in -*combe* (valley) and -*cot* (cottage) are particularly common in Devon, and places with the element -*hurst* are found in Sussex. The Old Norse place-name ending -*thwaite* is common in West Yorkshire, Lancashire and the Lake District, reflecting the Norwegian influence. East of the Pennines, the Danish ending -*thorpe* is more common.

There are many place-names that occur in more than one locality. Richard McKinley reminds us that place-names such as Drayton, Burton, Eccles, Bradley, Norton, Ashby, Newton and Kirkby occur in numerous locations.[10] Surnames derived from these place-names will have arisen independently from different sources, though not every place will have necessarily given rise to a surname.

While it is often easy to recognise that a surname is locative in origin, the obvious derivation is not necessarily the correct one. Many locative surnames originate not from the better-known large towns that now share their name but from tiny hamlets and villages. David Hey points out that the surname Sunderland derives not from the port of Sunderland in Tyne and Wear but from a farm in Halifax, Yorkshire.[11] Reaney informs us that the surname Brighton cannot be derived from the Sussex town, as the present-day form is a contraction of Brightelmestone. The contracted form, although recorded in the reign of Charles I, did not come into general use until the early nineteenth century. Reaney suggests that the surname is instead derived from Breighton in Yorkshire, which occurs as Bryghton from 1298 to 1567.[12] A map of the distribution of the 1,058 people with the surname Brighton in the 1881 census shows that the name is concentrated in Yorkshire, Norfolk and the West Country with only a few isolated occurrences in Sussex (Figure 1). It is interesting to note that there is a manor by the name of Brightston in the parish of Clyst Honiton in Devon and a small village by the name of Brighton in Cornwall, though there are no obvious candidates for the source of the surname in Norfolk.

The search for the home of a family name can sometimes be difficult because the place from which the name is derived no longer exists. McKinley comments:

> The number of villages and hamlets which existed in the period 1100 to 1350, but which were subsequently deserted is much greater than is generally appreciated. For instance, the number of villages known to have been depopulated in Leicestershire, a medium sized county, is over sixty. In some cases where villages have disappeared, farms or houses survive bearing the names of the lost settlements, but in other instances no such traces remain, and even the sites of lost villages are sometimes undiscovered. Most of the places that were lost were never more than hamlets or small villages.

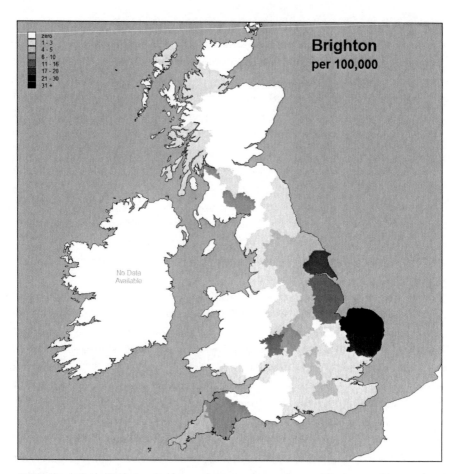

Figure 1. The distribution of the surname Brighton in the 1881 census. The northern Brightons probably take their name from Breighton in Yorkshire. The name in the south-west is possibly derived from the manor of Brightston in Devon or the village of Brighton in Cornwall. There is no obvious candidate for the source of the surname in Norfolk where the name is particularly prevalent.

McKinley further comments that:

> A considerable number of places were depopulated as a consequence of the fourteenth century pestilences, while in some parts of the country there were many further instances of villages being deserted because of depopulation caused by the conversion of arable to pasture and the enclosure of open fields, mostly in the period from about 1450 to 1550. [13]

There are now numerous online gazetteers and other resources that can help the researcher identify the names of even the tiniest and most insignificant places. A comprehensive listing of place-name resources is provided in Appendix F. For historical place-name references it is helpful to check the relevant published county histories. British History Online (**www.british-history.ac.uk**) has a large collection of county histories, including all the available volumes in the authoritative 'Victoria County History' series. The medieval sources described in Chapter 8, such as inquisitions post mortem and the feudal aids, are also invaluable for locating the names of obscure manors, though it is not always easy to identify their present-day location.

While a large stock of surnames are derived from place-names, the reverse situation can apply and some surnames have been incorporated into place-names in the form of a manorial affix: a double-barrelled place-name that includes the name of the individual or, more usually, the family associated with the place in question, either by tenure as lord of the manor or as a tenant. The affix was usually added to the place-name as a suffix to form names such as Compton Pauncefoot in Somerset, Milton Keynes (from the de Cahaignes family) in Buckinghamshire, and Melton Mowbray in Leicestershire. In a minority of cases the surname was appended as a prefix, as in Glanvilles Wootton in Dorset, or combined with the root name, as in Westonbirt, Gloucestershire. The use of the manorial affix was particularly prevalent in the southern and western counties of England, and especially in Devon, Somerset and Dorset, but it is absent in Cornwall and Northumberland. The majority of these double-barrelled names came into being in the thirteenth and fourteenth centuries, and although some of the affixes have now been lost, there are around 800 or so places in England that still bear the names of their medieval owners.[14] My maiden name, Cruwys, is still associated with the parish of Cruwys Morchard in Devon, where the family have been lords of the manor continuously from the twelfth century to the present day. The surname Cruwys was previously affixed to two other Devon manors held by the Cruwys family in North Devon: Rackenford Cruwys and Anstey Cruwys. When the manors changed hands the suffix fell into disuse and these villages are now known simply as Rackenford and East Anstey.

Topographical surnames

Topographical surnames are those that are derived from features of the landscape, whether natural (such as Ash, Hill, Marsh or Wood) or man-made (such as Bridge, Castle, Hall, Cross, Mills or Styles). This class also includes surnames that describe the position of a man's residence, such as Atwood, Bywater, Townsend and Underwood. A group of surnames ending in -er and -man (such as Bridger, Bridgeman, Brooker, Churchman, Crossman, Grover, Weller) appear at first glance to be occupational in origin, but are actually topographical surnames. Bridger and Bridgeman, for example, derive from a man who resided near a bridge.

The same topographical terms that appear in surnames are also found in place-names, and some surnames in this class will, therefore, be both locative and topographical in origin. Cross, for example, is a name denoting residence near a stone cross set up in the roadside or a market place, but there are also a number of places by the name of Cross, from which the name could be derived. Similarly, the surname Castle could refer to someone who lived near a castle or from someone who worked at a castle, but equally it could be derived from one of a number of places by the name of Castle in south-west England, Northumberland or County Durham.

McKinley found that most topographical surnames seem to have originated in England between about 1150 and 1350, but somewhat later in the north of England and in the Scots-speaking parts of Scotland. Topographical surnames are more common in the south-eastern counties of England than in any other region, and Sussex in particular has an abundant and varied collection of topographical names. The neighbouring counties of Kent and Surrey have a smaller but still relatively high proportion of topographical names. The topographical names ending in -er are mostly concentrated in the south-eastern counties of England. Topographical surnames are rare in Wales and in the Gaelic-speaking parts of Scotland.[15]

The topographical features of the English landscape have produced a rich vocabulary. Some of the terms are drawn from dialect words that are specific to particular regions or counties, and these surnames show distinct regional distribution patterns. There are some topographical terms that were familiar at the time of surname formation but are no longer in common usage, yet these words have been preserved in present-day surnames.

Surnames from given names and relationships

This category includes names that are derived from the given name of the father or mother, or sometimes the name of the grandparent or other kinsman. Such names are also used to denote membership of a clan. Surnames that originated from masculine given names are known as patronymics. Surnames from feminine given names are known as metronymics. Patronymic surnames usually denote the relationship to the father either by the use of the possessive form (for example, Andrews, Phillips, Rogers or Roberts) or by the addition of a prefix or suffix with the meaning of son (Davidson, Fitzpatrick, MacDonald or O'Neill). There are also surnames in this category that derive from given names without any prefixes or suffixes, such as John, Matthew, Owen and Peter. Patronymic surnames have consistently dominated the listings of the most common surnames in the British Isles and are particularly prevalent in Wales. Six of the ten most common surnames in Britain in 1881 were patronymic surnames that have a particularly high concentration in Wales: Jones, Williams, Davies, Evans, Thomas and Roberts.

Patronymics

Ireland

In Ireland, patronymics were the earliest form of surname and came into being in the eleventh century, although a few were formed before the year 1000. The early Irish surnames were formed by the addition of the prefix *Mac* (the Celtic word for son) to the father's given name or *O'* to the name of a grandfather or earlier ancestor to form names such as MacManus, MacShane, O'Connor and O'Neill. The *Mac* prefix, and occasionally the *O'* form, were later added to occupational surnames and sometimes nicknames.[16]

England

Surnames from given names were not common among the landholding classes of society, and consequently there is less information about their development. McKinley suggests that most such surnames were formed between 1150 and 1300.[17] The earliest patronymic surnames in England generally used the name of the father alone without any embellishment (e.g. Martin, Thomas, William). Some of the very early patronymic surnames include those derived from Old English and Scandinavian names such as Godwin (from the Old English name Godwine meaning good friend, protector or lord) and Elgar (from the Old English word *Æðelgār* meaning 'noble spear').[18] The Conquest introduced a new stock of given names to the country. The Old English and Scandinavian names started to become much less common from about 1150 onwards, and many had disappeared entirely by about 1350.[19] By about 1250 there was just a small pool of given names that were in general usage, and many of these names are still popular today: Edward, Henry, John, Robert, Richard, Thomas, William, etc. This reduction in the stock of given names coincided with the beginnings of patronymic surnames in England, and consequently these patronymic names are derived from a limited name pool. Distinct regional differences can be seen. Surnames with the suffix *-son* predominate in the north of England. Examples include Anderson, Ferguson, Harrison, Jackson, Richardson, Robertson, etc. In southern and central parts of England the genitive form ending in *-s* was preferred – Harris, Richards, Roberts, etc. The possessive form was most common in the south-west Midlands. The differences can clearly be seen in the distribution of the surnames Richards and Richardson (Figures 2 and 3). The reasons for the differences in usage are not fully understood, but are possibly explained by the later adoption of surnames in the north, when the *-son* form was more fashionable.

Patronymic surnames with the prefix *Fitz* – from the French *fils de* (son of) – (FitzGerald, FitzPatrick, FitzWilliam, etc.) arose in the twelfth and thirteenth centuries primarily among the land-owning classes. Some of these surnames were introduced to Ireland by Anglo-Norman families, and are now found in greater numbers in Ireland than in England. It is sometimes thought that *Fitz* surnames are associated with illegitimacy, but, as McKinley explains, this belief is mistaken:

> It seems to have arisen from the relatively late practice of royalty bestowing such names on acknowledged natural children. The first person to do this seems to have been Charles II, many of whose natural children were given the surname of Fitzroy. He was followed by his brother, James II, who called his illegitimate children FitzJames. The practice continued into the nineteenth century.[20]

Figures 2 and 3.
Surnames with
the suffix *-son*
predominate in the
north of England,
whereas in southern
and central parts
of England and
Wales the *-s* ending
was preferred. The
different usages can
clearly be seen in the
distribution patterns of
the surnames Richards
and Richardson in the
1881 census.

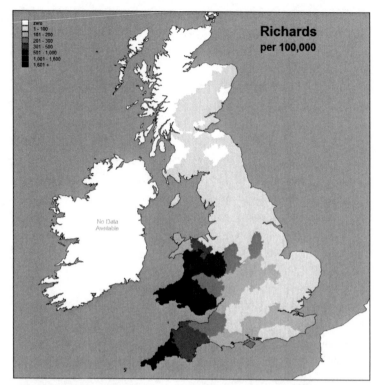

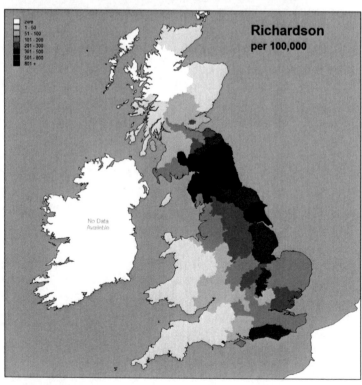

Scotland

In the Lowland parts of Scotland, where Scots (a Germanic language) was spoken, surname formation followed a similar pattern to that seen in the north of England. Surnames with the suffix -*son* are found from the thirteenth century onwards, though some of these names are derived from Gaelic given names such as Finlayson, Gilchristson and Malcolmson. New patronymic surnames with the addition of -*son* were still being formed in the fifteenth and early sixteenth centuries. These patronymic surnames are particularly prevalent in Orkney and Shetland (both technically part of the Lowlands) and the Hebrides, where many surnames have Norse origins.

In the Gaelic-speaking parts of Scotland surnames were often derived from clans rather than individual families. Many clan names are patronymics prefixed by *Mac. Mac* surnames are also written as *Mc*, *Mhic*, or *M'*. It is very common to find the same person's surname spelt *Mc* in one record and *Mac* in another. As in Ireland, the *Mac* prefix was also added to occupational names.

In earlier records, a person might be known not only by the name of his father but also by his grandfather's name. The prefix *Vc*, meaning grandson or granddaughter, was used to denote this relationship. The ScotlandsPeople website cites the example in 1673 of Dugall Mcdugall Vcean (Dugall, son of Dugall, grandson of Ean) who married Marie Camron or NcNdonochie Vcewn.[21]

Wales

Fixed surnames were adopted much later in Wales than in England, Ireland and Scotland. Welsh surnames were largely derived from the traditional Welsh patronymic naming system whereby a man was known by the name of his father. The prefixes *ab* and *ap* (derived from *mab* or *map*: the Welsh word for son) were used to denote the filial relationship. The general rule was to use *ab* before vowels and *ap* before consonants, though this rule was not always followed consistently. Hence, Robert *ab* Evan was the son of Evan, and David *ap* Richard was the son of Richard. With the adoption of fixed surnames the *ap/ab* was gradually dropped. In most parts of Wales the possessive -*s* form was adopted so that Robert *ab* Evan became Robert Evans and David *ap* Richard became David Richards. It is thought that the -*s* type of patronymic surname was used in Wales rather than -*son* because this form was popular in the border counties from the sixteenth century onwards at the time when Welsh surnames were developing. In some areas of Wales the *ap* and *ab* prefixes were subsumed into the surname, and so David *ap* Richard became David Prichard, and Robert *ab* Evan became Robert Bevan.[22]

Pet forms, diminutives and augmentatives

Given names often have many variant forms. The name Richard can, for example, be shortened to Dick, Hick, Rick and so on. All these pet forms, which are technically known as hypocoristic forms, have in turn given rise to surnames (Dickson/Dixon, Hickey, Hicks, Hickson, Ricks/Rix, etc.). Some pet forms are diminutives, that is, they include a suffix with the meaning of 'little'. The most common suffixes include: -*cock*, -*ett*, -*in*, -*kin* and

-ot. These diminutives have produced surnames such as Bartlett (from Bartholomew), Hitchcock (from Richard), Hopkins (from Robert), Hutchins (from Hugh), and Wilmot (from William). Augmentatives, meaning 'big', are much rarer, but are found both in French (*-at*) and Italian (*-oni* and *-one*). Ciccone, the maiden name of the American pop singer Madonna, is an augmentative form of the given name Francisco. Cicco is a pet form of Francisco and the surname literally means 'big Cicco'.

Metronymics

Throughout recorded history Europe has been a patriarchal society and, consequently, there are only a small number of surnames derived from feminine given names. The few metronymic names that have survived seem to be derived from the names of women who were widows for most of their adult lives or who were heiresses in their own right. Examples include Magson (son of Margaret), Emmett and Emmott (from a pet name for Emma), and Ibbotson (from the medieval pet name for Isabel). Emmott also derives from the place-name Emmott in Lancashire. The surname of the Belgian surrealist artist René Magritte is derived from the name Marguerite. Iceland still maintains a patronymic naming system, but metronyms are sometimes used instead. The Icelandic novelist Guðrún Eva Mínervudóttir takes her last name from her mother Minerva.

Surnames derived from kinship terms

There is a small group of surnames that are derived from terms used to describe varying relationships. The *English Surnames Series* places these kinship names in the additional category of 'surnames of relationship'. Hanks and Hodges describe this category as 'surnames from kin terms'. Surnames in this group include names such as Bastard, Brothers, Cousins, Fairbrother, Fathers, Husband, Kinsman, Widowson, Youngson and Younghusband. Some of these surnames probably have alternative derivations. McKinley believes that Cousins has become confused either with the medieval surname Cusaunce (derived from the French place-name Coutances) or the surname Cusson (signifying son of Constance or son of Cuthbert).[23] Reaney and Wilson suggest that the surname Husband is an occupational surname derived from husbandman (a farmer).[24]

Surnames of occupation, status or office

Surnames derived from occupations include some of our most prolific and recognisable surnames. Smith is not only the most common surname in both England and Scotland, but is also the most common name in the United States. There are a further twelve surnames, all of which have instantly recognisable origins in familiar occupations, that are among the top fifty most common surnames in England and Wales: Taylor, Wright, Walker, Turner, Clark, Cooper, Ward, Baker, Clarke, Cook, Parker, and Carter. Occupational surnames are more often found in England than elsewhere in the British Isles.

Reaney noted 'the surprising variety and specialized nature of medieval occupations'.[25] Many occupational surnames have their origins in obscure trades and occupations that are no longer in existence, and will not be immediately recognisable. Surnames are sometimes the only written record of long-forgotten occupations. Lexicographers working on the *Oxford English Dictionary* (OED) are now tapping this largely unexplored resource and using early surname forms to trace the history of words. In some cases it has been possible to antedate the existing entry by several hundred years. For example, the OED's entry for 'mould-maker' now includes a 1337 reference to Gilbertus le moldemaker, whose name appears in a register of the freemen of the city of York. The previous earliest quotation found dated from 1780.[26] The meaning of medieval occupational terms is not always readily apparent and some such names that are now known to be occupational were previously regarded as nicknames or were unexplained.

A preponderance of occupational terms can be found attached to given names in thirteenth- and fourteenth-century tax records, but it is very difficult to ascertain whether or not these bynames ever developed into hereditary surnames. The *London Lay Subsidy of 1332* includes references to Wills le Chaundeler, Wlatus le brewere, Robtus le fflourmakere and Wills le Stokfishmongr. But in the same volume we find references to Henrc de Braghing, stokfishmongere; Thomas de Dunstaple, ffelmonger; and Johes de Wynchestr, plomer.[27] In most cases it will probably be impossible to trace such surnames back by genealogical methods to the original bearer of the name, but there is still much to be learnt by studying and mapping the distribution of occupational surnames at various points in time.

Many occupational surnames have distinct geographical distributions. Baker is a quintessentially English surname that is found throughout the country but is markedly more prevalent in the south (Figure 4). The surname Baxter is derived from the Middle English word *baxter* (also *bakster, bacster*) meaning baker or female baker.[28] Baxter is found in East Anglia, and the north of England, and is particularly prevalent throughout Scotland with the exception of the extreme northerly counties and isles (Figure 5). In some cases the differing distribution patterns can be accounted for by the use of dialect words for different occupations. The best-known and most striking illustration of this phenomenon is the example of the surnames Fuller, Tucker and Walker. Each of these names describes someone who worked in the textiles industry and refers to the process of scouring or beating the cloth as a means of cleansing the fabric. Fuller is used in the east of England, Tucker in the west, and Walker in the Midlands and the north. The differing regional terms are clearly reflected in the distribution of the three surnames in 1881. The surname Tucker is highly concentrated in the south-west of England, and Fuller in the south-east (Figures 6 and 7). Walker is prevalent throughout England and Scotland but is much less common in the south-west and south-east of England (Figure 8).

Occupational surnames also have different words in other languages, and these names are often translated into their English equivalent. Without any familiarity with the language the connection might not be immediately obvious. For example, the surname MacGowan in Ireland is derived from the Gaelic *Mac an Ghabhann* meaning 'son of the smith'. McLysaght

Figures 4 and 5.
Baker and Baxter are related occupational surnames. The two surnames have very different distributions in 1881: Baker is more prevalent in the south; Baxter is more common in the north and in Scotland.

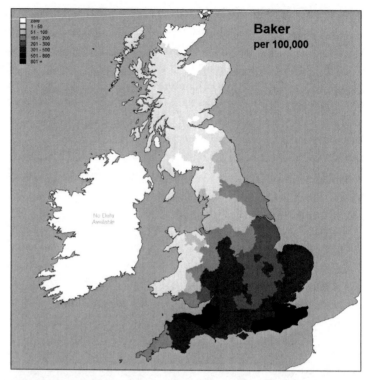

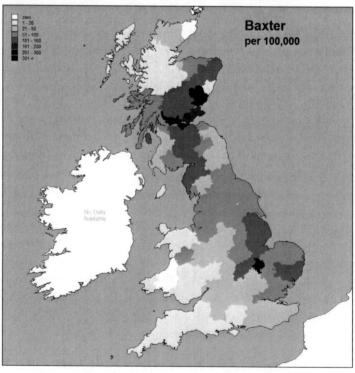

notes that the majority of MacGowan families in County Cavan anglicised their surname and became Smiths by translation.[29] Similarly, the Cornish surname Angove is derived from the Cornish word for Smith (*an* 'the' and *gof* 'smith').[30] Not surprisingly, the surname Smith is rare in Cornwall.

Some occupational names are thought to derive from the object associated with the activity of the original bearer, such as a tool used by the original name-bearer or a product that he sold (e.g. Bacon, Cakebread, Hammer, Last and Pick). These are known as metonymic surnames. However, there are many names that at first glance appear to fall into this category but that on closer examination could have an alternative origin. Hammer, for example, is also a topographical surname from the Old English word *hamm* meaning stream.[31] Bacon is possibly derived from the Germanic given name *Bac(c)o* or *Bahho*. The name was used by the Normans in the forum *Bacus*, the oblique case of which is *Bacon*.[32]

Surnames derived from status or office (Abbot, Burgess, Chamberlain, Freeman, King, Reeve, Sheriff, Squire, etc.) are often categorised with occupational surnames, but are sometimes treated as a separate category. While some of these surnames probably did originate with a name-bearer who held the status or office in question, it is likely that many more were nicknames, sometimes used in an ironic sense, or were perhaps derived from someone employed in the household of a person holding the office. Some names in this class, such as Abbot, Prior, and Monk, could not be hereditary because the holder was bound by a vow of celibacy. Other names of high status, such as King and Pope, occur at relatively high frequencies and could not possibly derive from the few people who actually held such positions. In the 1881 census there were over 65,000 people with the surname King, and over 10,000 people with the surname Pope. An alternative explanation for the origin of these names was offered by Camden:

> So the distinct Families of the *Constables* in the County of *York*, are said to have taken that name, from some of their Ancestours, which bare the office of Constables of some Castles. In like manner, the *Stewards, Marshals, Spencers*. That I may say nothing of such as for well acting on the stage, have carried away the names of the Personages which they acted, and have lost their own names among the people.[33]

Reaney uses the term 'pageant names' to describe such names, and cites a passage from the year 1377 that provides plausible origins for the surnames Squire, Knight, Emperor, Cayzer, Pope, Cardinal and Leggatt.[34]

Nicknames

The category of nicknames has become something of a catch-all category for surnames that don't immediately seem to fit elsewhere. The Registrar-General for England and Wales issued a special report on family nomenclature in 1856 and commented

Figures 6, 7 and 8. The occupational surnames Fuller, Tucker and Walker are derived from the textile industry and refer to the process of scouring or beating the cloth as a means of cleansing the fabric. Different dialect words were used to describe this occupation, which accounts for the strong regional distributions of the three surnames in the 1881 census.

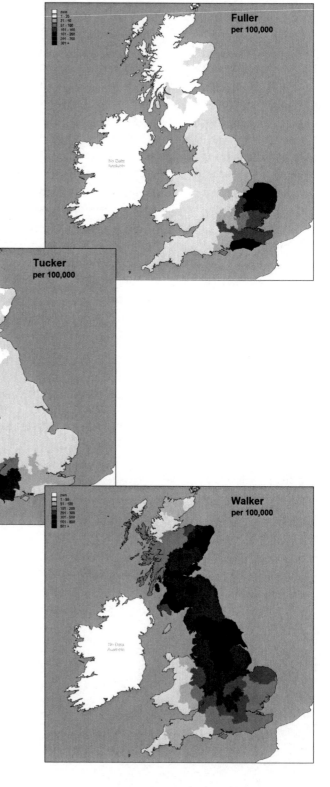

that: 'Some of the terms which swell the list are so odd and even ridiculous that it is difficult to assign any satisfactory reason for their assumption in the first instance as family names, unless indeed, as has been conjectured, they were nicknames or *sobriquets*, which neither the first bearers nor their posterity could avoid.'[35] The category includes surnames derived from moral characteristics (Faithful, Smart, Humble, and Proud) and physical features (Little, Long, Short). Early surname writers such as Camden and Lower included all manner of animals, birds, fish, flowers and colours in this class.

Surnames derived from nicknames are of early origin. Reaney observes that: 'Nicknames are common in medieval records, but comparatively few have given modern surnames. For many of them only a few examples of the nickname occur, and often enough there is only a single instance.'[36] Many of the nicknames that appear in medieval records are bynames that never developed into hereditary surnames. Of those names that were adopted the original meaning of the nickname might have been very different to the present-day meaning. It is difficult to understand why nicknames that were specific to one particular person should ever have been adopted as a hereditary surname by later generations, and it is almost impossible to trace a nickname back to its point of origin to find out the real reasons why these names were originally bestowed on an individual.

However, many surnames that at first glance appear to be nicknames often turn out, on closer examination, to have alternative meanings. For example, the surname Bear is not derived from someone who looks or behaves like a bear but is a locative surname from the Old English word *bearu*, meaning grove, which was particularly prevalent in the south-west of England.[37] In the *Devonshire Lay Subsidy of 1332* we find William atte Beare paying 3*s* 4*d* in Staverton and John atte Beare paying 8*d* in South Brent.[38] The present-day form of a surname is often very misleading. Surnames evolve over time and difficult-to-pronounce words have a tendency to become simplified and changed to something more meaningful or easier to pronounce. Hence the splendid Irish surname Mucklebreed, which to modern ears sounds like a character from a Harry Potter novel, is in fact a corruption of the Gaelic surname *Mac Giolla Bhrighde* (MacGilbride).[39] Haddock is seemingly not derived from a fish, but is more likely to be a corruption of the place-name Haydock, a parish in South Lancashire.[40] In 1881 the surname had a strong concentration in both Lancashire and Yorkshire, and had spread out to Yorkshire, the West Midlands, South Wales and East Anglia. Similarly, the surname Stammer is probably not a nickname for someone with a stammer. In 1881 the surname is concentrated in Sussex and the surrounding counties, but also has a second hotspot in Suffolk. The surname in Sussex is derived from the village of Stanmer near Brighton. Stammer has an alternative derivation from the Old English name *Stānmær*, which probably accounts for the presence of the surname in Suffolk.[41]

There are numerous supposed nicknames from the names of animals and birds. Some of these names are occupational in origin and derive from the work of looking after the animals in question. Some apparent nicknames are possibly derived from the name of a shop or inn, as Camden observed in 1605:

Neither is it improbable, but that many names, that seem unfitting for men, as of brutish beasts, &c. came from the very signs of the houses where they inhabited; for I have heard of them which said they spake of knowledge, that some in late time dwelling at the sign of the Dolphin, Bull, White-horse, Racket, Peacock, &c. were commonly called *Thomas* at the *Dolphin*, *Will* at the *Bull*, *George* at the *White horse*, *Robin* at the *Racket*, which names as many other of like sort, with omitting *At*, became afterward hereditary to their children.[42]

Lower devoted a whole chapter of *English Surnames* (1849) to the subject of 'surnames derived from heraldric charges and from traders' signs'. He tells us that signs:

… formed one of the most curious features of our towns and cities in the 'olden tyme.' Every quadruped from the *lyon* and *hee-cow* (!) down to the *hedgehogge*,—every bird from the *eagle* to the *sparrow*,—every *fysshe* of the sea, almost every object, in fact, artificial, natural, praeternatural, and supernatural, good, bad, and indifferent, from the *angel* to the *devil*, lent its aid in those days to excite the attention of passers-by to the various articles of commerce exhibited for sale.[43]

Reaney is more sceptical. He points out that most of the evidence produced for sign names is from the sixteenth and seventeenth centuries, by which time most surnames were already well established, and that there are only fleeting references to names that might be the precursors of sign names in medieval records (e.g. *John atte Belle*).[44] Reaney suggests that names derived from signs 'are usually late and less common than has been supposed. Some of the "signs" really refer to topographical features (*Ball, Cock*).'[45]

There are a number of curious classes of surname that tend to get bundled together in the nicknames category. Some surnames are derived from seasons, festivals, months and days of the week (Christmas, Winter, May, Friday, etc.) and are sometimes known as 'seasonal surnames'. Hanks and Hodges suggest that seasonal surnames might relate to the time of birth or baptism of the original name-bearer, or the day of the week on which feudal service was owed.[46] Rogers offers an alternative explanation and postulates that many of these names were given to foundlings.[47]

A small class of surnames are supposedly derived from phrases and expressions and include such names as Bidgood (pray God), Goodyear, and Pardew (from the French *par Dieu*: by God).

There is clearly much more research that could be done on the origin of nicknames, and family historians who undertake detailed studies of a single surname will have much to contribute, though the origins of many of these names will probably remain obscure.

3

VARIANTS AND DEVIANTS

And as to find out the true original of Surnames, is full of difficulty, so it is not easie to search all the causes of alterations of Surnames, which in former Ages have been very common amongst us, and have so intricated, or rather obscured the truth of our Pedegrees, that it will be no little labour to deduce many of them truly from the Conquest …

William Camden, *Remaines Concerning Britaine* … (1605, 7th impression, 1674), pp. 175–6

With any surname study a decision needs to be made as to how many other related or variant spellings to research. It is not always a straightforward choice and the number of legitimate variant spellings can differ from one surname to another. Some short surnames will only have a handful of variants, whereas longer surnames can have 100 or more possible different spellings. A surname that has been in existence since the 1200s might now survive in a multiplicity of forms, many of which will seemingly bear little relation to the original name. Alternative spellings also occur as a result of clerical errors or mistranscriptions. These spellings, which have conveniently been referred to as 'deviants', are of a transient nature and will appear only once or a few times in official records.

How surnames evolve

As we have seen in Chapter 1, the development of hereditary surnames was a gradual process. In Britain some families were already using surnames in the 1100s, and surnames were in general usage by the 1500s, though there were still some places where surnames did not come into being until as late as the nineteenth century. During the key period of surname formation very few people were able to read and write. Surnames were recorded in official documents by a clerk or scribe, who spelt a name as he heard it. There was no standardised spelling and there were no convenient reference books or dictionaries that the scribes could consult. Names were spelt inconsistently and it was common to find the same name spelt in a variety of different ways within the same document. Samuel Johnson's *Dictionary of the English Language*, the first authoritative English dictionary, was not published until 1755. The first surname dictionaries only started to appear in the middle of the nineteenth century, facilitated by the increasing availability on both sides of the

Atlantic of name-rich trade and street directories. Bernard Homer Dixon's *Surnames* was published in America in 1855 and reprinted in 1857, and was seemingly the first surname dictionary in the English language. Dixon noted that: 'The surnames in this work have invariably been given as they have been found written, although not in all their forms; for names are often variously spelled, sometimes even by descendants of the same branch.' A second American surname dictionary, entitled *An Etymological Dictionary of Family and Christian Names*, was published in 1857 by William Arthur. In England, Mark Antony Lower began his study of surnames in about 1836, publishing a sixty-eight-page pamphlet entitled 'The Book of English Surnames' in 1838 and a book of essays on surnames in 1842. His publications influenced both Dixon and Arthur. Lower's monumental 443-page *Patronymica Britannica*, was published in 1860, and was the first surname dictionary to focus on surnames in the United Kingdom.

The spelling and pronunciation of surnames only started to stabilise in the nineteenth century with the introduction of universal education. Nevertheless, the presence of a signature on a document should not necessarily be taken as a sign of literacy. When it is possible to view the original marriage registers it is sometimes found that a name is still spelt in different ways on the same certificate even when the bride or groom signed the register.

Generally speaking, the greatest diversity of surname spellings will be found in the earliest records and more consistent spellings will be found in later records, and especially from the mid-nineteenth century onwards. Some surnames will continue to evolve even in more recent times, as I have found when researching my own family tree. My grandfather's birth was registered in the name Kenneth Ratty in 1901, but by the time he married in 1923 he was known as Kenneth Rattey, and he had changed the pronunciation of his name to 'Ray-tee'. I have not been able to pinpoint the precise timing of the change, but his parents appear in the electoral roll for Greenwich in London under the surname Ratty through to 1915, but by 1918 the name was consistently spelt Rattey. Although the reason for the spelling change is not known I have always wondered if it is related to the publication of the much-loved children's book *The Wind in the Willows* by Kenneth Grahame in 1908. The book features a character by the name of Ratty, though he is actually a water vole and not a rat, and perhaps the association was responsible for much teasing and jocularity.

Surnames are especially vulnerable to change when the bearer moves to a new location, either within his home country or when emigrating for a new life overseas. In Britain, until the advent of the railways in the nineteenth century, most people only migrated short distances, staying within the neighbourhood with which they were most familiar and travelling no further than the nearest market town. Consequently, the local people would have an intimate knowledge of the core surnames of the neighbourhood and their pronunciation. However, if someone with a characteristic local surname moved to a big city far away from home or a new country overseas, their new neighbours would not be familiar with the name and might have trouble both spelling and pronouncing it, and their dialect might be difficult for people to understand. The name-bearer might have deliberately changed his name when the locals had difficulty spelling it or pronouncing it, or the name might have been changed for him if it proved particularly troublesome. It is easy to see how surnames could undergo quite dramatic changes under such circumstances. Often, as a result of emigration, a unique variant will arise that is only found in the host country. On the other hand, emigration can sometimes preserve an early spelling that has become extinct in the country of origin. A similar pattern can also be seen in the home country if the bearer moved a long way from his place of birth to find work in London or one of the new industrial centres. It is not uncommon to find that different members of the same family choose to use different spellings of their surname. For example, in my own family tree I have a relative by the name of Thomas Faithfull who emigrated to Australia in 1843 with his wife and seven children. His youngest son William went to seek his fortune in New Zealand in 1861. All the Faithfulls in Australia spell their name with two 'Ls', but William's descendants spell their name as Faithful with a single 'L'.

Sometimes evidence can be found in written records of the use of two alternative spellings or pronunciations for a surname in the form of an alias, such as 'James Roides alias Rodes', 'Simon Woodhouse alias Wydis', and 'John Clegge otherwise Clagge'.[2] Aliases were also used when families of the same surname proliferated in a small district. Popular forenames combined with numerous surnames led to confusion and ambiguities, so alias names became necessary, and in time some of these alias names became hereditary. Aliases were sometimes also used when names were changed for the purposes of inheritance, or when a widow remarried and her children adopted the surname of their stepfather. George Redmonds has made a detailed study of aliases in Yorkshire in *Surnames and Genealogy: A New Approach* (1997, 2002), and cites numerous examples. Mike Brown and M.D. Hooper have studied the use of the alias in Devon.[3, 4]

Unusual surname spellings can often be of quite recent origin and will eventually turn out to be a variant of a more common surname. In some cases the researcher will be able to link all the people with the same rare surname into one big family tree tracing back perhaps to the 1700s. The parish registers or other contemporary records will usually provide evidence of the prior forms of the surname, but in some cases the research will seemingly come to a dead end because no baptism or marriage can be found to take the line back any further. One reason for this can be a failure to consider all the likely variant and deviant spellings. The elusive baptism or marriage might possibly be hidden away in an index under a previously unconsidered form of the surname, or the name might have been transcribed in such a way that the connection was not immediately apparent. If all attempts to find earlier references to the surname have failed then it is possible that your ancestor arrived in the area as a result of an unexpected long-distance move. Research into the local history of the area can pay dividends in such circumstances. Look at the local road networks to see which towns and cities were within travelling distance. If there is a river nearby or the place is near the sea then the journey could have been made by water. A settlement examination might be found in the poor law records. These can sometimes provide extraordinary detail about the person's movements and give conclusive proof of a move from one county to another.

Spelling changes

The same letter sounds can be represented in many ways in the English language, and consequently some surnames can be spelt in a variety of different forms without having any effect on the pronunciation. Vowel sounds are responsible for the largest number of spelling variations, and care will need to be taken when searching in indexes or online databases to ensure that a possible variant has not been overlooked. For example, the names Heard, Herd, Hird and Hurd are pronounced identically, but will all appear on separate pages in an index. The letter 'e' in particular has a habit of attaching or detaching itself to surnames at random in names such as Clark/Clarke, Crew/Crewe, Davis/Davies and Davy/Davey. There are also a number of consonant sounds that result in identical pronunciations but different spellings in names such as Philby/Filby, Dickson/Dixon, and Wrigley/Rigley. A single consonant can change into a double consonant or vice versa in names such as Robin/Robbins and Faithful/Faithfull. Such changes are easy to anticipate and will present few difficulties for the researcher, though variants beginning with different letters of the alphabet will require more effort to extract from databases and indexes as a double search will be required. There are also some consonant sounds that are mute and result in different spellings such as the Scottish surname Cockburn/Coburn, which is pronounced '*coburn*' in both spellings. Not surprisingly, the single and plural forms of names can cause confusion, and the letter 's' is often added on or dropped in names such as Brook/Brooks, Crew/Crews, and Rigg/Riggs. Another feature of Scottish names was the interchangeability of 'u', 'v' and 'w', so that, for example, Irwyn changed to Irvine or Irving, and Methven can also be found as Methuen.

When a surname began with a vowel or started with the same letter as the given name, it was sometimes difficult for the clerk to work out where the given name ended and the surname began. A man by the name of John Noakes might perhaps be recorded as John Oakes, whereas a Thomas Sanderson might appear as Thomas Anderson. The technical term for the process in which new names are created by the changing of the boundaries between the words is meta-analysis.

When names are written down, adjacent letters, or sometimes whole syllables, can be transposed in a process known as metathesis. For example, in the parish registers of Ogbourne St George in Wiltshire, the names Curs(e) and Cruse/Cruce are used interchangeably until the late 1700s when the spelling stabilised as Cruse. The written records are unfortunately not able to tell us if the pronunciation of the name was affected or if the clerk was simply suffering from dyslexia.

Pronunciation

Languages are in a constant state of flux and none more so than the English language, which is the most widely published language and also the language with the largest and richest vocabulary. English has absorbed words from many different languages and a wide variety of sources, and is now a truly international language. Immigration, greater mobility and the influence of television and the cinema have helped to blur the differences in regional accents and change the way that words are pronounced. Scientists had the unique opportunity to document some of these changes by analysing the Queen's Christmas broadcasts to the Commonwealth from 1952 onwards. They found that the royal vowel sounds have undergone a subtle evolution, and that her pronunciation has changed from the cut-glass tones of what is known as Upper Received Pronunciation to the more democratic Standard Received Pronunciation and its close relative, Standard Southern British English.[5]

The pronunciation of surnames has evolved in a similar way. While twentieth-century changes in pronunciation can be documented in audio recordings and television broadcasts, we are reliant on spelling changes in the written record to reveal how pronunciation changed in earlier centuries. Once the family tree has been taken back as far as possible, it will be necessary to collect as many references as possible from medieval records in an attempt to document the changes and prove continuity of the surname in a given location. Vowel sounds are the most prone to change, but some consonants have very similar sounds and can easily be confused or altered as a result of a local dialect. The consonant sounds that are most prone to change are: B and P; D and T; D and TH; F and V; M and N; S and Z. George Redmonds cites some interesting examples from Yorkshire where he found explicit aliases to prove the relationship between names such as Bickerdike and Pickerdike, Vaux and Faux, and Dinsdale and Tinsdale.[6]

Suffixes are particularly prone to confusion because of the lack of stress on the final syllable. George Redmonds cites numerous examples from Lancashire and Yorkshire, which have again been positively confirmed by the discovery of aliases linking the two variants together. The suffixes Brook/Brough/Burn and Halgh/Hough were often used interchangeably. Other examples found by Redmonds include: Stansfield/Stancliffe, Burdwicke/Burdett and Summerscales/Summerskill.[7]

The beginnings of surnames can also change over time, often as a result of differences in local dialect. Wogan and Ogan can be used interchangeably, Earnshaw can change into Yearnshaw, and Eyre can become Hare. The addition of a letter or syllable at the beginning of a word is known in linguistics as prosthesis.

Sometimes the pronunciation of a surname is deliberately changed by the name-bearer. For instance, my own maiden name Cruwys is mostly pronounced '*cruise*' in the UK, but in Australia one branch of the family deliberately changed the pronunciation to '*crewiss*' during the Second World War, probably to make the name seem Welsh rather than Germanic. This same process also occurs with immigrant surnames, which were either changed by choice in order to blend in with the new neighbours or by default because the name was difficult for the locals to pronounce. Many well-known media personalities have anglicised their surnames in this way. For example, the actress Helen Mirren has a Russian father and English mother and was born Helen Mironoff, while the American business tycoon Donald Trump is the grandson of a German immigrant by the name of Friedrich Drumpf who became known as Frederick Trump on arrival in America.

The process can also work in the opposite direction and in some cases names have been changed for snobbish reasons or through social affectation in order to make them seem more important, with families often adopting contorted spellings or unusual pronunciations in the process. A classic example is the change from Smith to Smythe. In the BBC sitcom *Keeping up Appearances*, the fictional character Hyacinth Bucket is best remembered for insisting that her surname should be pronounced '*bouquet*'. The practice was pilloried in a memorable sketch from *Monty Python's Flying Circus*, the surreal BBC comedy series from the early 1970s:

INTERVIEWER: Good evening. I have with me in the studio tonight one of Britain's leading skin specialists – Raymond Luxury Yacht.

RAYMOND: That's not my name.

INTERVIEWER: I'm sorry – Raymond Luxury Yach-t.

RAYMOND: No, no, no – it's spelt Raymond Luxury Yach-t, but it's pronounced 'Throatwobbler Mangrove'.

INTERVIEWER: You're a very silly man and I'm not going to interview you.[8]

The surname researcher will need to bear all these different factors in mind during the course of their research. If research has stalled, try reading some of the variant spellings you have found out loud. Ask your family and friends to do the same, especially if you have friends who live in a different part of the country to you. The pronunciation of surnames is not always intuitive and a previously unconsidered alternative pronunciation might provide a lead to a new variant spelling.

Surnames, along with many place-names, are often pronounced in a most unexpected way, with the pronunciation bearing little resemblance to the spelling. Robert Charles Hope published a fascinating and informative book in 1883 that provides lists of place-names and surnames with unexpected pronunciations. He informs us that the name Marjoribanks is pronounced '*Marchbanks*', Anstruther is pronounced '*Anster*', and Bracegirdle is pronounced '*Breskittle*'. The book, grandiosely titled *A Glossary of Dialectical Place Nomenclature to which is Appended a List of Family Surnames Pronounced Differently from what the Spelling Suggests*, is now freely available in the Internet Archive. GenealogyMagazine.com has an interesting article by James Pylant and Gary R. Toms entitled 'Talliaferro is Tolliver: surnames sound a challenge for researchers', which looks at a selection of American names that are not pronounced in the way that might be expected. The article can be found online at **www.genealogymagazine.com/surnames.html**. It includes a link to a list of surnames collected by the authors that are not pronounced in accordance with their spelling.

Dictionaries and dialect dictionaries can be consulted to provide clues about the pronunciation of name components. Joseph Wright's seminal work *The English Dialect Dictionary*, published in six volumes between 1898 and 1905, is now available in the Internet Archive and provides a valuable snapshot of pronunciation in the closing years of the nineteenth century. Links to this dictionary and other linguistic resources can be found in Appendix E.

There are a couple of useful websites that allow the user to hear recordings of pronunciations of different words in a variety of accents. Forvo (**www.forvo.com**) has been online since 2008 and now claims to be the largest pronunciation guide in the world, with audio pronunciations of over 1 million words in more than 200 languages. It is a collaborative wiki-style venture that allows users to contribute their own recordings or add words that they don't know how to pronounce. Users can also rate the pronunciations provided. There are, for example, nineteen different pronunciations of the word 'coffee' with contributions from the UK, Spain, Sweden and America; pronunciations range from *coff-fee* to *caw-fee*. An app is available for the iPhone but is not currently available for Android users.

The website **www.howjsay.com** is a free curated 'Talking Dictionary of English Pronunciation' with audio files for over 150,000 words. The dictionary does not include surnames but it can be used to check the pronunciation of English words that are found as a component of a surname. Entries are read out in Standard British English with alternative pronunciations for some words (such as controversy and schedule) in World English. The dictionary is also available as an app for iPhone and Android, and there are versions of the dictionary available in German, French, Italian and Spanish.

Corruptions

Surnames have evolved in an unpredictable fashion, bringing about changes for which there are no rules. The peak period of surname formation occurred at a time when many words had different meanings to their present-day usage and when words that are now redundant were spoken on a daily basis. There is a general tendency for difficult-to-pronounce names to be simplified, a problem that Robert Ferguson wisely commented on as far back as 1883:

> I now come to corruptions which arise from the attempt to give to a name something of an apparent meaning in English. Let me observe that, almost as an invariable rule, corruptions are made towards a meaning and not away from it; the ancient name Irminger might be corrupted into Ironmonger, but Ironmonger could not be corrupted into Irminger. It is natural to men to try to get some semblance of meaning out of a name, and all the more that it approaches to something which has a familiar sound to their ears.[9]

Consequently, rather like a game of Chinese whispers, many surnames found today bear little resemblance to their original forms. It is often impossible to find the origins of the surname without checking all the transitional stages. The surname Kneebone, for example, has no connection with the medical profession or anatomy. It is instead believed to be derived from a place in Cornwall by the name of Carnebone in the parish of Wendron. The place-name was first recorded as Carnebwen in 1298.[10] However, Roger Kneebone, who has been researching his surname for over thirty years, is not so sure. He comments that Carnebone was formerly a burial place. It is on a high and desolate ground with rough grazing and he thinks it unlikely that many people would have lived there. He has, however, not as yet been able to find a more plausible explanation for the origin of the name.[11] Likewise, the surname Dangerfield is not as hazardous as it first appears. It is a Norman surname derived from one of a number of places in France called Angerville. The thirteenth-century spelling was most often represented as De Angervil(le). By the fourteenth and fifteenth centuries the preposition had become fused and the spelling was frequently expressed as Daungervil. By the time the name appeared in parish registers in the sixteenth century, the name had changed to its present form of Dangerfield, though sometimes the 'i' and 'e' are transposed and an additional 'e' occasionally appears at the end of the name.[12]

Deviant spellings

A deviant is a transitory spelling found as a result of a clerical error in recording or transcription. In contrast, a true variant spelling will have been perpetuated for several generations, even if the usage has not always been consistent. The term deviant spelling was coined by Derek Palgrave in a seminal article published in the *Journal of One-Name Studies* in 1984, and subsequently reprinted in 2004. He noted:

> All of us who specialise in a single surname are familiar with several versions of our name. We tend to refer to these different versions as 'variants' when, in fact, this may not be the case.
>
> In general, many of the versions are mistakes which have come about when the writer has written down what he thought he heard. If the speaker had a broad dialect or a speech impediment and the writer was hard of hearing, then the potential for deviation was considerable. When records are transcribed from original documents written in an unfamiliar hand, or from microfilm of such documents, there is scope for further distortion.

In Palgrave's own research he has come across over 100 different versions of the surname Palgrave, but he only regards a few of the spellings as genuine variants.[13]

The Guild of One-Name Studies recommends that members should not register deviant spellings as variants and should limit variants to those still found today. Variants and deviants are defined as follows:

> The Guild therefore defines a variant as a name spelling which varies from the primary name spelling (or another variant spelling) used by that person's ancestors and which is:
>
> • A name spelling that the person was known to have used, through signature evidence on wills, marriage bonds etc or other documents originating from the individual concerned, or
> • A name spelling used by officials on a consistent and persistent basis over a period of years.
>
> A deviant is any other spelling recorded, including cases where the spelling occurs in official records, but only randomly and inconsistently. Deviants will also include spellings derived from enumeration, transcription and indexing errors, both contemporary and modern.[14]

In practice, the boundaries between variant and deviant spellings will often become blurred, and especially when the research progresses into parish registers and then back into medieval records. The further back in time the research takes you, the greater the variety of spellings you will generally find. Consistent surname spellings often only began to be used from the beginning of the nineteenth century onwards and if there was no 'correct' spelling for a surname then there can be no 'deviant' spellings. The division of spellings into deviants and variants is, therefore, a more practical proposition when recording surnames from the nineteenth century onwards.

Spelling errors and mistranscriptions can occur at two different stages. A mistake can be made when the creator of the record misspells the name in the original record, which can occur when a vicar records a name in a parish register or when a scribe records a testator's wishes in a last will and testament. Further spelling errors can arise when original records are transcribed or indexed. The census forms for British censuses were filled in by the householder, and were only filled in by the census enumerator if the householder was illiterate or unable to fill in the form himself for some other reason. The census enumerator then copied these details into his own notebooks. The census records that have survived from 1841 to 1901 are the census enumerators' notebooks, not the original householders' schedules. These records are, therefore, already one stage removed from the original record. Further errors were introduced when these censuses were transcribed and indexed for publication on the Internet on websites like Ancestry and Findmypast. In contrast, for the 1911 census, it is the original householders' schedules that have survived, allowing us to see our ancestors' own handwriting on the census forms for the first time.

When searching indexes to censuses and other online datasets, the researcher will often find that a surname has its own characteristic mistranscriptions. I consistently find the name Tidbury mistranscribed as Sidbury in the censuses, and Cruwys is often transcribed as Crump. A Hempsall researcher reports that his surname commonly appears as Kempsall, while the surname Oates is often mistranscribed as Dates. It is useful to maintain a list of the deviant spellings – or mistranscriptions – of the surname you are researching (Table 1). After all, if you've found a surname mistranscribed in one record it's likely that it will be misspelt the same way in another record elsewhere. The main reason for failure to find someone in a census is usually because they are hiding under a previously unconsidered deviant spelling. With a certain amount of ingenuity and a lot of patience, missing people can usually be hunted down. William Benjamin Farmer Cruwys defied all initial attempts to be found in the 1901 census on Ancestry, but eventually turned up in Newport, Monmouthshire, with his surname indexed as Ommps! On looking at the census page the mistake is quite understandable and it would appear that the enumerator had in fact transcribed the surname incorrectly as Crumps. Thomas Faithfull and family were only found in the 1841 census by means of a careful search through the very faint images of the census pages for East Woodhay in Hampshire. His surname had been mistakenly indexed as Stuttefert! A transcription error can sometimes cause a person to be listed under the wrong surname altogether, as, for example, when a ditto sign is misinterpreted. The error could even originate on the original census page. I once spent a long time trying to find Thomas

Table 1. It is useful to maintain a list of deviant spellings found for the surname that you are researching. The list will help you to identify the letter sounds that are commonly misheard and the letters that are commonly mistranscribed. The two lists below are deviant spellings for the related surnames Cruse and Cruwys that have been collected by the author from censuses, General Register Office indexes, parish registers and various other sources. The list excludes misspellings that are legitimate surnames such as Crewe, Crews, Crewes, Cruice, Cruise and Cruze.

Deviant spellings of the surname Cruse

Amos, Ann, Anna, Aruse, Aure, Cause, Contes, Couse, Crase, Craske, Crass, Crease, Creede, Creese, Crewse, Crise, Crooce, Croos, Croose, Croosh, Crose, Crowse, Cru, Cruce, Crues, Crule, Crum, Crune, Cruser, Cruso, Crute, Cruye, Crvse, Cura, Curse, Curss, Cuss, Euse, Grise, Groves, Gruse, Guse, Oruso, Pruse, Ruse, Scruce, Trude

Deviant spellings of the surname Cruwys

Brewys, Cauwys, Cenings, Cenwys, Clewis, Coneys, Corewis, Cravys, Crawys, Creewys, Cremeys, Cremys, Crenny, Crenwys, Crerweys, Cressys, Creuse, Creuwys, Crewejs, Creweys, Crewse, Crewys, Crimmings, Crinorp, Crmoys, Crnwys, Crowys, Crucoys, Crues, Cruess, Cruings, Cruis, Cruiys, Cruloys, Crump, Crumys, Crungs, Crunys, Crurrys, Crurvys, Curoys, Crusse, Crurvys, Crusoys, Cruswys, Crute, Cruwiss, Cruwes, Cruwp, Cruwyd, Cruwyes, Cruyes, Cruyse, Cruyws, Crvwys, Crwoys, Crwes, Crwys, Crwwys, Crwye, Crys, Cumys, Curwis, Gemys, Gruwys, Le Crump, Omarys, Ommps, Oruwys

Hadlow and family in the 1901 census in London. It eventually transpired that the census enumerator had recorded his name as Hadlow Thomas rather than Thomas Hadlow. Ditto marks were used to record the surnames of his wife and children who were correctly listed with their given names first. Consequently, the transcriber quite rightly transcribed the whole family with the surname Thomas. There are also many people in the censuses who were living in institutions such as lunatic asylums who were recorded by their initials only. Sometimes an identity can be confirmed if the age, birthplace and occupation correspond to the missing person, but if only vague details are listed then a positive identification will not be possible without searching the relevant institutional records, if available. The various census providers each supply their own indexes. If someone does seem to have disappeared then they can sometimes be found in the index of an alternative provider.

Identifying variant and deviant spellings

As we have seen, changes in spelling and pronunciation can have a significant impact on the number of variant and deviant spellings associated with any given surname. All these factors present a challenge for the surname researcher starting out on a new surname study. First of all, there is the very practical problem of deciding which of the many possible spellings to research. Surname mapping (see Chapter 4) is a useful technique for checking the distribution of different variant spellings and there are many free tools available online. If two variant spellings are found in opposite parts of the country and with completely different distribution patterns then it is probably safe to assume that they are not related, and the research effort can then focus on the primary surname of interest. For all practical purposes, the variant spellings that need to be identified in the early stages of a surname study are variants that have survived to the present day. These are the variants that you will need to use when searching data collections or indexes, when advertising or promoting your surname study or when contacting living name-bearers. In order not to become too overwhelmed with data it is wise to restrict the number of variants collected in order to keep the workload at a manageable level, and especially when extracting references from large, easily accessible datasets. The study can easily be extended at a later date to include other variant spellings. However, if you have made a special visit to a distant record office to study records that are not available online then it would make sense to record all the possible variants while you have the opportunity. As research goes further back in time, the net has to be cast wider, and successful searches will require the identification of prior forms of the surname that are quite probably now extinct. Sometimes a reference to an alias will be found in a parish register or other document to provide definitive proof of a connection between two variants. As a surname study develops, it is usually possible to get a feel for the likely variant spellings simply by studying the matching variants that are generated when searching in the various online genealogical databases. However, there is no substitute for thorough genealogical research, tracing a line step by step back through each generation.

There are a number of tools that can be used as an aid to identify potential variants for a given surname. These tools might help the researcher to spot potential variants that have been overlooked or haven't been identified with other methods. Some of the tools can also be used to generate lists of deviant spellings or misspellings that could potentially be of use when trying to locate individuals who have previously eluded all attempts to find them in censuses and other large datasets. The various tools each have their own uses and the selection of the appropriate tools will very much depend on the individual surname that is being researched.

DNA testing

DNA testing can be an incredibly powerful tool for establishing whether or not two variant spellings are related, and the subject will be covered in more detail in Chapter 9. A DNA project provides an ideal opportunity to study a wider range of spellings in order to establish which variants are related. A fortuitous DNA match might also highlight connections between two seemingly unrelated surnames at an early stage of the research process. This situation is likely to become more commonplace as the DNA databases continue to grow in size. In my own DNA project an early match was found in America between the surnames Crews and Screws. In my Devon DNA project we discovered that the surnames Smale and Smalley were related, as were the surnames Widdecome and Withycombe. DNA testing does have to be used with caution. If two people with different variant spellings have closely matching DNA results, we can safely assume that the variants are related. However, if the results don't match it becomes more complicated and additional testing will be required to ensure that there has been no break in the link between the Y-chromosome and the surname. Furthermore, a potentially related variant can only be explored if a living name-bearer is available to test. Many early variant spellings have now become extinct.

Surname dictionaries and indexes

As your research progresses you will get a feel for the various spellings that are likely to be related. It is a useful practice to get in the habit of scanning through all the names in an index beginning with the first letter of your surname to see if there are any other variants that you might have missed. Surname dictionaries are a useful starting point as related variants will be grouped together, though different editors will not always be in agreement. The main surname dictionaries are listed in the Bibliography with links to many of the older dictionaries that are now available online in the Internet Archive.

For surnames that are found in Ireland, it will pay dividends to check the report by Robert Edwin Matheson, the former Registrar-General, on *Varieties and Synonymes of Surnames and Christian Names in Ireland* (1890, 1901). The report includes an alphabetical listing of selected surnames and for each surname a list of known variants and synonyms is provided. Matheson does not provide a comprehensive listing of all surnames found in Ireland and includes only those names that 'have been found to have been used interchangeably in the examination of the registration records, or that … have been reported to be so used by local officers'. The groupings are not always intuitive, as the following two randomly selected examples will demonstrate. The surname Coyne is listed with the variant names Barnacle, Coin, Kilcoyne, Kine and Kyne. The variant names found for the surname Quigley are Cogley, Kegley and Twigley.

Spelling substitution tables

The FamilySearch website has two very useful spelling substitution tables. One table provides a list of commonly misread letters. A second table provides a phonetics substitute table containing a list of vowels and consonants that might have been substituted when a record creator misunderstood what the informant had said. They are primarily designed for names in the United States and Canada but are equally useful for British surnames. Both tables can be found in the FamilySearch wiki at **http://tinyurl.com/spellingsphonetics**.

Selective substitution

The technique of 'selective substitution' was pioneered by Derek Palgrave, and is described in his landmark article in the *Journal of One-Name Studies* in 1984 (reprinted 2004).[15]

The known variant and deviant spellings of a surname are first identified. These variants are then split up into their constituent vowel and consonant sounds and listed in tabular form (Table 2). The resultant table can be examined to look for different permutations of previously unconsidered spellings. Andrew Millard has produced a very useful Excel spreadsheet that will automate the process and generate a list of all the permutations from the selected variants. The spreadsheet is available on GoogleDocs at **http://tinyurl.com/selectivesub**. It can either be edited online or downloaded to a computer for personal use. The selective substitution method is particularly effective for assessing the likely distortion of vowel and consonant sounds, enabling a more thorough scrutiny of the available databases. It does take a bit of practice to work out which combination of vowel and consonant sounds to use to generate likely variant spellings, but it is well worth the effort. The tool can be used when starting out on a surname study to assess the likely variants and it is also worth revisiting it when a more complete list of variants has been compiled to see if any possibilities have been overlooked. The tool can also be used to experiment with different permutations identified from the FamilySearch spelling substitution tables.

Table 2. The selective substitution method is used to represent optional spellings of the surname Palgrave in a concise tabular form illustrating the many possible permutations. They total more than half a million!

Optional spellings of Palgrave

P	U O I E A AR AU AW AY EA OW	LE LL (L) LD D	SE (S) Z X	GG G GGEG KE	R	E I O A AU AY IE	M M U V F FF W	A (E) T	(S)
I	II	6	5	4	I	7	7	4	2

Soundex

Soundex is a phonetic name-indexing system that was first patented back in 1918. A variation known as American Soundex was used in the 1930s for a retrospective analysis of the US censuses from 1880 onwards, and has since been used in many genealogy databases. Soundex uses a phonetic algorithm to group together similar-sounding surnames. Each surname group is allocated a unique numerical Soundex code. Although the Soundex system was state of the art when it was first introduced it is now somewhat primitive. It produces imprecise and unrelated matches but fails to detect genuine variants. Surnames that are pronounced the same but begin with different letters of the alphabet are assigned different Soundex codes, whereas unrelated surnames beginning with the same letter are grouped together. For example the surname Knowles is linked with the unrelated surnames Kanallakan and Kinlock, while the related variant Nowles has a different Soundex code altogether and is grouped with the surnames Nealis, Niles, Noles and Nowels.

There are now other tools, discussed below, that generate more plausible and accurate lists of variant spellings, but there are possibly some situations where Soundex could still provide clues to previously unconsidered variant spellings. A Soundex converter is available at **http://resources.rootsweb.ancestry.com/cgi-bin/soundexconverter**. This tool will provide the Soundex number for the surname and generate a list of all the other surnames sharing the same code. Dick Eastman has a useful article on his blog explaining how the Soundex system works: **http://blog.eogn.com/eastmans_ online_genealogy/2010/08/soundex-explained.html**.

A modified system for Jewish surnames, known as the Daitch-Mokotoff Soundex System, was developed in 1985 by Gary Mokotoff and this is now the standard indexing system used in all projects coordinated by Jewish genealogical organisations.[16]

Nominex

Nominex is a surname-matching system developed by British genealogist Stephen Archer, who is better known for his popular *British 19th Century Surname Atlas* CD (see p.80). The Nominex system was used in the surname search algorithms for the third edition of the *National Burial Index for England and Wales*. A demo version of Nominex, using names extracted from the *National Burial Index*, is available at **www.archersoftware.co.uk/ nominex**. The demo program can be used to generate a very useful and plausible list of variant spellings for any given surname, and is the tool of choice for checking variants of British surnames. The results are presented in ranked order from an exact match (100 per cent) down to an 80 per cent match.

The Name Thesaurus

The Name Thesaurus is a tool for finding variant spellings for both surnames and given names. It was developed by the British software company Image Partners and uses a proprietary technique called NameX.[17] Demo versions of the Surname Thesaurus and the Forename Thesaurus can be found at **www.namethesaurus.com** and

www.origins.net/namex/NameXSearch.aspx. A surname search provides three lists of variants ranked in percentages by match scores. The first list uses the NameX technology to provide more accurate matches. Two further lists are generated using the Soundex system and the Metaphone system, an improved version of Soundex. Soundex and Metaphone produce much lengthier lists, with many more irrelevant and unrelated spellings. The Surname Thesaurus contains 385,147,453 entries for 5,929,381 distinct surnames. Many of these 'surnames' are, however, mistranscriptions rather than genuine surnames. The Name Thesaurus is particularly helpful for non-British surnames that are not included in Nominex. It is also a potentially useful tool for casting the net wider in order to find further potential variants or to identify possible mistranscriptions in genealogy databases.

Standard Finder

Standard Finder is a free experimental utility provided by the Church of Jesus Christ of Latter-day Saints as part of its FamilySearch Labs project. The tool can be found at **https://labs.familysearch.org/stdfinder/NameStandardLookup.jsp**. Searches can be done on names, locations and dates. Name searches can be worldwide or restricted to specific cultures. The resultant list of surnames is quite short, but users can provide feedback to improve the system, and it could potentially develop into a very useful resource.

WeRelate variant names project

A new open source variant surnames project was launched in February 2012 as a collaborative venture between WeRelate, Ancestry and BehindTheName. A searchable variants database is hosted on the WeRelate wiki. A search generates a list of variant spellings for each surname or given name that has been indexed. Users are encouraged to remove non-matching names from the list, tick additional boxes or submit their own additional variants as appropriate. The project took as its starting point a database provided by Ancestry, which was supplemented with a list of given name variants provided by BehindTheName. Ancestry and WeRelate worked together to create the initial algorithm for the database to find similarly spelt names for the 200,000 most frequent surnames and the 70,000 most common given names. This includes every name that appears more than once in every 5 million names in Ancestry's database. The success of the project will depend on how many people contribute their knowledge, but it could also potentially develop into a very valuable resource over time. The database can be found at **www.werelate.org/wiki/Special:Names**.

Case studies

The study of variants is an ongoing process that requires diligent genealogical research over a long period of time. A few real-life case studies will help to demonstrate some of the difficulties that can be encountered when researching a specific surname and the potentially large range of variant spellings that will sometimes need to be considered, though not all surnames will turn out to be quite so complicated.

Phillimore and Fynmore

A very early and interesting surname study was published in the nineteenth century by the genealogist, publisher and solicitor William P.W. Phillimore (1853–1931), who is probably best known today for the publishing company that bears his name and the numerous volumes of Phillimore Marriage Registers which he transcribed and edited. Phillimore's life-long interest in genealogy began while he was a student at Oxford, where he made full use of the extensive collections in the Bodleian Library. After leaving Oxford, he practised as a solicitor in London. His office was conveniently located in Chancery Lane, close to the old Public Record Office. *The Family of Fynmore*, published in 1886, was a study of the surname Fynmore but also included a large group of related spellings such as Fynmore, Finnimore, Phillimore, Fillmore, and Filmer, which he noted were 'remarkable for numerous variations in spelling, by which their real origin has been much obscured'. The surnames are found in southern England, principally in Berkshire, Wiltshire, Hampshire, Gloucestershire and Devon. Fennymere has its origins in Shropshire, and Filmer is a variant form seen in Sussex and Kent. Phillimore documented 122 different spellings in the various sources he researched, with an astonishingly diverse range of variants such as Venmore, Binmore, Pilmoor, Belmer, Billamore, Filyemore and Fynymour. In the registers for Cam in Gloucestershire, he discovered that the forms Phinimore and Phillimore were used interchangeably until 1680, when Phinimore appeared for the last time and Phillimore became the accepted spelling. The forms Fenemore and Venemore were found to exist side by side in Oxfordshire. In Netheravon, Wiltshire, he cited the example of 'Phineas Philamore alias Fennymore' who 'in 1731 was party to a conveyance, which, he, however, signed as Phillomour'. Phillimore set an admirable example by publishing a list of all the different spellings 'to illustrate the difficulties attending an enquiry into the history of a surname of so changeable a form'. The list was subdivided into ten different phonetic groups or 'divisions'. He made a study of the Registers of Births for the period of 1877–81, noting the number of occurrences of each of the variant spellings, and recording the totals in the variant list. He found the most numerous spellings at that time to be Filmer, Phillimore, Finnemore, Fenemore and Finnemore. Many of the variant spellings he found were medieval forms that were by then obsolete. He noted that: 'The tendency seems to be for the lesser varieties to approximate to or adopt the spelling used by the most important family of the division to which they belong.'[18]

Rubery

Polly Rubery has been researching her family history for over thirty-five years and has specialised in a one-name study of the Herefordshire surname Rowberry. Polly encountered a wide range of spellings in the parish registers when researching her own

Rubery line, and the fortuitous discovery of an alias eventually led her research in an unexpected direction.

Polly had successfully been able to trace her line back to her great-great-great-grandfather, George Rubery, who died in 1845 in Bristol. His death certificate led her to his army records, which gave his birthplace as Hereford around 1773. A baptism was found at Hereford St Martin in 1773 for a George Rowberry, the son of Thomas and Mary. The research had then stalled because Polly had been unable to find a record of the marriage of George's parents. However, she had noticed that a Thomas and Ann *Robry* had baptised a daughter, Kate, in the same parish three years previously. As George had baptised his first daughter Catherine Rubery at Reading St Mary in Berkshire in 1800, it seemed likely that Kate was his sister and that Ann and Mary were one and the same person. However, a Thomas and Ann marriage also proved elusive. That problem was eventually solved when Polly was able to scan the Herefordshire Marriage Index at the Herefordshire Record Office and noted a marriage in 1755 in Eaton Bishop between Thomas *Robey* and Ann Parry in 1755, a spelling that had not been considered in a previous search of the index and that is not found in any other record for this family. A baptism for Thomas was then found in Thruxton in 1731, where he was described in the parish register as 'the son of John and Elizabeth Robery', but the research once again came to a halt because there appeared to be no record of their marriage. The breakthrough came in 1997 when Polly received a contact from Linda Hansen who was born in New Zealand but was living in Switzerland. Linda told Polly that she was descended from a family in Woolhope, Herefordshire, who, when they first appeared in the parish registers in the late 1600s, were recorded as 'Rowberry or Gomberry'. Both surnames were used interchangeably by this family right through until the early years of civil registration. With this new information Polly was eventually able to locate the marriage of John *Gumry* and Elizabeth Jones in 1720 in Holmer and a baptism for a John *Gomberry* in 1692 in Woolhope. It eventually transpired that she and Linda were sixth cousins once removed.

The research has since been confirmed by DNA testing. Y-chromosome DNA tests were done on a descendant of Henry Rubery and a modern-day Gummery. The two results matched very closely, confirming that the two men shared a common ancestor. The reason for the use of the alias has not yet been discovered, as unfortunately both surnames seem to originate just across the county border in Worcestershire, in the Tenbury area, where the early parish registers are lost and the post-1660 ones were badly damaged in a flood of 1770.

The full sequence of events can be seen in the following extracts from the parish registers and other records:

1692 John, son of Thomas and Elizabeth GOMBERRY baptised in Woolhope, Herefordshire
The parish registers give the parents of John's two eldest brothers, one of whom died in infancy, as GOMBERRY. Baptisms of the later siblings describe them as 'ROWBER(R)Y or GOMBER(R)Y' and 'ROWBERRY alias GOMMERY'.

1720 John GUMRY 'of Bridge Sollers' married Elizabeth Jones 'of Madley' in Holmer, Herefordshire

1731 Thomas, son of John and Elizabeth was baptised at Thruxton, Herefordshire
The parish register entry has ROBERY, but this surname has clearly been added over a deletion in the original (the parchment having been scraped). The bishop's transcripts give the surname as GOMERY.

1755 Thomas ROBEY married Ann PARRY at Eaton Bishop, Herefordshire
The children of Thomas and Ann were baptised as ROBERY, ROBRY and ROBREY, the last one being Kate ROBRY at Hereford St Martin in 1770.

1773 George, son of Thomas and Mary ROWBERRY, baptised at Hereford St Martin

1793 George RUBERRY enlisted in the Army in 1793 in Birmingham, giving his age as 20 and his birthplace as Hereford

1799 George RUBERY married Sarah NEWBURY at Caversham, Berkshire
Their children were baptised with the surnames RUBERY, ROWBREY and REWBERRY

1845 George RUBERY died in Bristol in 1845 aged 76

The discovery of a link with a seemingly completely different surname poses a particular challenge for the researcher. Polly did begin to wonder if she should really have been doing a Gomery one-name study, but she eventually managed to persuade Linda Hansen to do a one-name study of the Gomery surname instead. However, the DNA project that Polly set up includes both surnames and all the related variants.[19]

Sunley

Cecil Humphery-Smith, the genealogist and heraldist and the founder of the Institute of Heraldic and Genealogical Studies in Canterbury, Kent, shared with John Titford the extraordinary findings from a research project on the Sunley surname. The initial research efforts stalled because of a failure to take account of all the possible variants:

> The task was to trace the male-line ancestry of a man named James Sunley, son of Thomas Sunley of Thornton-le-Moor, who was baptised at North Otterington, Yorkshire, on 9th May 1824. A good deal of time was wasted in tracing an unrelated Sunley family … before the full story emerged. The surname of Thomas, the father of James Sunley, was given as Sunler, when he married Ann Wright by banns in 1823, and this Thomas himself, born in Newby and baptised at Kirby Wiske in 1803, was the third child of Isaac Sumner and Elizabeth (née Morland), who had married in 1796.[20]

As the research went further back in time, the name mutated again from Sumner to Summer. In earlier records the name was recorded as Somers. A surname evolution from Sunley to Somers could not have been anticipated at the outset of the research and was only proven by careful genealogical research.

Mitchelmore

Michael Mitchelmore from Sydney, Australia, first encountered the concept of variant spellings many years ago when searching the indexes at Somerset House in London for the birth of his great-grandfather. He came across a marginal note next to the Mitchelmore surname that said 'see also Michamore', which was exactly where he found him. An earlier ancestor used the spelling Michelmore and prior to that there were three generations of Muchamores.

Michael has since collected over 100 variant spellings of his surname. The earliest reference dates back to the thirteenth century when the name Richard de Muchelmore was recorded near Malborough, Devon, in 1243. Gradually, Mitchelmore and Michelmore became the two most common spellings, as they still are today. The spelling Muchmore originated in Cornwall and is still found quite often in England. By contrast, Muchamore was at one time common in the southern South Hams in Devon but is now quite rare, though the name is now familiar in the UK through the works of the children's writer Robert Muchamore, whose books have encouraged a love of reading in a new generation of teenage boys.

The most common spelling in North America, where the surname goes back to the seventeenth century, is now Muchmore (sometimes Muchemore), but there are also a fair number of Mitchelmores and Michelmores. The variants Mitchamore and Mitchmore are only common in the USA and can be traced back to three brothers, William, Richard and John Mitchelmore, who emigrated from East Allington, Devon, to Galveston, Texas, in 1872. William registered his children under the surname Mitchamore but Richard used Mitchmore, the shorter version of the name. Emigration has also preserved the unusual variant Mouchemore. It was carried to Australia in the nineteenth century when Daniel Mouchemore emigrated from Dartmouth in Devon to Melbourne, Victoria. Australia is the only country where the surname Mouchemore is to be found.

A DNA project was started in 2008 and, although the project is still in its infancy, the initial results show that the majority of the Mitchelmore trees from the southern South Hams share a common ancestor and suggest that they may have a common ancestor with the Michelmores from the northern South Hams.[21]

4

SURNAME MAPPING

I have been much impressed in my investigations with the manner in which surnames, scattered apparently indiscriminately over the country, fall into order and disclose in their arrangement a method and regularity which render their distribution a subject of curious interest both for the antiquarian and the historian, and sometimes, I may say, for the ethnologist.

Henry Brougham Guppy, *Homes of Family Names in Great Britain*
(Harrison and Sons, 1890), p. 5

Every surname has its own unique distribution pattern. Rare surnames will often cluster in a particular location near their point of origin. They will slowly diffuse over time into neighbouring areas and the large industrial conurbations. Even today, with increasing mobility, many of these rare surnames can still be found close to the place where they originated. Even the very common surnames do not have an even distribution pattern. The Joneses predominate in Wales, the Campbells in Scotland, the Sullivans in Ireland, and the Johnsons in England. Even Smith, the most common surname in both Britain and America, has its own distinctive pattern, being much less common in Wales and the south-west than elsewhere (Figure 9).

Mapping a surname at different points in time can provide clues to the home of a family name and the migratory routes of the name-bearers. The visual representation of a surname on a map can reveal patterns that are difficult to detect in spreadsheets and databases. Spatial relationships, such as migrations along the paths of major roads or rivers, are more easily discerned. Mapping is also a very useful tool to investigate variant spellings in order to decide which variants to include in your surname study.

There are now many websites that will provide free distribution maps of thousands of different surnames. The maps on these sites are a good starting point for a surname study and will provide a focus for the research in the areas where the name is predominantly found, and help to gauge the size of the task ahead. For more advanced researchers, there are also a number of commercially available websites and tools that can generate maps based on an underlying dataset or that can be used to input your own data and create your own maps. Maps can be plotted either using the *absolute* numbers – the actual number of events – or the *relative* distribution – the distribution in relation to the total population. If the data is not normalised to the region's population, heavily populated areas such as

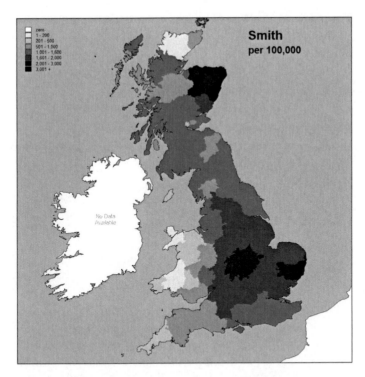

Figure 9. Smith is the most common surname in both Britain and America, but has its own distinctive distribution pattern in the 1881 census, being much less common in Wales and the south-west than elsewhere. The lack of Smiths in Cornwall is accounted for by the language difference. The Cornish word for Smith is Angove (*an* 'the' and *gof* 'smith'). The surname Angove is confined to Cornwall in 1881.

London and Manchester are exaggerated. The best utilities will provide options to view the data using both absolute and relative distributions.

History

It has long been recognised that some surnames cluster in specific regions or counties. There is an old Cornish rhyme, dating back at least to the early seventeenth century, which describes the distinctive elements of Cornish surnames:

> By Tre, Ros, Pol, Lan, Caer, *and* Pen,
> *You may know the most* Cornish *men.*[1]

Reverend George Oliver, writing in the *Gentleman's Magazine* in 1830, recognised that many surnames were only found in specific counties and cited the examples of the rare

surnames Ellerker, Legard and Wilberforce, which are 'peculiar to the county of York';
Carruthers and Burnside from the North of England; Poynder and Thwaite from
Lancashire; Tryce from Worcestershire; and Poyzer from Derbyshire.[2] Mark Antony Lower,
in the second volume of *English Surnames*, published in 1849, devoted a whole chapter to
'Provincialisms in surnames' and commented:

> Some counties and districts have peculiar surnames, which are rarely found beyond their
> limits. These are often of the local class, and the tenacity with which they cleave to the soil
> which gave them birth is truly remarkable.

He noted that names ending in *-hurst* (meaning wood), *-field* and *-den* were particularly
common in Kent and Sussex, whereas names ending in *-combe* were a 'favourite termination'
in Devon. He also cited an old folk proverb regarding the prevalence of certain surnames
in Cheshire, where there are:

> As many Leighs as fleas, Massies as asses, and
> Davenports as dogs' tails.[3]

The first attempt to plot a surname on a map seems to have been made by the historian
William P.W. Phillimore in 1886. His self-published book *The Family of Fynmore* included
as a frontispiece a wonderful hand-drawn map showing the distribution of the variant
spellings of the surname in the southern counties of England (Figure 10).

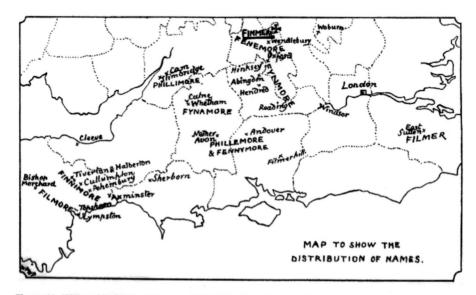

Figure 10. William P.W. Phillimore's map of the distribution of the surname Fynmore and variant spellings was
published in 1886 and is seemingly the first surname distribution map to appear in print.

Henry Brougham Guppy

The first person to consider the relative distributions of surnames was Henry Brougham Guppy (1854–1926), whose pioneering work, *Homes of Family Names in Great Britain* (1890), laid the foundations for all future surname geographers. Guppy was a respected botanist and geologist who spent his working life studying the flora, fauna and coral reef formations in a number of Pacific islands, but who also took a particular interest in surname distribution. He set out to 'ascertain the homes of familiar surnames and to ascertain the characteristic surnames of each county'.

   For the purposes of his survey, Guppy extracted the names of farmers from the Kelly's Post Office Directories for all the English counties. He devised a system using proportional numbers to represent the relative frequency per 10,000 of the farmers in each county, and he only noted names that 'exceeded, in their relative frequency, a rate of about seven per ten thousand amongst the farmers of that county'. Farmers were chosen because they were considered to be 'the most stable section of the community, both in the present as well as in the past', with their land being passed down from father to son and often remaining in the hands of the same family for five or six generations. Guppy divided the surnames into six different categories:

1. *General names*, occurring in from 30 to 40 counties
2. *Common names*, occurring in from 20 to 29 counties
3. *Regional names*, occurring in from 10 to 19 counties
4. *District names*, occurring in from 4 to 9 counties
5. *County names*, which are established in 2 or 3 counties, and have usually their principal home in one of them
6. *Peculiar names*, which are mostly confined to one county, and generally to a particular parish or division in that county

Guppy provided an alphabetical listing of all the more common names in England and Wales that fell into his first three categories with a description of their distribution patterns. He then provided geographical listings of surnames by county, with counts of all the surnames found in each county divided into the six separate classes. The survey was supplemented by snippets of information on county surnames extracted mostly from published sources such as county and parish histories. Wales, unfortunately, was not divided into counties but split into North and South Wales, with Monmouthshire treated as an English county. Surnames in Scotland were discussed separately in a brief appendix. Guppy identified seven distinct 'sub-kingdoms' in Britain based on the distribution of names, which he labelled: Caledonia, Lothian, Northumbria, Mercia, Anglia, Devonia and Wales. He found the highest proportion of 'peculiar names' in Devon and Cornwall, where they constituted around 40 per cent of the total.

   Guppy himself recognised the limitations of his work, which he said 'cannot be regarded as other than a preliminary exploration, or as the exemplification of a method'. He has been somewhat unfairly criticised by later researchers, and by Reaney in particular, who compared Guppy's lists with medieval lists for the same counties and found marked differences, with many of the names given by Guppy missing entirely from the early lists. However, it is now recognised that many of the names that appear in those early records are bynames that never developed into hereditary surnames. We know from the research of David Hey and George Redmonds, and from the experience of family historians, that nineteenth-century distribution patterns can often be a reliable indicator of the origin of a surname. Guppy's sampling was crude by today's standards, but his methodology was sound and his instincts were correct. With the benefit of hindsight it seems extraordinary that, for the greater part of the twentieth century, surname writers ignored Guppy's work and instead expended much time and energy in attempting to classify surnames into arbitrary categories based on presumed surname origins, which were in many cases derived from false etymologies, whereas a regional classification would have been of much more practical benefit as a pointer for future research.

Frank Leeson

Guppy's work was not followed through until the 1960s when surname researchers began to experiment with maps based on data from telephone directories and birth indexes. The genealogist Frank Leeson published what was probably the first ever article on the subject of surname distribution in the *Genealogists' Magazine* in December 1964. He explained:

> An obvious use for single-surname records is plotting of the distribution and movements of bearers of a name or name-sound as a means of indicating or confirming its geographical or etymological origins, multiple or otherwise, and its subsequent spread and intensity. The latter information can be of interest to demographers and social historians, and even of practical value to record searchers faced with an otherwise random search for a holder of a certain name.

Leeson plotted distribution maps of the 'surname-sounds' of Lee and Leeson. Births were extracted from the General Register Office indexes for 1850 for the Lee surname-sounds: Lea, Lee, Leese, Legh, Leigh and Ley. Births for the less common Leeson-sound surnames – Leason, Leeson, Leesing and Leesam – were collected from 1841 through to 1880 and mapped in ten-year blocks. Many of the variants were found to have their own distinctive distribution patterns. The distribution of Leeson-sound surnames was also studied in 1962 by extracting names from telephone directories. The distribution was found to be very similar to the nineteenth-century birth maps, though the rural nuclei in Northamptonshire and Lincolnshire had disappeared and there was a general drift to the south-east. He concluded: 'It seems that as a pilot distribution study telephone directories, easily accessible in any reference library, have something to recommend them.'[4]

George Redmonds

Telephone directories continued to be the staple of distribution studies throughout the 1960s and 1970s. George Redmonds included hand-drawn distribution maps with names taken from telephone directories in *Yorkshire, West Riding*, the first volume of the *English Surname Series*, published in 1973, though sadly the later volumes in this series did not continue the practice.

Surnames and genetic structure

In parallel with the work of genealogists and surname historians, from the 1960s onwards, human biologists, anthropologists and geneticists began to investigate the use of surname models to study the genetic structure of populations and to measure the gene flow between populations. The frequency of marriages between two people sharing the same surname (isonymy) was studied in an attempt to measure the amount of inbreeding within populations. Gabriel Ward Lasker (1912–2002), an English-born anatomist and anthropologist working at Wayne State University in Detroit, Michigan, published a number of the key surname studies of this period, many of which were in collaboration with C.G. Nicholas Mascie-Taylor, who worked in the Department of Biological Anthropology at the University of Cambridge.

In 1983 Lasker and his colleague Bernice Kaplan from Wayne State University studied the distribution of surnames derived from place-names. They extracted 13,209 listings for ninety-seven selected surnames from telephone directories that were in use in the summer of 1981. They found that: 'The distribution shows a tendency to some association [with the place-name] even after the whole span of time since the surnames were established in the Middle Ages.' However, the centres of high frequency were not always associated with the place where the name was thought to have arisen, and there were some intriguing anomalies. For example, there were appreciably fewer people of the corresponding surnames than would be expected at random in some places such as Sheffield, Birmingham and Derby. In contrast, high frequencies of some surnames were found at a considerable distance from the putative origin. There were more Bromleys than expected in Manchester, and more Yorks and Yorkes than anticipated in Birmingham. Kaplan and Lasker concluded:

> There is a tendency for surnames from place names to be found at or near the place from which the name was derived. Although the increased likelihood averages close to 100%, the great majority of persons with such surnames are now resident in a general distribution throughout the country. The distributions are not even; there are scattered areas of high and low frequencies. This unevenness of distribution ... is interesting because it contrasts with the usual pattern of distribution of genetic polymorphisms. In a study of the distribution of landholding farmers in the late 19th century, Guppy (1890) pointed out foci of high frequency of specific surnames in particular parts of the country. This pattern still holds in the late 20th century. Although more persons with these surnames than would be expected at random are at or near the place where the surnames probably originated, most such foci

of elevated frequency are scattered about the country. It seems apparent that no matter how many generations elapse, and after all associations with the original places of concentration have been lost, a very irregular pattern of geographic distribution will remain ...[5]

For some of their other interesting studies, Lasker and colleagues used a computerised dataset of all marriages in England and Wales for the first three months of 1975, which was acquired from the Registrar-General's office. Marriage records were chosen because in human population genetics it is the 'breeding population' that is of primary interest, and surnames were used as a 'biological marker' as a proxy for genes. Many of the individuals in birth and death records would never marry and would, therefore, never enter the breeding population. The dataset of marriages from 1975 yielded 32,457 different surnames. Rare surnames – those that occurred at a rate of 1 to 6 per 100,000 – accounted for 93 per cent of the surnames in the listings. It was found that the rarer the surname, the more likely it was to be localised and to recur in the same registration district. The probability of being listed in the same district decreased with increasing frequency of the same surname.[6]

In a 1984 study Mascie-Taylor and Lasker analysed the distribution of Smiths and Joneses in Great Britain from their sample of marriages in 1975. They found that:

> Jones is not only more frequent in Wales, but also tends to be frequent in nearby places in England, such as the Liverpool region, and declines to the north, south and east as far as London. Furthermore, even a generally distributed English surname, Smith, shows significant clines – albeit less pronounced ones – sloping down to lower frequencies from a high point at intermediate latitudes in the east of England. The patterns are essentially the same as those reported by Guppy so the distribution of the names may have been relatively unchanged since nearly a century ago.[7]

In a 1985 study using the same dataset, Mascie-Taylor and Lasker analysed the distribution of eighty-four common surnames in England and Wales and found distinctive geographical patterning. For this analysis they only used surnames that yielded samples of 200 or more. They concluded that: 'With samples sizes from 200 to 2,198 of each surname, almost all surnames have patterns of geographic distribution significantly different from that of a random sample of persons of all surnames.' Welsh surnames showed particularly strong groupings with specific surnames characteristic of North and South Wales. A distinct group of north of England surnames was found, including most notably those that end in -son.[8]

Lasker's 1985 book *Surnames and Genetic Structure* was a landmark in the history of surname mapping as it was the first publication to use computer-generated surname distribution maps. The appendix of this book features maps and distribution diagrams for 100 common surnames in England and Wales, with the data again taken from the dataset of marriages from 1975. The distribution patterns were compared with Guppy's descriptions of the same surnames from 1890. It is striking that many of the patterns detected by Guppy still persisted eighty-five years later. The main text of the book comprises a review of the history of surname studies in human biology and an evaluation of the key findings from the published literature. A formula known as the Lasker Distance is now used by geographers in comparative studies of regions and their surnames. The Lasker Distance is defined as 'a measure of similarity, or difference, between two populations in surname space … The greater the Lasker Distance the less similar the composition of surnames in the two geographic areas.'[9]

Lasker and Mascie-Taylor published a further selection of surname distribution maps in 1990 in their *Atlas of British Surnames*. The 154 maps featured in the *Atlas* were computer-generated from data collected from telephone directories. Most of the datasets were supplied by members of the Guild of One-Name Studies, and many of the maps were accompanied by brief comments about the origin or history of the surname provided by the Guild member who submitted the data. The title of the *Atlas* was somewhat misleading as there was no coverage of Scotland. The coverage of Wales was also very limited, with the whole of mid-Wales being covered by the Shrewsbury phone directory and south-west Wales by the Swansea directory. Despite the limitations of the data sources, the maps clearly demonstrated the great diversity and unique distribution patterns of British surnames, though as the authors commented: 'Ultimately the explanations of the distributions lie in the histories.'

The Surname Detective

The 1990s saw the publication of two seminal works in the history of surname distribution. The first of these, *The Surname Detective* by Colin D. Rogers, was published in 1995. Rogers investigated the distribution of 100 English surnames from 1086 to the present day. The book is split into three parts, each of which is liberally illustrated with surname distribution maps. In the first part, Rogers studied the distribution of surnames in the present day using modern telephone directories. The second part is concerned with the historical distribution of surnames in the last 500 years in order to see how much the surnames had been affected by geographical mobility, while the final section deals with the distribution of surnames in the medieval period. At the end of the exercise Rogers was able to conclude:

> With a few exceptions, common surnames of all types still appear to be concentrated where they were six hundred years ago. Furthermore, as there is nothing unusual about the hundred names investigated, the expectation is that this broad generalisation is true of most of the others.[10]

Some of the sources used by Rogers, such as telephone directories, would no longer be the sources of choice now that we have so many more records such as the censuses and civil registration indexes easily available online. However, the methodology employed by Rogers was sound and forms the basis for all modern surname studies. His book is still a worthwhile read because he highlights in detail the issues involved in selecting sources for surname distributions and the methods used to plot the distributions.

The Surnames of Wales

The second pioneering book from the 1990s is *The Surnames of Wales* (1996) by the family historians John and Sheila Rowlands, who had been researching their family history for many years and had been actively involved in transcribing and indexing documents. During the course of their research they had become aware of the local characteristics of Welsh surnames, and were curious to see if the patterns they had seen were also evident elsewhere. John and Sheila Rowlands decided to undertake a major survey of all the surnames recorded in the marriage registers of Wales between 1813 and 1837. They had already compiled indexes of marriages in Cardiganshire and Pembrokeshire for this period, and some indexes were available from other sources. The remaining information was extracted from the parish registers and bishop's transcripts at the National Library of Wales, a process that took them almost two years to complete. The survey yielded a total of 135,880 marriages and 271,591 surname records (the numbers do not tally because in a few instances no surname was recorded for one of the marriage partners). The period chosen was from a time when settled surnames were the norm in most parts of Wales, and the sample size covered a sufficiently lengthy period to ensure that it would give a good representation of the pool of surnames in each area. The book provided a fascinating insight into the diversity and regional distribution of surnames in Wales and showed that even common Welsh surnames have their own unique distribution patterns. For example, the incidence of the surname Jones, the most common surname in Wales, was found to be as high as 30 per cent in parts of North Wales, but as low as 1 per cent in some areas of South Wales. Beyond the small number of surnames that were present throughout Wales or only occasionally absent, John and Sheila Rowlands found that there were many names that had 'a strong regional presence which readily identified them with a particular part of Wales', and a few surnames that had a strong local presence. However, they noted that: 'the vast majority of individual surnames occurred only infrequently (often only a single occurrence within a hundred) and could not be considered as "having a presence", even at this relatively local level.' The book has a glossary with descriptions of over 250 of the surnames found in the survey and statistics on their incidence in Wales, and there are nearly forty maps showing the distribution of the more interesting surnames.

Surname regions

The first census to be made available as a complete transcribed and computerised dataset was the 1881 census, which was issued on CD in 1999 by the Church of Jesus Christ of Latter-day Saints (LDS). The 1881 census covered England, Wales, Scotland, the Channel Islands and the Isle of Man, and provided a complete listing of the population on the night of 3/4 April 1881. Although all the other British censuses have now been transcribed and made available online, the 1881 census is regarded as the most accurate in terms of its transcription quality. A team of dedicated volunteer genealogists from the Genealogical Society of Utah and family history societies throughout the UK worked on the transcriptions, whereas the work on many of the other censuses has been outsourced, often to overseas organisations that do not have the same local knowledge of place-names and surnames. The 1881 census has been used in a number of academic studies that have provided valuable insight into the distribution of British surnames.

Kevin Schürer, a professor of history at the University of Essex, embarked on a study of the 1881 census to see if surnames could be used to identify historical and cultural regions, and the results were published in 2004 in the journal *Local Population Studies*. For the purposes of his study, Schürer only used census data from England and Wales. The data was then further processed in order to standardise and classify the information and, most importantly, to link it to a parish-based geographical information system (GIS) so that the data could be mapped. The paper investigated issues such as surname density (the number of people per surname), and the separation distances of surnames (whether or not surnames clustered together in the same region or were spread out over a wide area). Schürer found marked regional contrasts, which to a large extent reflected customs relating to the origin of surnames. He also used a statistical technique known as cluster analysis to group together parishes with similar pools of surnames. The analysis was performed first on the top 1,000 surnames ranked nationally and, secondly, on the surnames ranked from 2,000 to 7,500. For both sets of surnames distinct surname regions were found. The paper was illustrated with fourteen striking colour maps that graphically demonstrated the regional differences. Two particularly revealing maps illustrate the differences in the distribution of patronymic and metronymic surnames ending in -*son* and the possessive -*s*. The -*son* surnames predominate in the north of England and -*s* surnames are concentrated in the south and particularly in Wales.[11]

With the increasing availability of digitally encoded name-rich datasets, surnames have now begun to attract the interest of geographers, and a new science of surname geography has evolved. Surname studies are being used to provide insight into the structure of populations, to study patterns of migration and to quantify the social and ethnic mixing within populations. The Centre for Advanced Spatial Analysis (CASA) and the Department of Geography at University College London (UCL) have been at the forefront of this research in the UK. The UCL researchers have published a number of interesting papers on surname mapping, and their research has also produced two very useful tools for family historians, the Great Britain Names Public Profiler and the World Names Profiler, which will be discussed later in this chapter. The comprehensive CASA working paper, 'Family Names as Indicators of Britain's Regional Geography', is a good introduction to the research. The paper looks at the surname regions of Britain, discusses the methodology in detail and provides a review of the literature. The paper also includes some very interesting maps.[12]

For the basis of many of their studies, the UCL researchers are using an enhanced version of the 2001 electoral register, which represents the 45.6 million people who were resident in the UK during October 2001. In a study published in 2010 in the *Journal of Maps*, Cheshire, Longley and Singleton used this dataset to explore the surname geography of Britain. A computer program was used to cluster the surnames together based on their distances from each other, and the results were plotted on a map. 'The

Surname Map of Great Britain', which accompanies the published paper, demonstrates very clearly the different surname regions, with Britain being split up into ten distinct regions. The south-west of England and Scotland both formed distinct regions. There was a clear divide in Wales, with the areas under English influence clustering into a separate region from the rest of Wales. The north-west and north-east of England formed another distinct region. There was a clear division between the West Midlands and the East Midlands, while the surnames in southern and south-eastern England formed one big mass. London, Birmingham and Leicester were all grouped into one region, largely as a consequence of the large number of 'non-British surnames' found in these places.[13] A more detailed and technical analysis of the data was published in *Geoforum* in 2011. It is interesting to note that even after the passage of over 100 years the surname regions identified using modern data correlate very closely with the surname regions proposed by Guppy in 1890.[14] Cheshire, Mateos and Longley used the same clustering techniques to explore the surname regions of Europe using data extracted from electoral registers and telephone directories for sixteen European countries.[15]

A surname map of Ireland

An innovative approach to the display of surname data was adopted by cartographers Kenneth Field and Linda Beale. They produced a visually stunning map showing the distribution of surnames in Ireland in 1890. The actual surnames were used to plot the distribution and the size of the font was adjusted in proportion to the number of people with each surname. Special software was used to disperse the surname markers and ensure that the names did not overlap. An article describing the methodology used was published in the *Journal of Maps* in 2010, and a high-resolution poster-sized version of the map can be downloaded free of charge.[16]

Germany

A six-year project at the universities of Freiburg and Mainz in Germany has looked at the distribution of surnames in Germany based on telephone directory data provided by Deutsche Telekom AG. A paper entitled 'The German Surname Atlas Project – Computer-Based Surname Geography', presented at the thirteenth International Congress of Onomastic Sciences, which includes a number of interesting maps, can be found online at **http://pi.library.yorku.ca/dspace/handle/10315/3961**.

Mapping resources

A number of useful websites and mapping tools are now available that can be used to map the distribution of a surname in various countries around the world. The datasets that are used to generate the maps all have their limitations but, nevertheless, these websites can provide a useful preliminary survey for the researcher who is starting out on the study of a surname, will help to indicate the countries and regions where more localised research is likely to be the most productive, and will also help to gauge the size of the task ahead.

Worldwide distribution

The World Names Public Profiler (**http://worldnames.publicprofiler.org**) is an outreach website created by Paul Longley and Pablo Mateos from the Department of Geography at University College London (UCL) and Alex Singleton from the University of Liverpool. The Profiler can be used to generate distribution maps and tables for over 8 million surnames in twenty-six different countries, with a particular emphasis on European surnames. The data the maps are derived from is mostly obtained from publicly available telephone directories and electoral registers from the period 2000–05.

Map Your Name (**www.mapyourname.com**) is a collaboration between three companies: OriginsInfo, Experian and Geowise. The software company OriginsInfo developed the website, the data was sourced from files held by the information company Experian, and Geowise provided the geographical data visualisation software. The website uses data from twelve countries: Australia, Denmark, France, Germany, Ireland, Italy, the Netherlands, Norway, Spain, Sweden, the USA and the UK. The datasets used to generate the maps are not defined, though they are likely to include modern telephone directories and electoral registers. Maps can be generated showing the distribution in Europe, Australia and the USA of any of the 60,000 or so most common surnames in these countries.

The subscription website Ancestry provides a number of free surname distribution maps. The maps are included in the 'What's in a name?' widget on the homepage of Ancestry subscribers, but can be accessed by non-subscribers at **www.ancestry.com/ learn/facts**. A map can be generated to show the distribution of a surname in England and Wales in 1891 and the number of households with the surname in each county. Separate maps are also provided showing the distribution of a surname in Scotland in all the censuses from 1841 through to 1901. Three maps can be generated for the US, based on the 1840, 1880 and 1920 US censuses, which show the percentage of people with the chosen surname living in each state. (Note that the US maps can only be accessed from the US Ancestry site at **www.ancestry.com**. The link to the US maps is not available from Ancestry.co.uk.) There is a link provided with a list of all the people in the relevant censuses, showing their names, approximate year of birth and residence, though a subscription is required to access all the additional census details and to view the original census images. The entries used to generate the maps are based on the Ancestry transcriptions but user-submitted corrections are also included in the lists. For example, a surname originally transcribed as Couse but corrected by a user to Cruse is included in the maps for both Cruse and Couse. Some users have also provided details of the maiden name of married women, so the numbers provided should be used with caution.

The genealogy social networking website MyHeritage provides surname distribution maps based on the number of people with a particular surname in its database. The company has a very international database with over 62 million members from around the world. While the maps will not be a reliable indicator of the present-day distribution of a surname, they might reveal occurrences in unexpected countries. The search menu can be accessed from **http://lastnames.myheritage.com/last-names**. It is then necessary to click on the appropriate letter of the alphabet and find the surname of interest. An alternative way of accessing the maps is by using the URL **http://lastnames.myheritage.com/last-name/Kennett** (the same URL as above but without the final letter S) and substituting your own surname after the final slash in the place of Kennett.

The British Isles

The Great Britain Family Names Profiler (**http://gbnames.publicprofiler.org**) is another website that has been produced as part of a project by a team at UCL. The GB Profiler has a database of 25,630 surnames in Great Britain from the 1881 census and the 1998 electoral register. Only surnames that have more than 100 entries are included in the list. Maps can be generated showing the distribution of the names in Great Britain in 1881 and 1998. The website also provides useful information on the frequency of the surnames.

Stephen Archer's *British 19th Century Surname Atlas* (**www.archersoftware.co.uk**) is an excellent software program that is an essential purchase for anyone with an interest in British surnames. It can be used to generate distribution maps for over 140,000 surnames found in the 1881 censuses for England, Wales and Scotland. The maps can show either the actual numbers of the surnames in 1881 or the frequency per 100,000 of the population, and can be aggregated either by county or by Poor Law Union (Figures 11 and 12). The display of the maps can be customised with a colour scheme of your choice, and the county names and actual numbers can also be displayed on the maps if preferred. The user can also zoom in on particular counties or regions, which can be very useful when generating maps of surnames with a strong regional distribution or for displaying the actual numbers in densely populated cities such as London. The four-map view is a very handy feature that can be used to generate maps of potentially related variant spellings to see if the distributions overlap (Figure 13). The program can also be used to generate a list of surnames ranked in order of frequency, and to produce a list of the characteristic surnames of each county in Britain.

Rootsmap (**www.rootsmap.com**) is a commercial service which offers distribution maps for Great Britain and Ireland. The maps for Great Britain are based on the 1881 census, but Rootsmap has developed its own methodology and, unlike the other services, which use place of residence in 1881, it extracts data on the place of birth of the heads of household in order to provide the closest match to the male line. However, if there are not enough heads of household then all individuals are used. The Irish maps are produced using Stephen Archer's GenMap software (see p.85) and are based on Griffith's Valuation of Ireland (1847–64).

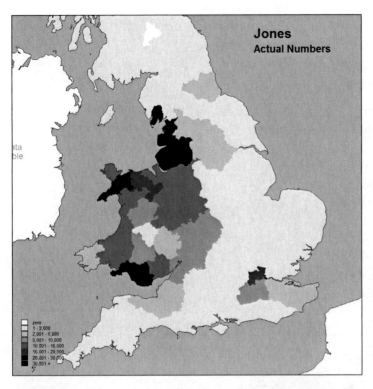

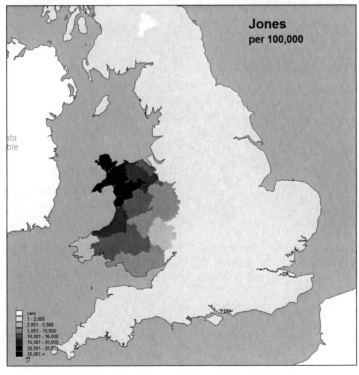

Figures 11 and 12.
Stephen Archer's *British 19th Century Surname Atlas* CD allows the user to plot the actual numbers in the 1881 census and also the relative distribution of the surname per 100,000 of the population. The actual (absolute) numbers can sometimes, as here, give a misleading picture of the distribution of the surname in heavily populated urban areas (Figure 11, top). When the distribution is normalised in relation to the general population the heartland of the Jones surname in Wales, and particularly in the north-west of Wales, becomes apparent (Figure 12, bottom).

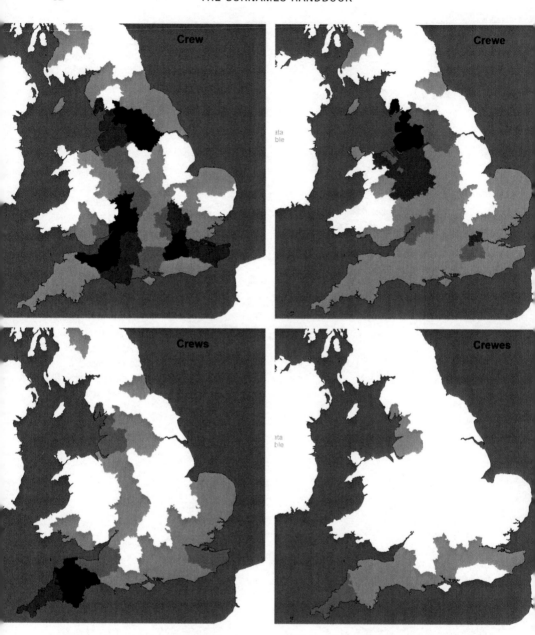

Figure 13. Stephen Archer's *British 19th Century Surname Atlas* CD allows the user to produce a four-map view, which is particularly useful for comparing the distribution patterns of variant spellings. The surnames Crew and Crewe have very different distributions to the surnames Crews and Crewes and there is little overlap, suggesting that these names are not related.

Continental Europe

The Belgian family name website (**www.familienamen.be**) produces distribution maps of surnames in Belgium based on data from the 1998 national register.

Geopatronyme (**www.geopatronyme.com**) is a French website that produces distribution maps of surnames in France for the following periods based on births by *départements*: 1891–1915, 1916–40, 1941–65, 1966–90. The names can also be seen in list form for the same periods, ranked by the number of births. Similar maps using the same datasets can also be found on the Genealogie website at **www.genealogie.com/ nom-de-famille/**. The latter website also has a list of the 6,000 most common surnames in France, and maps showing the characteristic surnames in each *département*. The maps are based on data collected by l'Institut National de la Statistique et des Études Économiques (INSEE). The institute collected data from 1970 onwards on the names, dates and places of birth of people born from 1945 onwards and of those still living from 1970 onwards. There are, therefore, significant gaps in the data as people born before 1946 and those who died before 1970 are not included in the database. The 1.3 million French people who died in the First World War and the 530,000 who died in the Second World War are also not included. In addition, some municipalities are missing or wrongly referenced. Despite the limitations of the underlying database these websites still provide a useful overview of the distribution of French surnames.

Geogen (**http://christoph.stoepel.net/geogen/en**) is a German surname mapping website that uses data extracted from telephone directories. It produces two different maps, one based on the absolute distribution of the surname, and the other showing the relative distribution of the surname in a range of bands per million of the population. The GoFeminine website (**http://nachname.gofeminin.de/w/nachnamen/ deutschland.html**) can also be used to generate distribution maps for German surnames, and has a list of the 289 most common surnames in Germany. The source of the data is not given.

GENS Italy (**http://gens.labo.net**) produces distribution maps for surnames in Italy and can also be used to produce maps of surnames in the US, though the source of the data is not provided.

The Dutch family name database (**www.meertens.knaw.nl/nfb**) produces distribution maps of surnames in 2007 and 1947. The 2007 data is taken from a database of 16 million people with 314,000 surnames who were registered as being of Dutch nationality. The 1947 census was used to provide data on about 100,000 surnames.

Surname Origins

Surname Origins (**http://surnameorigins.ca**) is a new bespoke mapping service offered by Howard Mathieson for a very modest fee. Surname distribution maps can be generated for England and Wales, Scotland, Ireland and the United States. The maps can be displayed at the national, regional or county level, and can be shown against the backdrop of the physical landscape or a historic map of the country. The Irish maps are based on the distribution of the surname in Griffith's Valuation. The maps for the other countries use census information. Surname Origins is also able to produce customised maps based on the researcher's own data.

Compiling your own maps

The mapping websites and tools can provide a useful overview of the distribution of a surname, but have a number of limitations. Most of the websites focus on the present-day distribution of a surname, which will not necessarily be the historical home of the name. The datasets used for these websites are of varying quality, and none represent 100 per cent of the population of any given country. The 1881 British census, which is the most widely available dataset, provides a valuable snapshot of the distribution of a surname in the late nineteenth century. However, the 1881 census was taken at a time when the British population was increasingly mobile, thanks to the growth of the rail network and the burgeoning industrial centres. Consequently, for some surnames the 1881 census will not present a true picture of the origin of the name. Furthermore, for the maps generated from names in historical censuses we are reliant on transcriptions of varying quality. For common surnames the larger numbers will probably smooth out any distortions resulting from mistranscriptions or increasing mobility, but for rare surnames these maps could potentially present a misleading picture of the origin of a name.

The dedicated surname researcher will not just want to study the distribution of a surname in the present day and in the censuses, but will also want to investigate distribution patterns in earlier centuries. However, prior to the censuses there are no national datasets that can be easily used for the purposes of surname mapping, and consequently there are no ready-made tools to facilitate the process. In order to map a surname in earlier centuries or to provide a more accurate picture from recent datasets, it will, therefore, be necessary to collect your own data and compile your own maps. The datasets that can be used for this purpose will be discussed in Chapters 7 and 8. For rare surnames, a more practical proposition is to focus principally on the region where the surname is found, and it will be more appropriate to compile regional rather than national maps.

At the most basic level a map can be hand drawn or distributions can be plotted on scanned copies of published maps. A fine example of a hand-produced map can be found on the Yeo Society website. The map shows the distributions of the surnames Yeo, Yaw and Yea in Devon, Cornwall and Somerset in 1569 and 1641 and can be found at **www.yeosociety.com/yeoroots/distributionmap.htm**. There are a number of useful software programs that can be used to generate maps based on your own data, which will make the process easier.

Google Maps

Google Maps (**http://maps.google.co.uk**) is a very useful tool for plotting simple surname distribution maps using modern place-names. Place-markers can easily be added to maps by searching for a location and right-clicking on the pin provided. The labels can be named, and descriptive text can be added to each label. If Google Earth (**www.google.co.uk/earth**) is installed on your PC you can also toggle between the earth view and the satellite view. The maps can also be embedded into your website or blog. The maps can either be open to the public or restricted to those who have the URL. A free Google account is required to create a personalised map. Tutorials for producing customised maps using Google Earth and Google Maps can be seen at **http://earth.google.com/outreach/tutorials.html**. Google Maps can be especially useful for plotting the locations of the earliest known ancestors for all the trees that have been documented for a particular surname. If all the trees cluster in a specific region this could indicate that the surname has a single origin. Linda Gant has made particularly effective use of Google Maps on her one-name study website (**www.gant-name.org.uk/maps.html**). If you wish to use Google Maps to plot large quantities of data then a batch geocoder such as BatchGeo (**www.batchgeo.com**) can be used to add geocodes to place-names before uploading the data to Google Maps. Experienced surname geographers will want to experiment with some of the advanced features of Google Earth that allow the user to upload historical photos as an overlay. Detailed instructions can be found in the Google tutorial at **http://earth.google.com/outreach/tutorial_earthoverlays.html**.

GenMap

GenMap is a Microsoft Windows-based program that can be used in conjunction with the user's own data to generate surname distribution maps for the British Isles using the historic pre-1974 county boundaries.[17] Data can be imported from a database file (Access or similar), a GEDCOM file or a CSV (comma-separated values) text file. The file should have one or more fields with geographical information such as parish names or county names. GenMap can be used in particular to plot surname distributions using data extracted from the IGI, census data, and births, marriages and deaths from the civil registration indexes (Figure 14). The program can be used to generate point maps with markers in the form of circles, triangles or squares showing the locations of the events. The markers can be scaled in size in proportion to the number of events at each location. Flood-fill maps can also be produced either at county level or by using the registration districts for England and Wales. The flood-fill maps work better than the point maps when a large number of events and places are being plotted. The maps are highly customisable and the user can choose the colours for the flood-fill maps and the numeric ranges to which each colour applies. The program has its own built-in gazetteer that has been pre-tagged with the appropriate map references for places in Ireland and Britain, but the user can also add extra place-names with the appropriate map references if required.

Family Atlas

Family Atlas is a Windows mapping program from the genealogy software company RootsMagic.[18] Although designed for use with RootsMagic, it also works with GEDCOM files produced by other family history programs. Family Atlas allows you to import your family data directly from your GEDCOM file, and then create markers based on that data to plot on a map. Places are automatically geocoded by matching them against the 3.5 million names in the built-in world place database. The maps can be customised by adding text, lines, shapes and pictures, and the colour schemes and map styles can also be personalised to suit individual preferences. There is also a timeslider that can be used to plot events over time. Family Atlas is also useful for converting genealogy files into the appropriate format (kml: keyhole mark-up language) for use in Google Earth and Google Maps. RootsMagic has produced a helpful webinar 'Mapping Your Family Tree with Family Atlas' (**www.rootsmagic.com/webinars**), which demonstrates the program's many features. Gerald Cooke has made good use of Family Atlas to produce a timeslider map that plots the births and baptisms of people with the surname Pimble from 1500 to the present. WM Recorder (**http://wmrecorder.com**) was used to record the events. The resultant video can be seen at **www.youtube.com/watch?v=cv9DmADQhDI**.

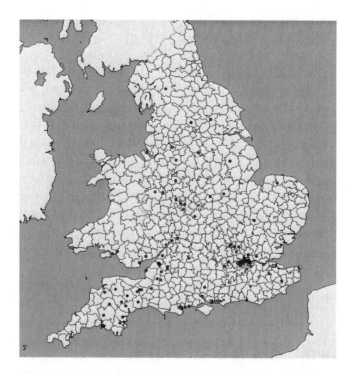

Figure 14. A map produced with GenMap showing the Cruwys births from 1837 to 2005 by registration district.

Surname Distribution Analysis

Surname Distribution Analysis (**www.wykes.org/dist**) is a free utility that can be used to plot the distribution of surnames in Britain and the US. The program was designed to be used in conjunction with the CDs produced by the LDS for the 1881 British census and the 1880 US census, but it can be used with any data if you produce an 'Aggregated Distribution File' in the appropriate format. Simple instructions are provided on the website. The program provides a handy free alternative to the more sophisticated paid programs, and is particularly useful for plotting distribution maps in the US.

Family history software

Some family history software programs, such as Family Tree Maker, Legacy, Family Tree Builder and Gramps, are now starting to integrate mapping features into their interface using either Bing Maps or Google Maps/Earth. However, the focus is on mapping the locations associated with individuals or small family groups rather than for a whole surname. Family Historian Version 5, which became available in March 2012, has introduced the ability to download free applications known as plug-ins that can be used to enhance the program and provide support for features such as mapping and timelines. Advanced users can write their own plug-ins using the built-in scripting tools. At the time of writing, plug-ins were available to map individual life events or to map life facts for selected groups of people. These plug-ins have the potential to be adapted by more knowledgeable users to provide surname mapping features.

Word clouds

There are a number of free utilities such as Wordle (**www.wordle.net**), which can be used to generate word 'word clouds' from user-provided data. The clouds give greater prominence to words that appear more frequently in the source text. The word clouds can be customised with different fonts, layouts and colour schemes. With Wordle it is also possible to input your

Figure 15. A word cloud showing the relative distributions of the surname Cruse and other related spellings based on their frequency in the 1881 census.

own weighted data into the program. This could, for example, be in the form of surname variants and the number of instances in a particular dataset. As a demonstration, I have used Wordle to generate a cloud of the variant spellings of the surname Cruse based on their frequencies in the 1881 census (Figure 15).

Word clouds have been used to great effect in a stunning map showing the distribution of the 181 most common surnames in the United States. The map was published in a double-page spread in the February 2011 issue of *National Geographic* magazine (pp.22–3), and an interactive version can be viewed online at **http://blogs.ngm.com/blog_ central/2011/01/whats-in-a-surname.html**.

James Cheshire has used Wordle to striking effect on his Spatial Analysis blog (**http:// spatialanalysis.co.uk/2010/02/great-britains-surname-cloud**) to produce a word cloud showing the distribution of the 500 most common surnames in Great Britain. The visual display clearly illustrates that there are only a minority of very common surnames, and that most British surnames are very rare. Cheshire employed a similar technique to produce word clouds of London surnames, which can be found at **http://spatialanalysis. co.uk/2011/01/mapping-londons-surnames**.

Websites

www.members.shaw.ca/geogenealogy Howard Mathieson's geogenealogy website has a comprehensive collection of links to genealogy mapping resources.
www.ancestralatlas.com Ancestral Atlas: a map-based genealogy website.
www.click2map.com An online map creator.
www.cyndislist.com/maps Map and geography links from Cyndi's List.
www.locatinglondon.org A website for plotting London events on historical maps.
www.maphistory.info A gateway site dedicated to the history of maps with a comprehensive listing of images of early maps available on the web.
www.ordnancesurveyleisure.co.uk/leisure Ordnance Survey Get-a-map.
www.oldmapsonline.org Old Maps online is a gateway to historical maps in libraries across the world.
http://sketchmap.co.uk A free online mapping program.

Blogs

http://bigthink.com/blogs/strange-maps Frank Jacobs' strange maps blog.
http://blogs.casa.ucl.ac.uk The CASA blog network is a multi-author blog with the latest outputs from the Centre for Advanced Spatial Analysis at University College London.
http://mappinglondon.co.uk The Mapping London blog.
http://spatialanalysis.co.uk James Cheshire's spatial analysis blog.

5

SURNAME FREQUENCY

If English Surnames are remarkable for their variety, they are no less so for their number. How great the latter may be it would be a hopeless task to attempt to ascertain: it is sufficient to say with the Rev. Mark Noble, that 'it is almost beyond belief.'

Mark Antony Lower, *English Surnames*, vol. I (1849), p.xii

Establishing the frequency of a surname in the present day and at various key points in the past is an important component of a surname study. In the early stages of a study a frequency analysis will help to establish how rare or common the surname is in its country of origin and throughout the world. It will help you to gauge the size of the task in hand, and to prioritise research in the areas that are likely to yield the most rewards. As a study progresses, many researchers like to do more detailed analyses of their data to examine aspects such as the growth or decline of their surname over time, patterns of immigration and emigration, and birth and death rates. The researcher will be interested in recording the absolute frequency of the surname – in other words the raw figures of births, deaths, census entries, etc. for the surname in question. It is also a worthwhile exercise to measure the relative frequency of the surname – that is the frequency of the surname in relation to other surnames in the same region or country.

In order to establish how rare or common a particular surname is in the general population, either in the present day or in a historical context, we need access to suitable surname-rich national databases. Censuses, electoral registers, telephone directories and civil registration indexes are the most useful sources for the purposes of establishing surname frequencies, and can be used to provide a snapshot of the surnames in a population at a given time. However, not all of these records have been transcribed, computerised and assembled into conveniently searchable databases, and some records, such as the modern censuses, are closed to public inspection and will only be released when the agreed closure period has expired, which varies from country to country. There are many other national surname-rich databases maintained by government departments and organisations such as, in the UK, HM Revenue and Customs (HMRC), the Department for Work and Pensions (DWP), the National Health Service (NHS) and the Driver and Vehicle Licensing Agency (DVLA), but these databases are not accessible to the general public for obvious privacy reasons.

The datasets that are available are invaluable when searching for records relating to individuals in your family tree or for extracting all the entries for a specific surname, but it is much more difficult to obtain statistics on the relative frequencies of different surnames from these databases. We are, therefore, reliant on the work of academic researchers, government employees and commercial organisations that have access to the computerised data and can perform the necessary analyses. In this chapter we will review the historical datasets that have already been analysed for surname frequencies, most of which have focused on the more common surnames. We will also look at some of the websites that can be used to provide frequency and distribution figures for your own surname. The datasets that can be used for more in-depth analysis of a surname will be discussed in depth in Chapters 7 and 8.

England and Wales

A civil registration system for births, marriages and deaths was introduced in England and Wales on 1 July 1837. Registration was undertaken at a local level by civil registrars with returns sent on a quarterly basis to the Registrar-General at the General Register Office (GRO) where they were entered into the national indexes. These indexes are a valuable resource for the surname researcher and their use within a surname study will be discussed in Chapter 7. The Registrar-General was required to submit an annual report to Parliament. Most of these reports were concerned with a statistical analysis of the births, deaths and marriages. However, for the surname researcher the 'Sixteenth Annual Report', published in 1856 by the then Registrar-General, George Graham, is of particular interest. In a section on 'Family nomenclature in England and Wales' the Registrar-General made the first ever attempt to estimate the size of the surname pool in England and Wales. He examined the returns for births in the first quarter of 1851 and deaths in the first quarter of 1853. He recorded 32,818 different surnames out of a total of 275,405 persons registered in these two quarters and thus calculated that there were 11.9 different surnames for every 100 persons, corresponding to an average of 8.4 people per surname. He extrapolated that the total number of surnames in England and Wales was between 35,000 and 40,000. He also noted the lack of surname variety in Wales, and estimated that nine-tenths of the Welsh population accounted for fewer than 100 different surnames. The report also contained a table listing the fifty most common surnames in England and Wales with data derived from nine quarterly returns of births, eight of deaths, and eight of marriages. The Registrar-General concluded: 'From this estimate it appears that the persons by whom these 50 surnames are borne amount to about 3,253,800, nearly one sixth of the entire population of England and Wales. On an average, it seems, one person in 73 is a Smith, one in 76 a Jones, one in 115 a Williams, one in 148 a Taylor, one in 162 a Davies, and one in 174 a Brown.'[1]

In 1983 the human biologist Gabriel Lasker published an interesting study on the frequencies of surnames in England and Wales (see also p.73–5). Lasker studied the index of all marriages registered in England and Wales during the first three months of 1975, which he used as a representative random sample of the 'breeding population'. There were

32,457 different surnames (including different spellings from the same origin) listed in the sampled period. Lasker found that rare surnames – those that occurred at a rate of one to six per 100,000 – accounted for 93 per cent of the surnames in the listings. Most of the surnames (19,828) occurred only once.[2]

The Office for National Statistics now publishes annual reports on the top 100 given names for baby boys and girls, but surprisingly there have not been any attempts to provide equivalent data for surnames. Anthony Camp reported on three government surveys of high-frequency surnames in the *Genealogists' Magazine* in 1997. In 1944 the Organisations and Methods Division of HM Treasury surveyed several indexes, ranging in size from 200,000 to 30 million entries, and analysed the data in a number of ways. Of particular interest was an analysis of the relative frequency of different surnames. A pilot study of the 0.5 million names in the Civil Service Central Staff Records was undertaken in 1964 and resulted in a list of the seventy-five most common surnames. In 1966 the relative frequency of the first forty-eight surnames was obtained as part of a study of National Insurance records. Camp published the lists of surnames from all three studies in tabular form, ranked in the order in which they appeared in the Treasury survey, and also included in his table the rankings and frequencies from the Registrar-General's study.[3] A table showing the 300 leading surnames in England and Wales can be seen on the Surname Studies website at **www.surnamestudies.org.uk/statistics/comparative.htm**. The table, compiled by the late Philip Dance, consolidates the surname rankings from the Lasker study, the government surveys reported by Anthony Camp, and the lists from the Registrar-General, together with data from the 1996 electoral register and deaths registered in England and Wales between 1984 and 1987. The data is not directly comparable, but it is nevertheless fascinating to see that the rankings of the majority of the common surnames have remained relatively stable. The Surname Studies website also has a more recent list of the top 500 surnames in England and Wales, which can be seen at **www.surnamestudies. org.uk/statistics/top500.htm**. The names are taken from a survey of the National Health Services Central Register in 1991/2000, which covers England, Wales and the Isle of Man. At the time of the survey the database included around 60 million names. The top 500 names represent 39.33 per cent of the people listed in the register.

John and Sheila Rowlands' 1996 book *The Surnames of Wales* (see also p.76), based on a comprehensive survey of Welsh marriages between 1813 and 1837, provides an informative insight into the distribution and characteristics of Welsh surnames. It was found that the ten most common surnames in Wales were carried by 55.85 per cent of the population. This is in marked contrast to England where the ten most common surnames account for just 5.15 per cent of the population (Table 3). The glossary of the book provides statistics on the incidence and distribution of over 250 Welsh surnames. Michael Williams studied the modern-day distribution of Welsh surnames by extracting names from the six British Telecom telephone directories for Wales. A listing of the top 100 surnames in Wales was published in his book *Researching Local History: The Human Journey* (1996). The Williams listing is reproduced on the Surname Studies website at **www.surnamestudies.org.uk/ statistics/wales.htm**.

Table 3. A comparison of the ten most common surnames in Wales and England in the early to mid-nineteenth century. Data extracted from *The Surnames of Wales* (1996) by John and Sheila Rowlands (p.4). (Reproduced by kind permission of the authors)

WALES		ENGLAND	
Surname	**%**	**Surname**	**%**
Jones	13.84	Smith	1.37
Williams	8.91	Taylor	0.68
Davies	7.09	Brown	0.57
Thomas	5.70	Jones	0.43
Evans	5.46	Johnson	0.38
Roberts	3.69	Robinson	0.36
Hughes	2.98	Wilson	0.36
Lewis	2.97	Wright	0.34
Morgan	2.63	Wood	0.33
Griffiths	2.58	Hall	0.33
Total	**55.85**	**Total**	**5.15**

Scotland

In Scotland civil registration began on 1 January 1855. Births, marriages and deaths are recorded locally by district registrars but copies of all records are kept centrally by the Registrar-General of Scotland at New Register House in Edinburgh. James Stark, the Registrar-General for Scotland, published a special section in his annual report to Parliament for the year 1860 on the 'Nomenclature in Scotland', in which he attempted to ascertain the number of distinct surnames in Scotland. Stark enumerated all the surnames in one year of the Index of the Birth Register, and counted a total of 6,823 separate surnames out of a total of 104,018 births. He calculated that: 'These numbers would give the proportion of 15.2 persons to every surname, or 6.5 different surnames to every 100 persons.' He concluded that: 'The above facts, therefore, appear to demonstrate that the effect of the Clan system of surnames in Scotland is to cause a much larger number of persons to hold the same surname; in other words, that, in proportion to the population, fewer surnames exist in Scotland than in England.' He also noted the effect of emigration from Ireland on the surname pool:

Within the last thirty years a very large addition to the surnames has been made in Scotland, in consequence of the immense immigration from Ireland. This immigration, beginning about the year 1820 did not assume gigantic proportions till about the year 1840, when the demand for railway labourers brought the Irish over in hundreds and thousands. Since that period, in addition to bringing over about a thousand names which are common to Scotland and to

Ireland, they have added to the Scottish surnames nearly a thousand surnames which till that period were peculiar to Ireland.

Stark also analysed the indexes of births, marriages and deaths for the years 1855, 1856 and 1858 in order to establish the fifty most common surnames in Scotland and their relative prevalence. He found that these fifty surnames constituted 29.6 per cent of all the names entered in the registers in the three years studied (180,748 out of 609,639 entries). He reckoned that thirty-two of the top fifty names either originated in Scotland or were 'peculiar to it – a very large proportion, considering all circumstances'.[4]

The General Register Office for Scotland, now part of the National Records of Scotland, has since published several surveys of surname frequency in Scotland and a useful summary can be found in the paper 'Surnames in Scotland over the last 140 years' published in 2003.[5]

Ireland

The first and only comprehensive study of surname frequency in Ireland was published in 1894 by Robert Matheson, the then Registrar-General for Ireland, as an appendix to his annual report. Matheson counted all the surnames that were represented by five or more entries in the Irish births index for 1890. From these data he produced a table showing the 100 most common surnames in Ireland and provided an estimate of the number of name-bearers for each of the top surnames. These estimates were ascertained by multiplying the number of entries by the average birth rate, which for the year 1890 was 1 in 44.8 persons. Matheson found that Murphy was the most common surname in Ireland with an estimated population of 62,600 persons (13.3 per thousand of the population). Kelly was in second place with an estimated 55,900 name-bearers (11.8 per thousand), and Sullivan was in third place with approximately 43,600 name-bearers (9.2 per thousand). Smith, which is consistently the most common surname in England and Scotland, was in fifth place in Ireland. While many of the names in the Irish top 100 are also found in England and Scotland, Matheson remarked that: 'most of the names in Ireland with the larger numbers are peculiar to this country, representing the names of Irish Clans and Septs, such as the Murphys, Kellys, Sullivans, O'Briens, Byrnes, Ryans, Connors, O'Neills, Reillys, Doyles, McCarthys, Gallaghers, Dohertys, &c.'

Matheson also provided a table showing the top twenty surnames in each registration county. He noted that even common surnames often had marked regional distributions. Murphy, for example, was the most numerous surname in the country as a whole, but it only occupied the leading position in a handful of counties. Many names were found to be peculiar to particular provinces or counties. In the final chapter of his appendix, Matheson provided an alphabetical listing of all the surnames with five or more entries in the births index for 1890. He noted the number of such entries in each of the four registration provinces (Ulster, Connaught, Leinster and Munster) and also provided counts for the registration counties in which the names were principally found.[6]

There is little information available on the modern distribution of Irish surnames. However, Sean Murphy, a genealogist in Dublin, Ireland, has published a useful draft paper on the Internet entitled 'A Survey of Irish Surnames 1992–9'. As the basis for the survey, the author used a CD-ROM version of the Irish telephone directory for 1997–98 and a hard copy of the Northern Ireland telephone directory for 1993. He has used the data to generate a range of interesting statistics on Irish surnames, including a list of the 100 most common surnames in Ireland, the estimated number of name-bearers of each surname, and their relative frequency. The study can be found at **http://homepage.eircom. net/~seanjmurphy/studies**.

1881 census

Censuses are one of the most useful sources for establishing the distribution of surnames as well as being an essential resource for tracing individuals and reconstructing family trees. Censuses provide a snapshot of a population on a specific date. In theory a census should cover 100 per cent of the population, but in practice there will inevitably be omissions as there will always be some people who will evade enumeration, either by accident or design. In many censuses people who are in institutions, such as prisons or lunatic asylums, will be recorded only by their initials. In boarding houses and lodging houses one can sometimes find tramps and other itinerant people who are simply listed by their gender with the name not known. Some historical censuses such as those for Australia and the early censuses for Ireland have either been lost or destroyed, and even for those censuses that have survived there are sometimes pages or sections that are missing.

The 1881 census was the first census to be made available as a complete transcribed and computerised dataset, and was first issued on CD in 1999. Kevin Schürer used a customised version of the 1881 dataset to investigate the surname regions of Britain (see Chapter 4). His study also provided an interesting insight into the historical frequency of surnames. For the purposes of his research, Schürer restricted his analysis to the 26 million or so individuals from England and Wales in 1881. A total of 396,776 unique surname strings were found in the dataset, though 158,876 of these surnames occurred just once, and were probably transcription errors or typing mistakes. For the purposes of his study Schürer focused only on those surnames with a total frequency of twenty-five or more, of which there were 41,203, equating to an average of one new surname per 630 persons across the whole population. He found that:

> the frequency distribution of these surnames was very far from even. Basically a large number of people shared a relatively small number of surnames, while, conversely, a large number of surnames were attributed to a small number of people. This exponential-type relationship is indeed common to most populations, both historic and modern.

He further commented that:

a fifth of the population shared just under 60 surnames, a half of the population were accounted for by some 600 surnames, while the top 10,000 surnames covered 90 per cent of the population. Conversely, ten per cent of the population, those with the rarest surnames, jointly accounted for some 30,000 surnames, more if those with frequencies of less than 25 are also considered.[7]

The 1881 census was also used as the basis of Stephen Archer's *British 19th Century Surname Atlas* CD. *Surname Atlas* was first released in April 2003, and the latest version became available in February 2011.[8] *Surname Atlas* is primarily a mapping tool (see Chapter 4) which can be used to generate flood-fill maps showing the historical distributions of the surnames found in the 1881 census of England, Scotland and Wales (sadly the 1881 census for Ireland was destroyed). It can, however, also be used to generate frequency data and rank orders for all the 400,000 or so surnames in the 1881 census. The entire list of surnames in the census can be viewed either in rank or alphabetical order. On perusing the surnames in rank order the typical long-tailed surname distribution can be seen. There are just twelve surnames with more than 100,000 occurrences in 1881. There are 428 surnames with a frequency of more than 10,000, and 3,921 surnames with a frequency of 1,000 or more. Even allowing for the large number of single occurrences that are likely to be mistranscriptions, it is clear that the vast majority of British surnames have a low frequency.

All the censuses for England, Wales and Scotland from 1901 to 1911 are now fully transcribed and indexed and have been made available online from a number of different commercial providers, but none of these databases can as yet be used to generate detailed statistics on the relative frequencies of different surnames in each census or to obtain overall figures on the number of different surnames found in each census. The censuses can, however, be used to generate frequency statistics for individual surnames, and this subject will be discussed further in Chapter 7.

Surname geography

As we have seen in the previous chapter, in the last ten years or so surnames have increasingly attracted the attention of geographers who have used surnames to explore the social and cultural structure of populations, and to investigate patterns of regional and international migration. In the UK this new discipline of surname geography has been pioneered by the Department of Geography and the Centre for Advanced Spatial Analysis (CASA) at University College London (UCL). UCL have published a number of interesting papers that have provided valuable statistics on the number and distribution of surnames in the UK in the present day. The UCL researchers used an enhanced version of the 2001 electoral register provided by a commercial supplier as the basis for their studies, which supplemented the names on the public version of the electoral register with further data from commercial surveys and credit-scoring databases. The full version of the register is only available to government and credit reference agencies under strict terms of confidentiality. In October 2002 people were given the right to opt out of the public version of the register that was sold to commercial organisations. The enhanced 2001 register is the last version before opting out was possible and is, therefore, the most comprehensive publicly available source of current data on names in the UK. The data represents 45.6 million people over the age of 17 who were resident in the UK in October 2001, with a total of 1,597,805 surnames. The researchers found that there were very few surnames possessed by more than 100,000 people, and the majority of names (1.45 million) had fewer than ten occurrences, creating an extremely long-tailed distribution. As might be expected, high densities of 'non-British surnames' were found in British cities, especially in London. London had the most atypical composition of surnames, and the highest number of unique surnames, reflecting its status as a global centre of immigration.[9, 10]

Table 4. The top twenty surnames by constituent country of the United Kingdom in 2001. The figures in parentheses indicate the percentage of the population with each surname. Adapted from: Fiona McElduff, Pablo Mateos, Angie Wade and Mario Cortina Borja, 'What's in a name? The frequency and geographic distributions of UK surnames' in *Significance*, December 2008, p.192. Available from: **www.ucl.ac.uk/paediatric-epidemiology/pdfs/Signficance_Surnames_Paper.pdf** (Reproduced by kind permission of the authors).

Rank	England	Northern Ireland	Wales	Scotland
1	Smith (1.26)	Wilson (0.75)	Jones (5.75)	Smith (1.28)
2	Jones (0.75)	Campbell (0.75)	Williams (3.72)	Brown (0.94)
3	Taylor (0.59)	Kelly (0.74)	Davies (3.72)	Wilson (0.89)
4	Brown (0.56)	Johnston (0.69)	Evans (2.47)	Robertson (0.78)
5	Williams (0.39)	Moore (0.62)	Thomas (2.43)	Thomson (0.78)
6	Wilson (0.39)	Thompson (0.61)	Roberts (1.53)	Campbell (0.77)
7	Johnson (0.37)	Smyth (0.60)	Lewis (1.53)	Stewart (0.73)
8	Davies (0.34)	Brown (0.59)	Hughes (1.23)	Anderson (0.70)
9	Robinson (0.32)	O'Neill (0.57)	Morgan (1.16)	Scott (0.55)
10	Wright (0.32)	Doherty (0.54)	Griffiths (0.96)	Murray (0.53)
11	Thompson (0.31)	Stewart (0.54)	Edwards (0.93)	MacDonald (0.52)
12	Evans (0.30)	Quinn (0.51)	Smith (0.85)	Reid (0.52)
13	Walker (0.30)	Robinson (0.50)	James (0.82)	Taylor (0.49)
14	White (0.30)	Murphy (0.49)	Rees (0.81)	Clark (0.47)
15	Roberts (0.28)	Graham (0.48)	Jenkins (0.69)	Ross (0.43)
16	Green (0.28)	Martin (0.45)	Owen (0.67)	Young (0.42)
17	Hall (0.28)	McLaughlin (0.45)	Price (0.67)	Mitchell (0.41)
18	Wood (0.27)	Hamilton (0.44)	Phillips (0.65)	Watson (0.41)
19	Jackson (0.27)	Murray (0.43)	Morris (0.63)	Paterson (0.40)
20	Clarke (0.26)	Hughes (0.41)	Richards (0.55)	Morrison (0.40)

The same 2001 electoral register dataset was used in a 2008 study by McElduff et al., who analysed data on 817,391 surnames from 434 UK administrative districts. The researchers appear to have removed the 'international' names from the dataset and focused exclusively on the surnames of UK origin but do not explain their methodology for doing so. They found that:

> Surprisingly, well over half of those [817,391] surnames were unique, borne by just one individual on the list; hence, 531,896 surnames represent 65.07% of the total number of surnames, but only 4.41% of the population. The percentage of the population with surnames that occur only twice is 4.93%. Turning to the other extreme, the most common surnames in the UK are Smith (1.22% of the population), Jones (0.93%) and then Williams (0.64%).

Northern Ireland, Scotland and, particularly, Wales were found to have lower proportions of unique surnames and a lower level of surname diversity than the English districts, largely because of their geographical isolation. The lack of diversity in Wales is, of course, also caused by the late introduction of surnames and the patronymic naming system, though this point is not considered by the authors. Clear patterns also emerged among the English regions. London, the south-east and the east of England were found to have higher surname diversity than the rest of the UK because the large urban areas attract 'international and domestic migration and generate a large and ethnically diverse population, with high population mixing'. The authors further found that the prevalence of the most common surnames had not changed between 1881 and 2001, and although the overall number of different surnames had increased 'the rank ordering of the most prevalent has remained relatively static'. The paper included a table showing the top twenty surnames in England, Northern Ireland, Wales and Scotland, which is reproduced in Table 4.[11]

Useful websites

Many of the mapping websites reviewed in the previous chapter can also be used to obtain frequency distributions for surnames and related variant spellings. Of these, UCL's World Names Public Profiler (**worldnames.publicprofiler.org**) is by far the most useful website for providing an approximate indication of the worldwide frequency and distribution of a surname. The website holds data from telephone directories and electoral registers for 300 million people in twenty-six different countries, representing a total population of 1 billion in those countries. They have 8 million unique surnames in their database, and 5 million unique given names. The site is free to use, but searches can only be performed if you provide your e-mail address and your gender. A map showing the global distribution of the surname is generated, and information is provided on the frequency per million (FPM) of the surname in the top ten countries and the top regions where the surname is found. The top ten cities are also listed, though the FPM is not provided. With a little effort it is possible to convert the FPM figures into approximate population figures for each of the ten countries. The methodology is described by James Irvine in Appendix B of his paper 'Towards improvements in y-DNA surname project administration' in the *Journal of Genetic Genealogy*.[12] The paper also includes a link to a downloadable pro-forma spreadsheet that will automatically convert FPMs into population figures for each of the countries covered.

British surnames

The Surnames of England and Wales website at **www.taliesin-arlein.net/names** has a useful search feature that provides an estimate of the present-day population of any given surname. The site uses an extract from an Office of National Statistics database, and contains a list of surnames in use in England, Wales and the Isle of Man in September 2002. Names shared by fewer than five people have been omitted from the list. It is suggested that 'multiplying the result for your surname by 0.93 will give a good idea of the living population for your surname'. Experience shows that the figure produced is a slight over-estimate, probably because the underlying database contains a number of duplicates. The site can also be used to generate a list of the top 250 surnames in the database.

The Great Britain Family Names Profiling website (**http://gbnames.public profiler.org**) is the product of a project at UCL and is primarily used to generate surname distribution maps (see Chapter 4). The site is, however, also very useful for obtaining information on the relative frequency of the more common surnames in 1881 and 1998. Data is provided for 25,630 surnames in Great Britain. The frequency of each surname in 1881 and 1998 is shown along with the rank order of the surname and the occurrences per million names.

The British Surnames website (**www.britishsurnames.co.uk**) provides estimates of the number of current name-bearers in Britain, historical figures from 1881, including breakdowns by county, and estimates for the USA and Australia. The site originally extracted data from a cached copy of the Great Britain Family Names website. The data extraction was presumably unauthorised and British Surnames was asked to remove the data. The site has now been rebuilt 'using data obtained from other sources, including public domain information, material available under redistributable licences and data used with permission by the suppliers'. No information is provided on the sources of the underlying databases used by the website. The site also carries some words of warning to advise that: 'All of these are approximate figures, and the current figures especially so … This data is aggregated from several public lists, and some stats are interpolated from known values. The margin of error is well over 100 per cent at the rarest end of the table!' The site is useful as a rough and ready guide to the distribution of British surnames, but the figures should be used with caution. The corresponding data from the UCL GB Names website should be used instead as a more reliable source.

Ireland

As we have already seen, the key resource for surname frequency and distribution in Ireland is the 'Sixteenth Annual Report' by Robert Matheson, the Registrar-General, published in 1894. A digital copy of the Matheson report is available online in the Internet Archive at **http://archive.org/details/cu31924029805540**. The Matheson table of the top 100 names in Ireland in 1890 has been reproduced on the Irish Names website at **www.ireland-information.com/heraldichall/irishsurnames.htm**. Ancestry Ireland, the website of the Ulster Historical Foundation, has provided a free searchable database of the Matheson surname listings that can be accessed at **www.ancestryireland.com/database.php?filename=db_mathesons**. A similar searchable database can be found on the *Irish Times* website at **www.irishtimes.com/ancestor/surname**. The *Irish Times* website can also be used to obtain surname distribution data from the Griffith's Valuation Survey (1847–64). A fee is required to access the county information from the *Irish Times* but it should be noted that the full text of the Griffith's Valuation is available free online on the Ask about Ireland website at **www.askaboutireland.ie/griffith-valuation/index.xml**.

Irish research is somewhat complicated because until 1921 Irish population data related to the whole of the island of Ireland, whereas from 1922 onwards the Republic of Ireland data excludes Northern Ireland data, which is to be found in the population data for the UK.

USA

A list of the top 1,142 surnames derived from a 1 per cent sample of the 1850 Census of Free Populations can be found at **www.buckbd.com/genea/1850freq.html**. Names with fewer than twenty-six occurrences were not included in the survey.

The US census bureau has compiled listings of the most frequently occurring surnames in the 1990 and 2000 censuses ranked in order of frequency. The frequency is also expressed as a percentage of the sampled population. The spreadsheets can be downloaded from **www.census.gov/genealogy/www/freqnames.html**. For the year 2000 there is a spreadsheet with a list of the 1,000 most frequently occurring surnames and a larger file containing a list of all surnames that occur more than 100 times. The surnames are further subdivided into percentages based on ethnicity. For 1990 a list showing the top 88,000 or so surnames is provided.

American Surnames (**www.americansurnames.us**) is a companion website to British Surnames. The site provides estimates of the number of people with a given surname in America in the present day and an historical comparison from the 1880 census. The surname ranking is given along with the percentage of people with the surname per million of the population, and the top five states by frequency. Comparative figures are provided for Australia and the United Kingdom. The UK totals are the same as those shown on the British Surnames website, and the figures are probably for Great Britain rather than the UK. The source of the data is not shown, and the figures should again be used with caution, but the website does provide a useful overview of a surname, which can be especially helpful in the early stages of a surname study. The US census data is also presented in a more accessible and easily searchable form on the Mongabay website at **http://names. mongabay.com**.

The How Many of Me website (**http://howmanyofme.com**) will not help to establish the number of people with your surname in the US but it can be a fun exercise to see how many people in the US share your name.

Other countries

Many of the mapping websites described in Chapter 4 will provide statistics on surname frequency for a selection of other countries. Some of the sites will give actual surname counts in particular countries, whereas others will give the frequency of a surname per million of the population. Some of the sites also provide lists of the most common surnames in the country in question. Most of the online mapping tools produce present-day frequencies using data from telephone directories and electoral rolls, but some will also generate historical surname frequencies. Two further websites will also be of interest to anyone researching the origins of a surname in Italy or Norway.

The Italy in Detail website provides a search service for Italian surnames and can be found at **http://italia.indettaglio.it/eng/cognomi/cognomi.html**. Searches have to be conducted by region. A list is then produced of the towns and provinces in that region where the surname is found, with an estimate of the number of name-bearers in each town in descending order of frequency.

A name search from Statistics Norway at **www.ssb.no/navn_en** allows the user to search for a surname and see how many times it occurs in Norway. There are also alphabetical listings of the top 100 surnames in Norway.

How many surnames are there?

Surprisingly, despite the proliferation of information now available online, there is no easy answer to the question of how many surnames there are, either within the British Isles or worldwide, and we can do no more than make an educated guess. As we have seen, numerous studies have been published in the last 150 years or so with details of the frequencies of surnames in the British Isles at different points in time. However, all of these studies have looked at a snapshot of the distribution of surnames at a specific date, either by analysing registrations of births, marriages and deaths for particular years or specific quarters within a year, or by looking at national datasets such as electoral registers or censuses for a given year. It is much easier to generate statistics on the approximate frequency of common surnames, and it is interesting to see that the high-frequency surnames appear to have been remarkably stable over the last 150 years with few changes in their rank order. The rarer surnames are much more difficult to quantify. Analysis of the electoral register and the 1881 census has shown that there are huge numbers of surnames that occur only once or a few times in the national datasets for any given year. Without doing comparisons with datasets in other years it is very difficult to establish how many of these singletons are phantom surnames created by mistranscriptions, fantasy surnames provided by the respondent either as a joke or to evade detection, or genuine rare surnames that are on the brink of extinction.

In the analysis of the 1881 census of England and Wales, 396,776 unique surnames were found in a population of around 26 million. If we subtract the 158,876 surnames that only occurred once and were probably the result of mistranscriptions, we are left with a total of 237,900 surnames in 1881, which is the most accurate figure currently available for the historical surname pool prior to the period of mass immigration. The enhanced 2001 electoral register studied by the team at UCL, which also included data for Scotland and Northern Ireland, recorded a total of 1,597,805 surnames shared among 45.6 million people. Some of these names will again be mistranscriptions, but immigration will undoubtedly have introduced many thousands of new rare surnames into the surname pool, and there will also be many transient surnames registered by workers and students who are temporarily residing in the country. We do not have comparable figures for the number of surnames that occurred only once in 2001, though we do know that there were 1.45 million names that had fewer than ten occurrences. If we exclude these names from the total we are left with a 2001 surname pool of 147,800 names, which seems remarkably low in comparison with the 1881 figure of 237,900. If we assume that the singleton surname rate was 40 per cent as it was in 1881 then we are left with a total of 958,683 surnames in 2001, which seems surprisingly high. The real figure probably lies somewhere in between these two extremes, and there are now possibly up to half a million surnames in the British Isles, with perhaps over half of these surnames having been introduced in the last 100 years or so.

With the exception of the Matheson study of Irish surnames, all these published surname studies treat variant spellings as separate surnames. Clark, Clarke and Clerk are, for example, all counted as different surnames, as are Davis and Davies. As we have seen in Chapter 3, it is not always easy to establish which surnames are related, and variant spellings can only be confirmed through diligent genealogical research. The number of extant variants for any given surname can vary considerably. Some surnames might only have survived with a handful of different spellings whereas an old surname that has been in existence since the 1200s might now have survived in a multiplicity of forms. If we were to group surnames into surname families the number of surnames would be greatly reduced and we might have a UK surname pool of between 50,000 and 100,000 core surnames, each with their own unique group of related variants.

It is even more difficult to establish how many surnames there are on a global basis, as there is no public database that provides listings of all the world's surnames. The most comprehensive global name database in the world is probably the Global Name Reference Encyclopedia from IBM, which is incorporated into its Master Data Service. This product incorporates IBM's proprietary InfoSphere Global Name Recognition technology to classify, analyse and match names.[13] This database is, however, designed for use by financial and government organisations to detect fraud and to fight crime and is understandably not available to the family historian. IBM unfortunately does not provide any indication as to the number of surnames in their database.

The UCL World Names Public Profiler holds data from telephone directories and electoral registers for 300 million people in twenty-six different countries. They have 8 million unique surnames in their database, and 5 million unique given names.[14] The UCL team claim that their data represent a total population of 1 billion in the countries surveyed, but this figure constitutes only around a seventh of the total world population, which is now running at over 7 billion. If we multiply the 8 million surnames by a factor of seven we derive a total world population of 56 million surnames. This is, however, likely to be an overestimate. There are still some countries in the world, such as Iceland, which do not use surnames at all. There are also other countries that have only a small pool of surnames in general usage. China, the most populous country in the world, has a very limited stock of around 7,000 surnames. The true figure is probably somewhere in between 8 million and 56 million, and if we pick the halfway point we can make an educated guess that the world surname pool is somewhere in the region of 24 million. Of those surnames, a few really common surnames are shared by hundreds of millions of people. In a list of ten of the most common surnames of the world published by the World Geography website, the Chinese surnames Li/Lee, Zhang and Wang took the top three places, while the Smiths, with an estimated 4 million name-bearers worldwide, were in eighth place (Table 5).[15]

Table 5. Ten of the most common family names in the world. The Silvas of Brazil and the Patels of India should probably also be included though no reliable figures are available. Adapted from 'Ten of the most common surnames in the world', The World Geography website (**www.theworldgeography.com**), 12 April 2012.

Surname	Number	Origin
Li/Lee	100 million	China, Korea, Vietnam
Zhang	100 million	China
Wang	93 million	China
Nguyễn	36 million	Vietnam
Garcia	10 million	Spain
González	10 million	Spain
Hernández	8 million	Spain and Portugal
Smith	4 million	England
Smirnov	2.5 million	Russia
Müller	1 million	Germany

Generating your own distribution data

In this chapter we have considered some of the historical datasets that have been analysed for surname frequencies and looked at the tools that can be used to generate instant figures for your surname. These sites are very helpful when you first start to research a surname and will give you an idea of the scale of the work you are taking on. The dedicated surname researcher will want to study the distribution of a surname in more detail at various points in time, which will involve extracting all references to the surname from national-level datasets. The sources that can be used for this purpose are discussed in Chapters 7 and 8. In order to put surname frequencies in context, the researcher will need to make comparisons with historical population figures. A range of resources on population statistics is provided in Appendix G.

6

HAS IT BEEN DONE BEFORE?

The time is opportune for the vast numbers of people who have an interest in a particular surname (usually their own), or in all the names of the families in a chosen locality, to make a contribution, either by proving the dictionaries right or by suggesting other explanations for the 'homes' of family names.

David Hey, *Family Names and Family History* (2000), p.18

Before starting out on any research it is good practice to check the published literature and online resources to see what research has already been done. Research is a cumulative process and each new generation builds upon the work of its predecessors. An increasing amount of material has now been digitised and made readily available online. Out-of-print books, including many of the old surname dictionaries, can be browsed online or downloaded to read at leisure in the comfort of your own home. Even if the source material is not readily available, indexes or catalogues to published works are now accessible online, and will tell you where the publications can be located. In order to avoid any duplication of effort it is a good idea to find out if anyone else is researching your surname. There are many websites that allow people to advertise their surname interests, and other researchers will often post their family trees online. You might be lucky and find that a lot of the hard graft has already been done. If you are able to collaborate with other genealogists the workload will be shared and the journey of discovery will be all the more enjoyable.

The preliminary survey of the published literature on the surname is only the first part of the research process. The information found will need to be evaluated both in the light of the person who provided the evidence, the date when the research was done and the records that were available at that time. In pedigrees, each link in the chain will need to be reviewed to ensure that the conclusions drawn are valid. Be particularly careful of any pedigree or narrative that does not provide dates for deaths and burials, or that does not give the dates or places where the events took place. This lack of information is often the sign of hasty and sloppy research. There are many false pedigrees claiming descent from an ancestor who died in infancy! Be wary too of trees that jump around from one county to another. This is often an indication that, in an attempt to take a pedigree as far back as possible with a minimal amount of effort, a researcher has cherry-picked names and dates from easily accessible sources without any understanding of the local geography or recognition that even in a small district there may be two or more contemporaneous neighbours with identical names. Many of the records are still not available online, and sometimes the missing jigsaw pieces can only be found in local archives. The most helpful and diligent researchers will provide details of the sources they used to construct their pedigrees so that other genealogists can verify their research. A well-referenced pedigree is usually a hallmark of good-quality research. Wherever possible, pedigrees should be verified in the original records, but this process is now easier than ever as so much original source material is easily accessible online.

Making connections

There are a number of websites that allow family historians to list the surnames that they are researching, and there are also many genealogy forums, message boards and mailing lists where surname interests can be advertised. A list of surname resources is provided in Appendix B. Family history societies often publish members' interests in their journals, and some have made their members' interests available online. It is worthwhile joining the family history societies in the areas where your surname is predominantly found so that you can connect with other people with an interest in your surname. Not all of the members of family history societies are necessarily online and a notice in a journal will be an effective way of reaching the offline members. Most of the family history societies have their own research centres where books and files about local families, often in typewritten and manuscript form, can be found. The Federation of Family History Societies (FFHS) (**www.ffhs.org.uk**) has lists of all its member societies in the British Isles and Australia. Genuki (**www.genuki.org.uk/ Societies**) has a full listing of all the societies relating to the British Isles, including some that are not affiliated with the FFHS. The Guild of One-Name Studies (**www.one-name.org**) maintains an online register of surnames that are being studied by its members. The subject of one-name studies will be discussed in greater detail in Chapter 10. Some of the commercial family history journals such as *Family Tree* magazine allow their readers to publish notices of surname interests. Family historians are increasingly using social networking websites, such as Facebook, Twitter and Google+, to make connections with other researchers. There are many surname groups on Facebook, which effectively serve as mailing lists but also allow group members to upload photographs and documents and to share links.

Thousands of family trees of varying degrees of accuracy and completeness have been published online. These trees should be treated with caution but they can be a useful starting point and you will eventually be able to follow up the research and verify all the names and dates in original records. The main sites that host family trees include: FamilySearch (**www. familysearch.org**), RootsWeb WorldConnect (**http://wc.rootsweb.ancestry.com**), Ancestry (**www.ancestry.co.uk**), Genes Reunited (**www.genesreunited.co.uk**), Geni. com (**www.geni.com**) and MyHeritage (**www.myheritage.com**). For some of these sites a subscription is required to contact other researchers.

Books and journals

Thousands of pedigrees and family histories have appeared in printed sources in books or journals published by local history societies, record societies, antiquarian journals and all manner of other obscure sources. In America, any work published prior to 1923 is out of copyright, and much of this older material has now been digitised and made available online either in the Internet Archive (**http://archive.org**) or on Google Books (**http://books. google.co.uk**). In addition, FamilySearch's Family History Books website (**http://books. familysearch.org**) provides access to over 40,000 digitised genealogy and family history books and journals from the archives of the large American family history libraries.

George W. Marshall attempted to list every pedigree he could find in printed sources that included a minimum of three generations, and he published a comprehensive index in *The Genealogist's Guide* (1903). This work is now available in the Internet Archive, and is a useful finding aid for early pedigrees. Marshall's work was continued by Major J.B. Whitmore who published *A Genealogical Guide* (1953), which indexed all the printed pedigrees published in the first fifty years of the twentieth century, and some missed by Marshall. Geoffrey Barrow published a third volume, *The Genealogist's Guide* (1977), covering the ensuing twenty-five years. T.R. Thomson's *Catalogue of British Family Histories* (1980) contains an index of family histories and where they are located. Many printed and online pedigrees are listed on the relevant country, county or parish pages on Genuki (**www.genuki.org.uk**), but the coverage varies considerably from county to county.

The pedigrees of the aristocracy and gentry are generally the best documented, and their family trees are also recorded in works such as *The Complete Peerage*, *Burke's Peerage*, *Burke's Landed Gentry* and *Debrett's Peerage and Baronetage* (initially published as two separate volumes). Older editions, often with many errors, are freely available in the Internet Archive and other online resources. More recent editions will be found in large reference libraries. Up-to-date pedigrees can be accessed for a fee from Burke's Peerage and Gentry (**www. burkespeerage.com**) and from Debrett's (**www.debretts.com**). A list of suggested corrections to *The Complete Peerage* is maintained at **www.medievalgenealogy.org.uk/cp**. Care should be taken even when consulting the more recent published pedigrees as they are not infallible, and only minimal checks are made.

In the sixteenth and seventeenth centuries, heralds from the College of Arms travelled around the country collecting pedigrees from families with an entitlement to bear arms. These pedigrees were published in a series of publications for each county known as the heralds' visitations. Most of these volumes are now freely available online. Helpful information on the use of the visitations and links to all the online versions can be found on the Medieval Genealogy website at **www.medievalgenealogy.org.uk/guide/vis.shtml**. Some of the visitations were later embellished and expanded, and not always very accurately, by antiquarian writers in the nineteenth century, and these later editions in particular should be used with care. *A Visitation of England and Wales*, edited by Joseph Jackson Howard, Maltravers Herald Extraordinary and Frederick Arthur Crisp, was published in over thirty volumes from 1893 onwards, and provides detailed and accurate pedigrees of all the armorial families going back no more than 200 or 300 years. Some of the later volumes contain abstracts of wills, marriage settlements and other documents to back up the pedigrees. Howard and Crisp also published *A Visitation of Ireland* in four volumes between 1897 and 1904. These books were all privately printed in low numbers, but digital versions of most of the volumes can now be found in the Internet Archive and a list of links is provided at **www.heraldry-online.org.uk/Archivebookslinks.htm**.

The printed bibliographies have now been largely superseded by the numerous online library catalogues. WorldCat (**www.worldcat.org**) provides a searchable online catalogue of the holdings of over 10,000 libraries worldwide but with a particular emphasis on North America. The COPAC library catalogue (**http://copac.ac.uk**) gives free access to the merged library catalogues of the major research libraries in the UK and the Republic of Ireland. The British Library's catalogue (**http://explore.bl.uk**) has details of nearly 60 million items in the British Library's collection. The National Library of Scotland (**www.nls.uk**) has a searchable catalogue to the more than 4 million items in its printed collections, and a number of other searchable databases are also provided. The National Library of Ireland (**www.nli.ie**) has an integrated online catalogue that gives details of the holdings in its printed and manuscript collections, and additional indexes and lists are in the process of being uploaded. The National Library of Wales (**www.llgc.org.uk**) has an online catalogue to over 4 million books, maps, photographs and other materials in its collection. The catalogue of the extensive holdings of the Family History Library in Salt Lake City, Utah, can be searched online at **www.familysearch.org/eng/library/fhlc**. If your surname is concentrated in a particular county or region then it can often be worthwhile searching the online catalogues of the local libraries in that area. If a book of interest is found in one of these catalogues and it is not stocked in your local library it is usually possible to borrow the book for a small fee via an inter-library loan. Second-hand books can often be picked up on Abebooks (**www.abebooks.co.uk**) or Amazon, or can be bought in an online auction on Ebay (**www.ebay.co.uk**). On Ebay it is possible to set up a saved search so that you can receive an email notification when the title you are looking for comes up for sale. Older out-of-copyright books will often be found in the Internet Archive or on Google Books. Some books and general reference works such as the peerage titles can be purchased on CD.

JSTOR (**www.jstor.org**) maintains an archive of digitised back issues of over 1,000 academic journals, and provides a fully searchable index. Most of the content is only accessible via subscribing libraries at universities and elsewhere. Content published prior to 1923 in the United States and before 1870 elsewhere is available free of charge. PERSI, the PERiodical Source Index, indexes articles in over 11,000 genealogy and local history journals in the US and worldwide. Articles are indexed by surname or location and are arranged in over twenty different subject headings. The index can be searched online at Ancestry (**http://search.ancestry.com/search/db.aspx?dbid=3165**) but is only accessible with a worldwide or US subscription. PERSI is also available through the US subscription service Heritage Quest (**www.heritagequestonline.com**). If articles of interest are identified through these catalogues the cheapest option is usually to order a copy of the article from your local library rather than paying the much higher fee to buy a digital copy online.

All pedigrees found in books and journals, however reliable or authoritative the source appears to be, should be considered as a starting point for your research, and should always be verified in the original sources wherever possible. Errors can creep into even the most meticulously researched pedigrees, and the appearance of a pedigree in print is not a guarantee of its accuracy.

Society of Genealogists

The Society of Genealogists (**www.sog.org.uk**) in London has a huge collection of books, journals, manuscripts and CDs in their extensive library, including many family histories and archival collections contributed by genealogists that are not available elsewhere. Members of the society can use the library free of charge; non-members are required to pay hourly or daily search fees. Work to digitise some of the society's collections has started and various databases are now available online in MySoG, the members' area of the website. The online records include parish registers, poll books, marriage licences, monumental inscriptions, indexes to wills and one-name-study material. SoGCAT (**www.sog.org.uk/sogcat/sogcat.shtml**) is an online searchable catalogue of all the

Figure 16. Surname resources at the Society of Genealogists in London.

published, printed and bound material in the society's library. The society's webpage on surnames and families (**www.sog.org.uk/library/surnames_and_families.shtml**) provides an introduction to the various surname-related records at the SoG, which include the surname document collection, the pedigree collection, members' birth briefs, and the great card index (Figure 16). A limited search and copy service is available but a personal visit is recommended if you are within easy travelling distance of London.

Famous name-bearers

As part of a surname study it can be an interesting exercise to investigate the lives of the famous name-bearers. A surname search on Wikipedia will often reveal a list of notable people who have been the subject of a Wikipedia article. The articles are of varying levels of accuracy, but will serve as a starting point for further research. Many databases of biographical resources have now been made available online and can be accessed free of charge from the comfort of your own home with your local library ticket. These databases include the new *Oxford Dictionary of National Biography*, which has entries for over 58,000 people. The sixty-three volumes of the first edition of the *Dictionary of National Biography* can be found in the Internet Archive and on Google Books. A list of links to all these volumes can be found at **http://onlinebooks.library.upenn.edu/webbin/metabook?id=dnb**. The Oxford Reference collection, which includes *Who's Who in the Twentieth Century*, as well as specialist dictionaries on artists, writers and scientists, is usually included in local library subscriptions. The online database of *Who's Who* and *Who was Who* is available online with some library tickets. The History of Parliament website (**www.historyofparliamentonline.org**) is in the process of publishing biographies of members of parliament. Numerous specialist biographical dictionaries for musicians, sportsmen and so on, will be found in your local reference library. Newspaper obituaries are also a rich source of biographical detail. Your library ticket will give you access to *The Times Digital Archive*, which has digitised and indexed copies of the entire content of *The Times* newspaper from 1785–1985. The British Newspaper Archive (**www.britishnewspaperarchive.co.uk**) is available in a variety of subscription packages, but is also available free through some local libraries. If your library doesn't subscribe to all the online resources, it can sometimes be worth registering with a library in a different local authority that offers a wider selection of databases.

DNA projects

DNA testing has been used by genealogists for over a decade and there are now over 7,000 surname DNA projects run by volunteer project administrators, which are using DNA testing as an integral part of their surname research. DNA projects can, therefore, acquire a significant body of genealogical research over the years. One of the very early steps when starting out on a surname study is to check to see if a DNA project has already been registered for your surname. Most of the surname projects will be found at Family Tree DNA (**www.familytreedna.com**), but some will also be found at Ancestry DNA (**http://dna.ancestry.com**). If there is already a project for your surname you will want to become involved with the project and share your genealogical research. DNA projects are of varying sizes: the largest projects now have over 1,000 project members, whereas some newer projects only have a few members. The amount of genealogical information held will vary from project to project. Some projects publish pedigrees on the testing company's website while others maintain an independent website. For the rarer surnames the project administrator will often do most of the genealogical research himself. If there is no project for your surname, you should consider setting up a project of your own. Even if you are not yet ready to start actively recruiting people to take a DNA test it is a good idea to register a project so that you can reserve the name. A project can be started with zero participants and run on a passive basis until you are ready to take the plunge yourself. DNA testing will be covered in greater detail in Chapter 9.

Surname dictionaries

Numerous surname dictionaries have been published in the last 150 years or so that have endeavoured to describe the origins and meanings of thousands of different surnames. The compilers of these dictionaries were necessarily restricted by the resources that were available to them at the time of writing, and the magnitude of the task meant that it was not possible to study any surname in depth. The better dictionaries will record the earliest references of a surname in an attempt to explain its origins, but none of the dictionaries published to date have made any attempt to use genealogical methods to study the distribution and evolution of the surname over time and to establish continuity between the historical references and the living name-bearers. In the light of recent research, many of the published etymologies are now known to be untenable. Some of the surnames included in such dictionaries are names that have been extinct for centuries or bynames that never developed into hereditary surnames. In contrast there are many rarer surnames that have persisted to this day that are not even mentioned. Nevertheless, surname dictionaries can be a useful starting point for research into the origins of a name.

For English surnames, P.H. Reaney's *A Dictionary of British Surnames* has been the standard reference work since its publication in 1958. Dr Percy Hide Reaney (1890–1968) was a grammar-school teacher who spent much of his spare time studying surnames and place-names. He explains in the preface to the first edition of his dictionary that: 'The present work is based on an independent collection of material begun in 1943 to beguile the tedium of the quieter periods of fire-watching.' A second edition, edited by Professor Richard Middlewood Wilson, and incorporating an additional 700 names, was published in 1976 after Reaney's death. A third edition, now retitled as *A Dictionary of English Surnames*, and again edited by Richard Wilson, was published in 1995. An additional 4,000 names were included but many Scottish, Welsh and Irish names were omitted unless they were found in English sources. It has since been found that a significant proportion of the names added by Wilson were bynames or surnames that had been extinct for centuries. The revised third edition of the dictionary contains a total of over 16,000 surnames, and has been in print ever since.

The Oxford Dictionary of Surnames (1988), compiled by the lexicographers Patrick Hanks and Flavia Hodges, took a somewhat different approach and focused not just on the indigenous surnames of the British Isles but also included immigrant surnames found in Britain that originated elsewhere in Europe. It was probably the first systematic survey of surnames with the names selected on the basis of their present-day distribution in telephone directories rather than on the whims of the compiler. The dictionary contains entries for over 10,000 surnames and their related variant spellings. It also includes a useful introductory section on surnames from different countries and cultures. The dictionary was republished in 2002 in a compilation volume entitled *The Oxford Names Companion*, which also included *A Dictionary of First Names* and *A Dictionary of British Place-Names*, but which unfortunately did not include all the introductory notes.

The Oxford Dictionary of Surnames has now been largely superseded by *The Dictionary of American Family Names* (2003), a monumental three-volume work edited by Patrick Hanks. The dictionary contains over 70,000 entries for surnames from all over the world that are found in America today. The entries include information about the frequency of the surname, its origins and meaning, and in some cases the name of the earliest known bearer in North America. There are more than 100 pages of introductory material including a very interesting section titled 'Introductions to Surnames of Particular Languages and Cultures', which contains fourteen essays written by experts on surnames from around the world. At a cost of £280 it is beyond the budget of the average family historian but is well worth checking out if it is available at your local reference library. There is also an online edition that is available to subscribing institutions. The general introduction is available online at **www.casa.ucl.ac.uk/surnames/papers.htm**. Partial entries for individual surnames can be searched free of charge at **www.ancestry.com/learn/facts**, but the frequency counts are excluded, as is the information on the earliest forebear. Much of the introductory material can be viewed on Amazon, and if your surname appears in the first volume, which covers the letters from A to F, it is also possible to perform limited searches inside the book to extract information on a particular surname of interest.

The Penguin Dictionary of British Surnames (2009), edited by John Titford, is an updated version of a dictionary compiled by Basil Cottle and first published in 1967. Titford used Cottle's text as the foundation of his new edition, but, with the benefit of Steve Archer's *British 19th Century Surname Atlas* CD, he was able to provide more accurate information on the origins of surnames derived from place-names, and he also took the opportunity to remove the entries for surnames that had disappeared by 1881, though with a few exceptions. Titford recognises the importance of the genealogical approach to surname study and it is clear that some of the more detailed entries have been provided in consultation with genealogists. He has also incorporated the published research from writers such as George Redmonds and David Hey. Importantly, this is also the first dictionary that makes any mention of DNA evidence (see, for example, the entries for

Brooking and Sykes). The book is clearly aimed at the popular market, and is written in an accessible style, with the text enlivened in places by brief bibliographies of famous name-bearers and a few incidental anecdotes. The author has also made a special effort to 'feature surnames, no matter how rare, borne by friends, acquaintances and former students, especially if they have posed something of a daunting challenge'. For the serious surname scholar the downside is that no early references are included. The entries are of varying lengths: some entries for surnames that clearly did not capture the compiler's imagination consist of just a short sentence whereas others, such as the entry for his own surname, Titford, take up a lengthy paragraph. The result is something of a mixed bag, and it is the more detailed entries that are likely to be of most value.

There are many other general surname dictionaries that were published from the middle of the nineteenth century onwards, as well as a range of specialist dictionaries for Wales, Scotland and Ireland or for specific regions or counties within the British Isles, such as the Isle of Man and Cornwall. A full list is provided in the Bibliography. Copies of the more recent dictionaries will usually be found in local libraries. The Society of Genealogists has an extensive collection. The older dictionaries will often contain fanciful and imaginative etymologies, and they have effectively been superseded by the more recent publications. However, as these dictionaries are out of copyright, most of them have been digitised and they are now readily available online in the Internet Archive or on Google Books. They can easily be searched in a matter of minutes or downloaded and searched on your computer. While the meanings presented will in most cases not necessarily be of much assistance, there is always the chance that they will provide valuable clues to the origins of a specific surname, if, for example, they have provided an early reference to the surname that is not found in a later dictionary or a reference to a place-name as the possible point of origin that has been overlooked by later surname dictionary compilers. Even if the derivation is wrong it can be an interesting and amusing exercise to see what other writers have said about your particular surname. If you are able to find a plausible alternative derivation for your surname you will also be given the satisfaction of proving that the experts were wrong!

The *English Surnames Series* is a set of county volumes published as part of the English Surnames Survey, though not every county was surveyed. The books are not light reading, and are aimed at an academic audience rather than the family historian. The editors did not set out to provide etymologies for all the surnames in each county but instead adopt a thematic approach, and are concerned with the historical origins, evolution and spread of surnames. The format is not standardised and each editor has approached the subject in a different way. The books benefit from extensive lists of references that are valuable pointers for further research in medieval records if your surname is concentrated at the county level.

Family Names in the UK

Family Names in the UK (FaNUK) is a major four-year research project, which is being carried out at the Bristol Centre for Linguistics at the University of the West of

England (UWE) under the direction of Richard Coates. Patrick Hanks, who is a visiting professor at UWE, is the lead researcher. The project will explore the origin, meaning and geographical distribution of over 44,000 surnames. The researchers are collecting information from published and unpublished sources from the eleventh century onwards that will be used to show how names were recorded and how the spelling has changed over time. The project will also draw on some of the more obscure sources that have been overlooked by other surname lexicographers, such as articles published in local history journals and other scholarly publications. Members of the Guild of One-Name Studies have been invited to contribute their specialist knowledge via an electronic questionnaire. The research is scheduled to be completed by the spring of 2014, and the database will then be made available online, and possibly in book form, some time in 2015 or 2016.

All surnames found in the UK today that currently have more than 100 living name-bearers will be included in the database. In addition, the project will include all the surnames that were included in Reaney and Wilson's *Dictionary of English Surnames* which still have living name-bearers, regardless of whether or not they meet the 100-name threshold. Stub entries will be provided for recent immigrant surnames such as Patel, which is now the thirty-second most common surname in the UK. Each entry will provide information on the current distribution of the surname, and the geographical location of the surname in the 1881 census. There will also be extensive lists of the early name-bearers for each surname. Further information about the project can be found at **www1.uwe.ac.uk/ cahe/research/bristolcentreforlinguistics/fanuk.aspx**. An article by Simon Draper and Patrick Hanks in the *Journal of One-Name Studies* provides further details.[1]

While Family Names in the UK will undoubtedly be a seminal contribution to surname research and will effectively make all the previously published surname dictionaries for the British Isles obsolete, there will still be plenty of scope for more detailed research on the origins of the surnames that are listed. Furthermore, as the database will exclude all surnames with fewer than 100 name-bearers (other than those already listed in Reaney and Wilson), there will also be thousands more surnames that are not listed, and whose origins will still need to be explored.

Online resources

In addition to the published surname dictionaries there are a number of online databases of varying quality that provide information on the etymology and history of surnames. The etymologies are often dubious, sources are rarely cited, and often the sole purpose of the database is to encourage the reader to purchase a scroll or a coat of arms, but nevertheless these databases can sometimes provide clues about early references which can then be followed up in the original records. Some of the more useful sites are listed in Appendix B.

7

LAYING THE FOUNDATIONS: THE KEY DATASETS

Genealogical methods have to be used to link modern names with those recorded in historical sources and to establish the variant forms of a surname before plotting them on distribution maps.

George Redmonds, Turi King and David Hey,
Surnames, DNA and Family History (2011), p.6

The records used in a surname study are the same as those used in traditional family history research, but the surname researcher will use the records in a different way. The family historian is interested in reconstructing his or her own family tree and will want to collect as much information as possible on every aspect of the lives of the people who feature in that tree. The surname researcher is interested in the bigger picture and will want to collect not only the data relating to his or her own family but all of the references for the surname of interest in the key genealogical datasets. The focus will be on breadth of coverage rather than depth. The websites and resources described in the earlier chapters on surname mapping and surname frequency are useful starting points for establishing baseline figures, but the dedicated researcher will want to invest time in collecting and analysing data from a range of datasets in order to build up a more detailed picture of the surname. It will be necessary to mine contemporary datasets, such as telephone directories, electoral registers and social networking websites, in an attempt to establish a reasonable estimate of the number of living name-bearers. If the surname being studied is not too large it can be a worthwhile exercise to make contact with as many living name-bearers as possible. The initial focus of the historical research will be on extracting data from birth, marriage and death (BMD) indexes and from the nineteenth- and early twentieth-century censuses in order to build up a picture of the frequency and distribution of the surname over time. Standard genealogical methods can be used to reconstruct the family trees for the surname, but the level of reconstruction achieved will depend on the size of the surname being studied. For more common surnames a collaborative approach, with different researchers taking responsibility for research in particular regions or countries, will be more practical. If the surname is very rare it might well be that all the individuals can be assembled into one tree. With more common surnames there will be multiple unrelated trees. The direction and nature of the research will be dictated by your own interests and the time you have available. Some researchers are more interested in studying the lives of all the people who bore their surname and may want to make a special study of the men who lost their lives in the two world wars or might get distracted researching a particularly illustrious or interesting bearer of their surname. Other researchers will be more interested in the process of reconstructing the trees for the surname or analysing the data and looking at the distribution and frequency of the surname or patterns of migration.

The censuses and records of births, marriages and deaths form the backbone of a surname study. Once this groundwork has been completed the research can be extended further back in time by collecting data from parish registers. The process of reconstructing trees now becomes more difficult, but probate records, if available, will help to verify family relationships, and other records can be used as census substitutes to measure the distribution of the surname in earlier centuries. The main focus of this chapter is on the research process in England and Wales, where research is facilitated by a rich range of records and a centralised system of civil registration of births, marriages and deaths from 1837 onwards. The basic principles will, however, also apply to research in other countries. The key datasets, such as the censuses and indexes of births, marriages and deaths, are hosted on a number of different subscription and pay-per-view websites. Of these, Ancestry and Findmypast have by far the largest range of records and a subscription to both of these services will almost certainly be required at some point during your research. A full list of all the subscription and pay-per-view websites for Britain and Ireland is provided in Appendix A, together with listings of all the main genealogy websites, with an emphasis on name-rich databases and genealogy portals.

Living name-bearers

When starting out on your family history research it is good practice to begin by making contact with your living relatives. They will often have a wealth of knowledge and information to share with you, much of which will not be found in any written records. They might also have certificates and other documents, or even a family bible, that will help to advance your research, and save you the expense of buying your own certificates. When studying a surname the research is focused not just on your own immediate family but extends to all the people who bear the same surname. If the surname is not too common it will pay dividends to make contact with all the living name-bearers. Traditionally this was done by letter, having first identified addresses in telephone directories or electoral registers. Such an approach is now increasingly difficult as more and more people choose to opt out of the published electoral register, have ex-directory telephone numbers or use a mobile phone instead of a landline. The people who are not listed in the telephone directory or who have opted out of the electoral register will instead often be found on the various social networking websites, such as Facebook, LinkedIn and Google+, which have become increasingly popular in the last few years. Facebook now has over 900 million users, and in some countries, such as the UK, Australia and the United States, around half of the population is on Facebook. A variety of tactics will, therefore, need to be deployed to contact as many people as possible with your surname. If you have a postal address a letter is often the best way to make the first contact. If no address is available then messages can be sent via the various social networks. Peter Amsden has written a very helpful booklet entitled *A Guide to Making Contact with Relatives* (1999). Although some parts of the book are now inevitably out of date, much of the basic common sense advice he offers still applies. The use of social networking sites and the more traditional genealogical methods that can be used to contact living people are discussed in detail in *DNA and Social Networking* (Kennett, 2011).

The surname researcher will also be interested in collecting information on living name-bearers in order to study the present-day distribution of the surname. Some of the websites on mapping and surname frequency described in the earlier chapters of this book can be used to obtain estimates of the number of living name-bearers, but for a more accurate figure the dedicated researcher will want to extract his or her own data. Telephone directories and electoral registers can be used for this purpose but are incomplete, though information obtained from civil registration indexes can help to fill in the gaps.

Telephone directories

A public telephone service was introduced in Britain in 1879 and the first telephone directories were published in 1880. Telephones were initially a luxury afforded only by the privileged few, but gradually came into more general usage. By 1975, 52 per cent of the population had a telephone. By 1985 the figure had risen to 81 per cent, and in 1998 96 per cent of the population had a telephone.[1] In the days before the Internet it was rare for people to have ex-directory telephone numbers, and consequently the telephone directories of the 1980s and 1990s provide comprehensive listings of most of the people living in the country at that time. Genealogists from this period often made use of telephone directories to extract the listings for everyone with their surname in order to measure the current distribution of the name. With growing concerns about privacy, the number of people who choose to have ex-directory telephone numbers has increased considerably in the last decade, and by February 2011 58 per cent of the population had opted out of the directory.[2] In addition, with the increase in the use of mobile phones and now smart phones, there are many people who choose not to have a fixed landline at all. British Telecom's current online directory contains just 17 million entries to represent a population of over 60 million people. Telephone directories are, therefore, no longer a satisfactory method for measuring the present-day distribution of a surname, though they can be a valuable resource for extracting details of living name-bearers. The telephone directory for Great Britain and Northern Ireland can now easily be searched online on the BT website (**www.thephonebook.bt.com**) and is also available on many other directory websites. However, it is not possible to do a blanket nationwide search for a specific surname, though searches can be done by county so long as the surname is not too common. There is a certain amount of overlap, and a search for Somerset, for example, will also yield results for Bristol and parts of Devon. It would be a practical proposition to extract all the references for rarer surnames, but a difficult task for the more common surnames. The subscription website Ancestry has put a collection of historic British phone books covering the years 1880–1984 online, which can be found at **http://search. ancestry.co.uk/search/db.aspx?dbid=1025**. This database can be useful for extracting details of individuals who are of particular interest but is not designed in a way to make mass extraction of names a viable proposition.

Electoral rolls

Electoral rolls can be an alternative way of gauging the present-day distribution of a surname, if the records are held at a national rather than a regional level. National datasets are available for the UK but it is not possible for members of the public to have access to the full database. From 2002 onwards electors were given the chance to opt out of the published register, and the number of people who have exercised this option has steadily increased in the last decade. The website 192.com (**www.192.com**) maintains an online database that includes the current edition of the edited register for the UK and historical electoral registers going back to 2002. The online edited version of the 2012 electoral roll contains 26.5 million records, representing just under half of the population. A surname search on 192.com will reveal limited details about the people on the current register bearing a particular surname, and will also reveal the names of the other people living in the same household, but credits need to be purchased to view the full details, including the address. However, in order to view the historical registers for the previous years going back to 2002 an Extended Archive Membership is required at a cost of £149.99 and credit must be purchased on top of this. The cost is, therefore, unlikely to be within the budget of the average family historian. Eroll (**www.eroll.co.uk**) is an alternative website that can be used to search the UK electoral register, but similar charges apply.

192.com, in their previous incarnation as i-CD Publishing, used to publish the UK electoral roll on a CD known as the UK Info Disk. Occasionally, copies come up on Ebay but the bidding can often be frenzied, and the CDs usually sell for around £50. However, a pre-2002 version of the UK Info Disk is still a good investment and cheaper than using the online services.

Births, marriages and deaths

Records of births, marriages and deaths are the basic building blocks of family history research, and the acquisition of the relevant certificates is essential for the construction of an accurate and detailed family tree. When studying a surname as a whole it will not be a realistic or practical proposition to purchase every single certificate for all entries relating to the surname, but instead much useful information can be gleaned from the indexes of births, marriages and deaths. The family historian is only interested in extracting the entries for his or her own particular family, whereas the surname researcher will want to collect all the references to a surname from the relevant indexes. These records can then be used to analyse the data by studying the distribution patterns of the surname and can also be used as an aid to reconstruct the family trees of the surname.

A system of civil registration was introduced in England and Wales on 1 July 1837. All records of births, marriages and deaths from this date onwards are held centrally by the General Register Office (GRO), which is now part of the Identity and Passport Service. The records are also held locally at the relevant register office. The entries in the registers held by the GRO and the local register offices are not available for public inspection and, in order to see the full details of a birth, marriage or death, it is necessary either to order a certificate from the General Register Office or from the local register office. However, marriages that took place in a church were also recorded in the church register, and these records will usually be found in the county record office, though there are some churches that have not yet deposited their parish registers and still retain the records locally. Many of the historical parish registers, and especially those for London, are being indexed, digitised and made available online on subscription websites such as Ancestry and Findmypast, and it is now often possible to view digital images of the original parish register rather than purchasing an expensive marriage certificate. It is sometimes possible to obtain details of baptisms and burials from post-1837 parish registers, which will usually provide sufficient information for the construction of family trees, though not all the detail found on the birth and death certificates will be included. It is not necessary here to provide a full account of the civil registration system but if you are not familiar with the process a full account and all the relevant links can be found on Genuki (**www.genuki.org.uk/big/civreg/index.html**).

All the births, marriages and deaths (BMDs) for England and Wales have been indexed by the GRO, and the indexes were issued in four quarterly volumes each year. These indexes were previously available for public inspection in London at the old Family Records Centre, and prior to that at Somerset House. Alternatively, the researcher could consult copies of the indexes on microfilm or microfiche at a few local record offices and selected Latter-day Saints (LDS) FamilySearch Centres. It was, therefore, necessary to travel to London or some other repository and laboriously transcribe the index entries by hand. The research process has been transformed in the last decade because all the BMD indexes up to 2005 have been transcribed and made available in searchable online databases, which also offer access to images of the original pages in the printed volumes. Complete transcriptions of the indexes from 1837 through to 2005 are available on a number of subscription and pay-per-view websites (see Appendix A). Findmypast also has births and deaths for 2006 but, as yet, no marriages. In addition, the FreeBMD project (**www.freebmd.org.uk**) is in the process of transcribing all the indexes from 1837 to 1983 and making them available online in a free searchable database. The project has transcribed nearly all the births, marriages and deaths up to 1950 and is starting to transcribe the indexes for the remaining years up to 1983. FreeBMD very conveniently allows the user to search for the births, deaths or marriages for a surname and then download the results of the search into a text file. The text file can then be opened in a spreadsheet (in Excel this can be done by using the 'data/ from text' menu) and all the search results will be placed into columns. A small amount of tidying up will be required to remove extraneous information. Searches on FreeBMD are restricted to a maximum of 3,000 results, so for more common surnames the search will need to be subdivided until all the entries have been extracted. Some tidying up will be required, but with a minimum of effort it is possible to create a large database of births, marriages and deaths that can then be manipulated as desired. Any gaps can be filled in by checking the coverage charts and extracting the missing data from one of the subscription websites. The subscription websites will also have to be used to extract the BMDs for the remaining years up to 2005. Extracting the data from Ancestry and Findmypast is a somewhat more laborious process. The data has to be copied and pasted and a considerable amount of tidying up is required, but it is still much quicker than transcribing by hand. Some of the additional information, such as the name of the marriage partner and the age at death for the later records, has to be transcribed by hand as it does not show up in the search results and has to be viewed separately. The process will need to be repeated for each variant spelling that is of interest. The post-2005 BMD indexes (with the exception of the 2006 births and deaths on Findmypast) are not currently available online. The recent indexes can be viewed at the following seven locations:

- Birmingham Central Library
- Bridgend Reference and Information Library
- City of Westminster Archives Centre
- Manchester City Library
- Newcastle City Library
- Plymouth Central Library
- British Library

These repositories also hold records of civil partnerships from 2005–10, and the adoption indexes from 1927 to 2010. Up-to-date information on the availability of the indexes can be found on the DirectGov website (**www.direct.gov.uk**). The GRO overseas records (regimental indexes, consular births, marriages and deaths, etc.) are available free of charge on the Family Relatives website (**www.familyrelatives.com**).

The basic BMD data from the indexes can often be supplemented by cross-referencing with other indexes and databases. Many local register offices have now produced their own indexes to the locally held registers. A full listing of all the online local indexes is maintained on the UKBMD website (**www.ukbmd.org.uk**). The local indexes often include additional information that is not shown in the GRO indexes, such as the spouse's name for a marriage record and the mother's maiden name for a birth record. Also, as the local indexers are working from original records rather than the copies that were supplied to the GRO, the number of transcription errors is reduced. Parish registers (see below) can also be used to supplement the basic index details, and many nineteenth-century parish register records are now freely available online on FamilySearch (**https://familysearch. org**) or one of the genealogy subscription websites (see Appendix A).

Once you have a complete set of BMDs in a spreadsheet, the data can be used for analysis purposes. The researcher might, for example, want to use the data to investigate the distribution of the surname by using one of the map programs such as GenMap (see Chapter 4) to plot births, marriages and deaths by registration district. It will also be possible to generate statistics for the total number of births, marriages and deaths for the surname and all the related spellings. Most importantly, the data can also be used to reconstruct family trees, though such an approach is only practical for lower frequency surnames. Using just the basic data from the BMD indexes the reconstruction process is easier with the twentieth-century records because additional information was included in the indexes. From the third quarter of 1911 onwards the mother's maiden name was recorded against all birth records. From 1912 onwards the surname of the spouse was shown in the marriage index. From 1866 onwards the age at death was included in the death index, and from the second quarter of 1969 onwards the deceased's date of birth was provided. Consequently, it is often possible to match a death record with the corresponding birth record, and to attach birth records to the corresponding marriage record. The male partner in the marriage record can often be linked with a matching birth record as only one viable candidate with the same given name will be found in the indexes. The matching can be made more confidently if the marriage and birth took place in the same registration district or if the male has an unusual forename or two or more forenames. For births, marriages and deaths from 1841 to 1911, the family groupings can be confirmed by cross-referencing with census records (see below). The methodology of the linkage process as used in the Pomeroy one-name study is explained in two detailed papers by Chris Pomery.[3,4]

The methods used to record the reconstructed family trees will vary from one person to another. Some researchers prefer to maintain their entire database in an Excel spreadsheet, while others like to use a relational database such as Access. Some researchers use a family history program called Custodian (**www.custodian3.co.uk**), which was designed for one-name studies. Other researchers record their family trees in one of the many commercial family history programs. For my own one-name study and family history research I use Family Historian (**www.family-historian.co.uk**) to reconstruct the family trees. I maintain a separate Excel spreadsheet with all my BMD data from the GRO indexes, and this acts as a master index and is cross-referenced to my family history program. One of the advantages of the whole-surname approach is that over time it is often possible by a process of elimination to work out which pieces of the jigsaw puzzle go where. For example, if you have two Johns who are a candidate for a particular entry in the death index, once you have one death certificate, you can confidently assign both GRO references to the right people. As the study progresses, you will also find that other researchers will be able to share details of their family trees with you which will help you to assign more of the records in the indexes to a specific tree.

Censuses

A census has taken place in England and Wales every ten years from 1801 onwards with the exception of 1941. The early censuses from 1801 to 1831 were intended to provide a statistical account of the population, and names were not usually recorded. The censuses from 1841 through to 1911 are one of the most valuable genealogical resources for they provide not only names and ages but also a range of other information of value to the genealogist such as family relationships, occupations and place of birth, though the precise details provided vary from one census to the next. All the censuses from 1841 to 1911 have now been transcribed and indexed, and they are all available online on a range of subscription and pay-per-view websites that also provide access to digital images of the original census pages. The 1921 census is expected to be released in 2022, but the 1931 census was destroyed in a fire in 1942. Thanks to the detailed genealogical information provided in the censuses, they can be used, in conjunction with the BMD records, to reconstruct all the family trees for the surname right through to 1911 when the more detailed BMD indexes start to become available. The census information is also useful to analyse the distribution of the surname over time, and can be used to generate maps. Some excellent examples of maps showing the distribution of the surname Adamthwaite in the censuses from 1841 through to 1901 can be seen on the Adamthwaite Archive website (**www.adamthwaitearchive. org.uk/#/distribution-maps-for-the-uk/4531948844**).

Parish registers

Parish registers are the most important source of genealogical information for the three centuries before the introduction of civil registration in England and Wales in 1837. The earliest parish registers date back to the reign of Henry VIII. Following the split from Rome, Thomas Cromwell, the vicar general of the new Church of England, ordered all the parishes to keep a record of baptisms, marriages and burials. The survival of the early parish registers is patchy. Not all the parishes complied with the new order, and early records were often kept on loose sheets that have not survived. From 1598 onwards a bound register was introduced and each year copies of the registers were sent to the diocesan office and recorded in what is known as the bishop's transcripts. Some registers have been damaged or lost, and there are inevitably gaps in many of the registers, particularly during the English Civil War and the ensuing Commonwealth Period. Nevertheless, the surviving records provide a remarkably complete genealogical record of the population of England and Wales. There are around 11,000 ancient parishes of varying shapes and sizes in England and Wales. The records of English parishes are now mostly held in the relevant county record office, though some registers are still retained by the incumbent. Nonconformist and non-parochial registers are held at The National Archives. Indexes are available at **www.bmdregisters. co.uk**, where images of the register pages can be purchased for a small fee. The surviving registers for Wales are found at the National Library of Wales or in the local record offices.

FamilySearch has indexed a large number of parish registers in two record collections known as the International Genealogical Index (IGI) and the British Vital Records Index. These two indexes are now available on the FamilySearch website, and FamilySearch is also in the process of slowly uploading digitised images of the registers in its collection. There are many gaps in FamilySearch's coverage. Somerset and Huntingdonshire are, for example, poorly represented. In Devon, around a third of the parishes are not included in the IGI. Large collections of transcribed and indexed parish registers are now being made available on the subscription websites, and especially on Ancestry and Findmypast. In many cases digital images of the original register pages are also available online. Family history societies have transcribed and indexed many of their local records and will often have CDs of indexed records for sale. Many of the indexes produced by the various family history societies have been included in the Findmypast database. Some transcriptions of parish registers have been made available online and will be linked from the relevant parish page on Genuki. FreeReg (**www.freereg.org. uk**) has a large database of freely available parish register transcriptions. Some parishes have volunteer online parish clerks who will answer individual genealogical enquiries. Details of the online parish clerk project can be found at **www.genuki.org.uk/indexes/OPC.html**.

There is, therefore, a wealth of information available from parish registers, but without a single centralised database, the extraction of the data required for a surname study becomes more complicated. However, for most surnames, once the research has been taken back to the beginning of the nineteenth century it will be found that the surname is localised in just one county or in just a few counties. The focus of the research will now shift to the county level, and using the variety of resources available it is usually possible to extract sufficient indexed data to get a good overview of the distribution of the surname in each county where the name is found. The process of linking the records of baptisms, marriages and deaths to reconstruct the family trees now becomes more difficult as less information is provided in the parish registers than in the records of civil registration. The marriage register does not provide the names of the parents so the process of linking a marriage to a baptism relies largely on geographical proximity and finding a matching candidate of the right age. Burial records do not always provide the age of the person being buried, and if there is more than one burial record for someone with the same name it can be impossible to assign the burial records with any confidence. The process is easier with a rarer surname and if the name is concentrated in small rural parishes, but much more difficult with more common surnames and in the large towns and cities. It is also easier if the families remain in the same parish for a sustained period, which tends to happen more often with the gentry and yeomen classes. Care should be taken when using FamilySearch records in isolation. Burial records are rarely included in the FamilySearch indexes, and if baptisms aren't matched up with corresponding burial records it can be very easy to follow a false trail and mistakenly link a tree to the baptism record of someone who died in infancy. Information from other genealogical sources, such as wills, newspapers and poor law records, will need to be used to help the reconstruction process. A date of death found in a will can be cross-referenced with a burial record, and family relationships described in wills can be confirmed in the parish registers. Other baptism and burial records can then be assigned correctly by a process of elimination.

A particular difficulty that will be encountered when searching in parish registers is the lack of consistent spelling, which can sometimes confound searches in indexed records. The meticulous genealogical approach will, however, yield dividends and in some cases a careful search through parish records will often provide first-hand evidence of the evolution of a surname. Sometimes it is even possible to identify the precise point when the spelling of the surname stabilised. Evidence might also be found in the parish registers of the use of an alias that will provide definitive proof either of a change of surname or the use of a different variant spelling.

It is essential to have an understanding of the local geography when trying to assemble the different parts of the family trees for a surname. In the past people did not often move far from their place of birth. If you are unable to find a baptism in the parish where a marriage took place, the search should first be extended to the neighbouring parishes. Particular care needs to be taken if the surname is found close to a county boundary. The individual might well have been baptised in a neighbouring village just a few miles from where he married, but if the baptism took place in a different county then a search will need to be done in a separate set of indexes. The process is easier now that so much material is indexed and available online but it is important not to jump to hasty conclusions without first checking which parishes are missing from the online datasets. County boundaries have changed considerably over the years. In the local government reorganisation of 1974, parishes that were once in Berkshire moved to Oxfordshire, while the historic county of Huntingdonshire was subsumed into Cambridgeshire, and Rutland became part of Leicestershire. The situation in London is particularly complicated. Maps are an essential tool for parish register research. Most family history societies have county parish maps available for their members either to download or purchase. The Institute of Heraldic and Genealogical Studies (**www.ihgs.ac.uk**) has produced a particularly fine set of large colour maps for every county of England, Wales and Scotland, which give the name of each pre-1832 parish, showing parochial boundaries, probate jurisdictions and the dates of the commencement of registers. Their maps of the City of London, Middlesex, Surrey, Kent and Essex are particularly helpful for an understanding of the pre-1832 parishes in London. Cliff Webb's booklets *Genealogical Research in Victorian London* (8th edn, 2009) and *Genealogical Research in late Victorian and Edwardian London* (5th edn, 2004) list all the parishes in London and provide details of the availability and present-day location of the registers. The booklets are each accompanied by large black-and-white maps of the London parishes, cross-referenced with the text. *The Phillimore Atlas and Index of Parish Registers* (Humphery-Smith, 2002) reproduces the IHGS maps, on a much smaller scale, requiring the use of a magnifying glass to pick out the details. *The Phillimore Atlas* also includes topographical maps of each county from 1834, and provides details of the survival and present-day location of all the parish registers in the UK. Increasingly, however, the information on the present-day location of parish registers will be found on the website of the county record office or on the relevant parish page of Genuki.

Maps and a knowledge of local history are also useful for understanding long-distance migrations. If a baptism is not found in a nearby parish then the registers of the nearest market town should be searched. A look at the transport links – by road, rail and river – might provide further clues or an explanation for a documented migration. London has long been a magnet for the young and the adventurous, and there can be few surnames that cannot be found in London at some point in their history. Bristol, Norwich, Manchester and other large towns and cities similarly attracted people from much further afield than the nearby parishes. The research is much more challenging in the large towns and cities, and especially in London. With some trees it is possible to trace the line right back to the start of the parish registers. Other lines seem to get stuck in the late eighteenth century and, despite much diligent searching, no further progress can be made. DNA testing can sometimes help to provide a breakthrough in such a situation and is also useful to verify trees or to link trees together for which no documentation can be found (see Chapter 9).

Wills

Wills are an important resource as they provide genealogical evidence of family relationships. Although wills are more likely to be found for the wealthier classes, there are also many wills that can be found for the more ordinary members of society, such as farmers, butchers and mariners. Transcribing wills can be a time-consuming but enjoyable exercise, and it takes time to master the art of reading old handwriting (see Chapter 8). However, for the purposes of a surname study much valuable information can be gleaned from the many will indexes that are now publicly available. From 1858 onwards probate record-keeping in England and Wales became the responsibility of the State rather than the Church. Since that time, all wills and letters of administration have been held centrally by the Principal Probate Registry in London. Calendars that provide details of the name and place of death of the deceased, the names of the executors and the value of the estate were published annually. Ancestry now has the probate indexes from 1858 to 1966 available online as part of its subscription service. The Probate Service has promised for some years to make the calendars available online free of charge, and it now appears that the launch will finally happen towards the end of 2012. The calendars will not be fully indexed but will be made available as images that can be navigated by browsing through the first few letters of a surname.

Prior to 1858, wills were dealt with by a bewildering number of ecclesiastical courts. There is no unified index and the records are mostly held in the local county record offices, though indexes to many of the will collections are now available online, and on some sites it is possible to view or purchase images of the original wills. The Prerogative Court of Canterbury (PCC) was the most important of the ecclesiastical courts, and over 1 million wills were proved in this court between 1384 and 1858. The original records are held at The National Archives. The entire collection has now been digitised, and the indexes can be searched free online at **www.nationalarchives.gov.uk/documentsonline/wills.asp**. Images of the wills can be purchased and downloaded for a small fee. British History Online has a small collection of wills and inventories at **www.british-history.ac.uk/catalogue.aspx?type=2&gid=73**. Over 190,000 Welsh wills can be viewed free online on the website of the National Library of Wales (**www.llgc.org.uk/index.php?id=487**). The Genuki page on probate records (**www.genuki.org.uk/big/eng/Probate.html**) has information on locating probate records and links to the various indexes and databases that are available online.

Hearth tax returns

The hearth tax was introduced in England and Wales in 1662 to provide a regular source of income for King Charles II, the newly restored monarch. Each household in England and Wales was required to pay 2s a year for every hearth, fireplace and stove in his or her dwelling. The money was to be paid in two equal instalments on Lady Day (25 March) and Michaelmas (29 September) by the occupier or, if the house was empty, by the landlord. Only those whose house was worth more than 20s a year and who paid church and poor rates were liable for the hearth tax. The tax collectors had to collect an exemption certificate from those who were not eligible to pay. Lists of householders were compiled for each parish and maintained for each county. From 1663 onwards the exempt householders were included in the listings. The authorities experimented with a number of methods of collecting the taxes as the yields in the early years were disappointingly low. The only returns of genealogical value are those for 1662 to 1666 and 1669 to 1674. These returns were audited by the Exchequer auditors and are held at The National Archives. The collection of the taxes in the remaining years was administered by salaried commissioners and officials, and the returns were not sent to the Exchequer. The tax was very unpopular and was finally repealed in 1689 at the start of the reign of William and Mary.

At least one complete list seems to have been preserved for every county in England and Wales, and because the listings include not just property owners but also the inhabitants of the houses and the exempt taxpayers, the hearth tax returns provide a comprehensive list of the population of England and Wales in the seventeenth century. Prior to the year 2000, transcripts of seventeen hearth tax returns were published by a number of different individuals and organisations. The Centre for Hearth Tax Research, based at Roehampton University in London, is now collaborating with the British Record Society (BRS) to publish transcripts for those counties without a published version. The first volume was published in 2000, and there are now seven BRS volumes in print. Details can be found on the British Record Society's website (**www.britishrecordsociety.org/hearthtax.htm**). Essex is due to be published in the summer of 2012. London is expected to be published within the next two years, and other counties will follow. The Centre for Hearth Tax Research also maintains the Hearth Tax Online website (**http://hearthtax.org.uk**), which serves as a platform for the publication and dissemination of research and analysis on hearth tax records, and also provides a searchable index to the names that appear in some of the published volumes (Figure 17). Transcripts of the hearth tax returns for Leicester (1664) and Pembrokeshire (1670) are available in the Internet Archive (**http://archive. org/search.php?query=hearth%20tax**). The hearth tax returns for the City of London

(1662), Westminster (1664), and the City of London and Middlesex (1666) are available on British History Online (**www.british-history.ac.uk/catalogue.aspx?gid=54**). CDs of the hearth tax returns for Devon (1674), Cornwall (1660–64) and Somerset (1664–65) can be purchased from West Country Books (**www.westcountrybooks.com**). The Suffolk (1674) and Somerset (1664–65) returns are available on CD from S&N Genealogy Supplies (**www.genealogysupplies.com**). The Suffolk returns can also be purchased from Archive CD Books Ireland (**www.archivecdbooks.ie**), and are available to Ancestry subscribers. They are somewhat misleadingly catalogued in a collection entitled 'Suffolk, England, Extracted Parish Records'. Details of the other printed hearth tax returns can be found in the COPAC (**http://copac.ac.uk**) and WorldCat (**www.worldcat.org**) catalogues. The printed volumes are expensive to buy but can be borrowed from your local library via the inter-library loan scheme.

When the publication programme has been completed the hearth tax returns will be a valuable and unparalleled resource for assessing the distribution of a surname in seventeenth-century England and Wales. As yet, there is no centralised index, so apart from the few volumes that are indexed online, each printed volume has to be consulted separately. However, most surnames tend to be concentrated in just a few counties by the time the research gets back to the 1600s, and a scan of the relevant county volumes, if available, will

Figure 17. The hearth tax returns can be used to plot the distribution of a surname in the seventeenth century. The returns for many counties can now be searched on the Hearth Tax Online website.

be a worthwhile exercise and can be used as a supplement to the surviving parish registers to measure distribution at the county level. Where countywide parish register indexes are not available, the hearth tax returns can also serve as an effective finding aid by helping to prioritise research in the parish registers where the surname is most likely to be found.

The National Archives has published a useful guide to the hearth taxes, which can be found at **www.nationalarchives.gov.uk/records/research-guides/hearth-tax.htm**. *The Hearth Tax, other later Stuart Tax Lists and the Association Oath Rolls* (Gibson, 1996) has a full list of the surviving hearth tax returns.

Protestation returns

In 1641 Parliament passed a bill requiring all men over the age of 18 to sign an oath of allegiance to King Charles I and to 'promise, vow and protest to maintain and defend as far as I lawfully may, with my Life, Power and Estate, the true reformed Protestant Religion expressed in the Doctrine of the Church of England, against all Popery and Popish Innovations within the realm …'. Lists of all the men who signed the oath were compiled for each parish, and these lists were sent to Parliament in 1642. The original returns are held at the House of Lords Record Office. The returns are incomplete and only cover about one-third of English parishes and just three Welsh boroughs. Devon has the largest return, in terms of the number of parishes, and the return for Cornwall is probably the most complete. In contrast, there are no surviving returns for the City of London, Bedfordshire, Gloucestershire, Herefordshire, Leicestershire, Norfolk, Northamptonshire, Rutland or Suffolk, and only incomplete returns for some other counties. However, for the counties where returns do survive these records provide a treasure trove of surnames and effectively serve as a census of the male population over the age of 18 in 1641. Most of the protestation returns have been transcribed and published at the county level. There is no overall national index, and it is therefore necessary to search on a county-by-county basis in the parts of the country where your surname is likely to be found. The returns are arranged by parish and grouped in hundreds. The protestation returns for West Sussex are available in the Internet Archive (**http://archive.org/details/publications05suss**). The surviving returns for Wiltshire were published in *Wiltshire Notes and Queries Volume 7* (1911–13) and are also available in the Internet Archive (**http://archive.org/details/ wiltshirenotesqu07deviuoft**). Transcripts of the protestation returns for Cornwall and Somerset are available on CD from West Country Books (**www.westcountrybooks. com**). The Lincolnshire returns are available on CD from the Lincolnshire Family History Society. The other printed volumes are only available in a limited number of large reference libraries. The COPAC or WorldCat catalogues can be checked to identify if a published volume is available for the county of interest, and the book can then be borrowed on an inter-library loan. Gibson and Dell (1995) provide a list of all the surviving protestation returns in the House of Lords Record Office and elsewhere.

Other sources

It has only been possible to cover the major datasets that are of particular importance for a surname study here. The researcher will also want to make use of all the standard genealogical resources such as newspapers, monumental inscriptions, occupational records, poor law records and directories. A comprehensive guide to genealogical sources for the British Isles can be found in *Ancestral Trails* by Mark Herber (2nd edn, 2005). For Welsh family history research the definitive guides are *Welsh Family History: A Guide to Research* (2nd edn, 2009) and *Second Stages in Researching Welsh Ancestry* (2010) by John and Sheila Rowlands. Colin Chapman's booklet *Pre-1841 Censuses & Population Listings in the British Isles* (5th edn, 2002) is a useful guide to the lesser-known name-rich lists that survive mainly at the local level from 1086 to 1841, but is strongest on sources from 1600 onwards.

Ireland

The civil registration of births, marriages and deaths commenced in Ireland in 1864, but Protestant marriages were registered from 1845 onwards. The Irish BMD indexes through to 1958 are available on the FamilySearch website. From 1922 onwards, with the partition of Ireland, separate indexes were maintained in Northern Ireland and the Republic of Ireland, and only a small proportion of the post-1922 Northern Ireland BMDs are on FamilySearch. The Irish census returns from 1861 to 1891 were destroyed by the government, and the early census returns from 1821 to 1851 were lost in the fire in 1922 at the Four Courts in Dublin, which was at that time the home of the Irish Public Record Office. The Irish censuses for 1901 and 1911 have been indexed and digitised and are freely available on the website of the Irish National Archives. Griffith's Valuation Indexes, which were published between 1847 and 1864, serve as a census substitute, and are available free online at Ask About Ireland (**www.askaboutireland.ie/griffith-valuation/index.xml**). An alternative index is available at **www.failteromhat.com/griffiths.php**.

The Irish Genealogy website (**www.irishgenealogy.ie**) has a collection of almost 3 million pre-1900 church records available to view free of charge. These records currently include Roman Catholic and Church of Ireland records from Counties Carlow, Cork, Kerry, Monaghan and Dublin City. Some church records are available on FamilySearch, though the coverage is patchy. Many Irish records are available on the subscription websites, such as Findmypast Ireland and Irish Origins, which are listed in Appendix A. The Irish Family History Foundation's Roots Ireland website (**www.rootsireland.ie**) has a huge collection of almost 19 million records available on a pay-per-view basis. The records include parish registers, gravestone inscriptions, tithe applotment books and passenger lists.

The *Irish Times* website (**www.irishtimes.com/ancestor/browse/records/wills**) has a useful guide to Irish wills. The Public Record Office of Northern Ireland (**www.proni.gov.uk**) has an index to wills dating from 1858 to 1943 with some gaps. Images of the wills from 1858 to 1900 can be viewed free online. The National Archives of

Ireland has digitised the calendars of grants of probate of wills and letters of administration for the years 1922–82 and these can be found at **www.nationalarchives.ie/2012/04/ will-calendars-1922-1982-online**. The wills from 1858–1922 will eventually be added to this collection. The Irish probate calendars are difficult to navigate on the website. Chris Paton has provided a user guide with direct links to the PDF files for each year at **http://britishgenes.blogspot.co.uk/p/ireland-probate-calendars.html**. Many of the early wills were destroyed in the fire of 1922 but published indexes and abstracts have survived, and these are available on some of the subscription websites.

Claire Santry's Irish Genealogy Toolkit website (**www.irish-genealogy-toolkit. com**) is an excellent guide to family history research in Ireland. The Bowes one-name study website has a useful list of Irish records that can be used to measure the distribution and frequency of a surname in Ireland over time (**www.bowesonenamestudy.com/ findings_2/distribution_and_frequency/ireland-2**). Extracts for the Bowes surname are provided, which give a good idea of the type of information that is available from each record. For more detailed advice on Irish records John Grenham's *Tracing Your Irish Ancestors* (4th edn, 2012) is the most comprehensive and authoritative guide.

Scotland

Scotland has a very similar set of BMD and census records to England and Wales. Civil registration in Scotland started in 1855, and all the Scottish BMD and census records, along with parish registers, wills and testaments and other records, are held centrally on the ScotlandsPeople website (**www.scotlandspeople.gov.uk**). In order to view the full index entries and the original images it is necessary to purchase credits. A cheaper option if you live in Scotland or plan to visit the country is to spend a day at the ScotlandsPeople Centre in Edinburgh. A daily search fee of £15 is charged, but it is possible to view not just the indexes but also all of the original digitised historical records (births over 100 years ago, marriages over seventy-five years ago and deaths over fifty years ago). Scottish certificates provide much more detailed information than their English counterparts.

The National Archives of Scotland (NAS) (**www.nas.gov.uk**) has an online catalogue. NAS was merged with the General Register Office for Scotland in April 2011 to form the National Records of Scotland, and a new website is under contruction at **www. nrscotland.gov.uk**. The Scottish Archive Network (**www.scan.org.uk**) has an integrated catalogue to the holdings of fifty-two Scottish archives.

There are numerous books on Scottish genealogy, but no single definitive guide. The most useful books include Bruce Durie's *Scottish Genealogy* (3rd edn, 2012), Anthony Adolph's *Tracing Your Scottish Family History* (2008), and Kathleen B. Cory's *Tracing Your Scottish Ancestry* (3rd edn, 2004). Rosemary Bigwood's *Tracing Scottish Ancestors* (1999) in the Collins Pocket Reference series, though from the pre-Internet era and now out of print, still remains a valuable guide. *Tracing Your Scottish Ancestors: The Official Guide* (2011) looks specifically at the records held at The National Archives of Scotland.

Other countries

A similar process of data extraction can be undertaken in other countries where your surname is found, but it is beyond the scope of this book to give an overview of these sources. FamilySearch has hundreds of datasets of births, marriages and deaths from all around the world, and is a good starting point for an investigation of the overseas distribution of a surname. The collections are of varying degrees of completeness and it is necessary to consult the description of each individual record collection to see what records are included. The FamilySearch wiki (**www.familysearch.org/learn/wiki**) is an increasingly valuable resource, and has many pages on international sources. Many other international datasets can be accessed with an Ancestry worldwide subscription. WorldGenWeb (**www.worldgenweb.org**) is a gateway to international genealogy websites.

8

SURNAME ORIGINS: PRE-1600 RESOURCES

… there is probably no person capable of the least degree of reflection, who has not, in an idle moment, amused himself with some little speculation on the probable origin of his own name.

Mark Antony Lower, *English Surnames: Essays on Family Nomenclature*,
'Preface to first edition' (1842), p.viii

As surname research progresses beyond parish registers, the records become sparser. We no longer have records of births, baptisms, marriages, burials and deaths covering the bulk of the population, though wills continue to be an important source of genealogical information. The early records that are available largely relate to the administration of government, taxation, the inheritance of land and property, and the records of the courts. Nevertheless, there is a rich variety of sources available to work backwards from the beginning of the parish registers to the time when surnames began to be adopted. If the people with your surname are from a landed family, it is often possible to obtain a good deal of genealogical information from the medieval records and to trace the line back for many more generations. Even for people of lesser status, many incidental references to ordinary people will be found, particularly in court records, manorial records and in some of the tax records where the threshold was set at a low level. Many of the sources are now in the form of lists of names – such as tax lists and muster rolls – that provide no clues to family relationships. The aim of the surname study is now to locate as many early surname references as possible. Even if the records do not provide confirmation of the genealogical links between each generation, it will often be possible to prove continuity of a surname in a particular location. The accumulation of evidence can then be used to explain the evolution of a surname and to pinpoint its likely origin or origins. If the surname is derived from a place-name, a search of early references might provide clues about the manor or farmstead from which the name was derived. With all surnames there will inevitably be lots of loose ends with isolated surname references that are impossible to fit into the bigger picture. Without corroborating information it will also be impossible to tell whether these single references are actual surnames or simply transitory bynames that never became hereditary.

Only a few medieval records are as yet available in conveniently searchable online databases, but many of the important records were transcribed and published in the late nineteenth and early twentieth centuries. These books are now out of copyright and many have been digitised and made available online in the Internet Archive and on Google Books. The medieval records are usually collected and published at the county level, but most surnames, even the most common ones, tend to have a strong regional concentration, so the best course of action at this stage is to focus the research on the counties where the surname is predominantly found, but to make use of online databases wherever possible to search for early references in other counties.

Spellings now become much less predictable, and it is difficult to anticipate the spellings that the medieval scribes might have used. When searching printed volumes, whether online or offline, it is always a useful exercise to scan the index, if available, in order to make a note of all the likely variant spellings that have been listed. The texts that have been uploaded to the Internet Archive and elsewhere can be searched by keyword, but the optical character recognition technology used to convert the books into searchable text is not always successful and key references might be overlooked if the index is not checked. In order to avoid duplication of effort, it is vital to keep a research log of the books that you have searched so that you don't waste time and energy searching the same book twice. An additional problem is that many of the early surname references are in Latin, and often in heavily abbreviated Latin, making it more difficult for the non-specialist to understand the meaning of the references found, though the records are written in a formulaic fashion and, even with the most basic knowledge of Latin grammar, it is usually possible to crack the code.

The key pre-1600 sources have been discussed in this chapter in chronological order for ease of understanding, but for all practical purposes the best strategy at this stage is to search all the online databases first. The remaining sources should then be searched in reverse chronological order. For some surnames it will not be possible to find references earlier than the 1500s or possibly the 1400s. For other surnames, and especially those with links to the landed classes, there will be an abundance of references going right back to the thirteenth or twelfth centuries. More and more medieval resources are now being digitised and made available in searchable online datasets, and it is becoming easier than ever to find early surname references and to elucidate the origins of your surname.

Anglo-Saxon names

The Ardens and the Berkeleys are widely believed to be the only families who can reliably trace their descent in the male line before the Conquest. The Ardens are descended from Aelfwine, an Anglo-Saxon nobleman who was Sheriff of Warwickshire.[1] The Berkeleys are reputedly descended from Robert FitzHarding, the grandson of Abnod, or Eadnoth, who was a horse thane to Edward the Confessor. Berkeley Castle in Gloucestershire has been in the possession of the Berkeley family for over 800 years, and is best known for being the scene of the murder of King Edward II in 1327.[2] There are, however, many other English surnames that are formed from Anglo-Saxon names, but the original bearer of the name would probably have lived in the twelfth or thirteenth centuries and it is unlikely that it will be possible to prove a direct line of descent. P.H. Reaney provides an extensive list of surnames and bynames derived from Anglo-Saxon names in the *Oxford English Dictionary of Surnames*,[3] and discusses the subject in detail in *The Origins of English Surnames*.[4] It is not clear how many of the names he lists actually developed into hereditary surnames and survived to the present day. An extensive list of Anglo-Saxon names is also provided by George William Searle in *Onomasticon Anglo-Saxonicum* (1897). If your surname is thought to be of Anglo-Saxon origin a wonderful database has now been made available online by King's College London. The PASE database (**www.pase.ac.uk**) provides information on all the recorded inhabitants of Anglo-Saxon England from the late sixth to the late eleventh century. PASE is an acronym for Prosopography of Anglo-Saxon England. Prosopography involves the systematic collection of all available biographical data for a particular group of people. Regardless of whether or not your surname is of Anglo-Saxon origin, it is fascinating to browse through the list of names to get an insight into the names of the Anglo-Saxon world.

Domesday Book

Domesday Book is England's oldest and most famous public record. The great land survey, commissioned by William the Conqueror and completed with remarkable speed between 1085 and 1086, describes in astonishing detail the landholdings and resources of England twenty years after the Norman Conquest. It was effectively the first census of England, though it does not provide full coverage of the country as some of the most northerly counties were not surveyed and major cities such as London and Winchester are missing completely. It is not clear if these cities were surveyed and omitted from the final copying up or never surveyed at all. Domesday provides the first evidence of surnames in Norman England, but only a handful of those surnames are still in use today and, as we have seen in Chapter 1, it is only believed to be possible to prove a line of descent from just one of those names: the surname Mallet. However, Domesday Book is a rich resource for place-names. Over 13,000 settlements are described, and over 90 per cent of these places are still found today. Many of our modern surnames are derived from place-names that were recorded in Domesday Book.

There are now numerous online resources for Domesday Book. The National Archives has an online database (**www.nationalarchives.gov.uk/domesday**) that can be searched by place-name and person (Figure 18). For a small fee you can download colour images of the folios together with a translation from the authoritative Editions Alecto. The Open Domesday project (**http://domesdaymap.co.uk**) provides a free online copy of Domesday Book that can be searched by place-name or by postcode. The Domesday entries for each individual place are provided and there is a link to a colour digital copy of the original handwritten folio pages in Latin as well as a map showing the present-day location on Google Maps. Phillimore (**www.phillimore.co.uk**) has published comprehensive Domesday editions for each English county with detailed notes. The entire

Figure 18. Domesday Book is England's oldest and most famous public record, and is stored at The National Archives in London. It is readily accessible from a number of online and offline resources.

set is also available on an Explorer CD, which unfortunately is not compatible with newer 64-bit computers. Background information on Domesday Book, together with a list of the major landholders, can be found at **www.domesdaybook.co.uk**. The historian and Domesday expert David Roffe has a summary of all the available Domesday texts and CD versions together with a comprehensive list of resources on his website at **www. roffe.co.uk/dbonline2.htm**. A summary of online resources can also be found on the Medieval Genealogy website at **www.medievalgenealogy.org.uk/guide/dom.shtml**.

Pipe rolls

After Domesday Book there is a big gap in the English public records until the middle of the twelfth century when a series of records known as the pipe rolls becomes available. The earliest surviving pipe roll dates from 1129–30 and is the second-oldest public record in existence after Domesday Book. No pipe rolls have survived for the next twenty-five years, but from 1155 onwards the pipe rolls continue in an almost unbroken series until 1833. They are the earliest series of English government records. The pipe rolls contain accounts of the royal income for each financial year arranged by county. The first thirty-seven volumes of the pipe rolls through to the year 1187 can be found on FamilySearch Books (**http://books.familysearch.org**) and in the Internet Archive. A chronological listing of links to all the online volumes can be found on the Medieval Genealogy website (**www.medievalgenealogy.org.uk/sources/pipe.shtml**). A full list of the published pipe rolls can be found on the website of the Pipe Roll Society (**www.piperollsociety. co.uk**). The indexes to each volume can be easily checked for surnames of interest but interpreting the records is more difficult as they are all written in Latin, and the early pipe rolls are written in very abbreviated Latin. The National Archives has a research guide to *Pipe Rolls 1130–c.1300*, which can be found at **www.nationalarchives.gov.uk/records/ research-guides/pipe-rolls.htm**.

Domesday People and *Domesday Descendants*

Two important and authoritative publications by Katharine Keats-Rohan, a medievalist at the University of Oxford, have brought together all the major sources on people found in English and French administrative records in the hundred years after the Conquest. The work is in the form of a prosopography – a biographical register – of all the major landholders in England of Continental European origin from 1066 to 1166. The first volume, *Domesday People* (Keats-Rohan, 1999), synthesises the information provided in Domesday Book, the pipe rolls and the *cartae baronum* (a baronial survey carried out in 1166) to provide comprehensive listings of all the persons occurring in Domesday Book. The second volume, *Domesday Descendants* (Keats-Rohan, 2002), draws on additional resources such as surveys and thousands of royal and private charters found in British and French archives to provide biographical details of over 7,500 people. A third volume in the series, *Domesday Names: An Index of Latin Personal and Place Names in Domesday Book* (Keats-Rohan and Thornton, 1997), provides an all-Latin index to Domesday Book, comprising two indices *personarum* and one index *locorum*, and is only likely to be of specialist interest. The books were the output of a major research project known as the Continental Origins of English Landholders 1066–1166 (COEL). The COEL database is available on CD and complements the material available in the books, though the three-figure cost of purchase is likely to be beyond the budget of most family historians. Further details can be found on the COEL website (**www.coelweb. co.uk**). Katharine Keats-Rohan has published some corrections in PDF files that are available at **http://users.ox.ac.uk/~prosop**. Rosie Bevan has compiled a much more extensive list of corrections, which is maintained in a searchable online database on the website of the Foundation for Medieval Genealogy (**http://fmg.ac/Projects/Domesday**).

Hundred rolls

The hundred rolls were enquiries into the rights of the Crown over land and property which were conducted between 1255 and 1280. The hundred rolls that were known to be extant in 1818 were published in two enormous bulky volumes, *Rotuli Hundredorum*, by the Record Commission in 1812 and 1818. The returns for 1279–80 were particularly detailed and list the names of all tenants. Unfortunately, not all counties were surveyed, and not all the returns have survived. There are surviving returns for 1279–80 for the following twelve counties: Bedfordshire, Buckinghamshire, Cambridgeshire, Huntingdonshire, Leicestershire, Middlesex, Norfolk, Oxfordshire, Rutland, Shropshire, Suffolk and Warwickshire. The hundred rolls are all written in abbreviated Latin, but are good sources for names at a key period of surname formation. They are available on CD or as a download from TannerRitchie Publishing (**www.tannerritchie.com**) but otherwise are currently only accessible in some university libraries and a few large reference libraries. A translation of the Kent hundred rolls for 1274–75 has been published online by the Kent Archaeological Society at **www.kentarchaeology.ac/khrp/hrproject.pdf**. Five further county volumes are available: *Economy & Society in Medieval Buckinghamshire: The Hundred Rolls 1254–1280* (Bailey, 2006); *Oxfordshire Hundred Rolls of 1279: Bampton and Witney Borough* (Stone and Hyde, 1969); *The Staffordshire Hundred Rolls* (Wrottesley, 1880); *The Hundred Rolls and Extracts Therefrom ... County of Suffolk* (Hervey, 1902); and *The Warwickshire Hundred Rolls of 1279–89: Stoneleigh and Kineton Hundreds* (Trevor, 1992). Hundred rolls discovered since 1818 and not in print are currently being edited by the Sheffield Hundred Rolls Project at the University of Sheffield (**www.roffe.co.uk/shrp.htm**).

Thirteenth- and fourteenth-century lay subsidy rolls

Early taxation records can be a very useful source of surname information. Taxes were usually levied when the king needed extra money to support military operations, and consequently more records tend to be available from the more turbulent periods of English history. The lay subsidies of 1290–1332, from the years leading up to the Hundred Years War, are the earliest taxes for which comprehensive returns survive. Lay subsidies were based on the moveable personal property of individuals rather than on the land that they owned and the buildings they lived in. These taxes are known as lay subsidies because they were only payable by the lay population, and the clergy were exempt. For many centuries the clergy were taxed separately from the rest of the population, and the corresponding returns can be found in the clerical subsidies. The lay subsidy of 1332 was the last one in which the names of individuals were recorded. There was no subsidy in 1333, and from 1334 onwards it was left to the local population to apportion the sum of money that had to be raised in a manner that seemed equitable. The subsidy rolls from 1334 onwards are good resources for place-names but contain no surnames. There is, however, one exception. In Kent, detailed lists of the individual taxpayers were kept in 1334 and names continued to be recorded in the Kent assessments in later years. The subsidies only record the names of the heads of household, and over 90 per cent of the taxpayers were men. It is thought that most of the women who appear in the tax lists are widows. Nevertheless, the subsidy rolls are a rich source of surnames, providing details of all the taxpaying inhabitants of each village at a key point in English history in the decades preceding the Black Death, which wiped out over a third of the population and led to the extinction of many surnames. The subsidy roll for Devon alone contains around 10,000 names. Many of the early tax lists have been transcribed and published by local record societies and archaeological societies, and most English counties have at least one taxation return in print for the period 1290–1332. Wales was not normally subject to parliamentary taxation during this period but was expected to make contributions in times of need. A subsidy was granted for the first time in Wales in 1291, with payments levied in 1292–93. Only a few of the Welsh rolls have survived and most of the names are of the patronymic form, but the rolls nevertheless provide a fascinating insight into the names in use in Wales at this time. There is no centralised index to the lay subsidies and it is therefore necessary to search each county volume separately, though in practice many surnames are very localised, and it will only be necessary to consult a few of the volumes. A list of all the printed subsidy rolls is provided in Appendix C, with links to online sources where available. The volumes for other counties will be found in large reference libraries, and can also be borrowed via inter-library loan.

Poll taxes

The poll taxes of the late fourteenth century were part of an experiment to increase the number of people paying taxes by shifting the basis of taxation from property to the individual. Three poll taxes were levied in 1377, 1379 and 1381 to finance the continuing war with France. The first poll tax of 1377 was a poll tax in the true sense of the word. The tax was levied at a flat rate of 1 groat (4d) per capita. Every lay man and woman, married or single, of 14 years of age and over, was required to pay the tax. The only people exempt were 'true and genuine mendicants' (members of a religious order whose members originally lived solely on alms). By 1379 the idea that individuals should be taxed according to their resources re-emerged. This second tax was levied on all lay married and single men and all single women of 16 years of age and over. The amount of tax payable varied from 4d to 10 marks (£6 13s 4d) as set out in a schedule. Only genuine paupers were exempt. The third and final poll tax of 1381 was payable by all lay men and women, married and single, of 15 years of age and over. Genuine paupers were once again exempted. The administration of the tax was somewhat more complicated. Everyone was required to pay 3 groats (1s) such that:

- the number of shillings should equal the number of taxpayers in each vill and
- everyone should be charged according to his means and
- the rich should help the poor, but
- no single person or married couple should pay more than 60 groats (20s) or less than 1 groat (4 pence).

The 1381 poll tax was one of the causes of the Peasants' Revolt, which began in June that same year. The failure of this unpopular tax led to its abandonment until the seventeenth century when it was intermittently revived between 1641 and 1703, although only a few nominal returns of these later poll taxes survive.

The poll taxes have now been transcribed and published by Dr Carolyn Fenwick in three monumental volumes: *The Poll Taxes of 1377, 1379 and 1381* (1998–2005). As Fenwick comments in the introduction to volume I: 'The documentary records of the English poll taxes of 1377, 1379 and 1381 are unique in that they provide information about people who are rarely, if ever, mentioned in other documents. They yield data about wives, servants, dependants, occupations and relationships in a way that no other material from the period does.' For the surname researcher the poll taxes provide a unique opportunity to assess the distribution of a surname in the fourteenth century. Unfortunately, the survival of the returns is not comprehensive. There are no returns for some counties, and only a few pages of names for other counties. For some counties such as Devon, where the poll tax coverage is sparse, the lay subsidy rolls are a much better supply of names. However, where the records have survived the poll taxes are a valuable source of information on surnames and their distribution in fourteenth-century England. Each volume of the series costs £95, which is likely to be beyond the means of the family historian. However, the books are available in some large reference libraries, and it is also possible to borrow the individual volumes on inter-library loan. A place-names index was published in volume 3, but no name index is currently available. It is, therefore, a very time-consuming process to trawl through the tiny print on each page in turn looking for the references to your surname, though because of the comprehensive nature of the coverage it is a worthwhile exercise if the counties are available where your surname is prevalent as you are likely to find people who will not appear in any other records.

In the past, historians and county record societies have published a number of transcriptions of the poll taxes for individual counties. An 1879 transcript of the Yorkshire poll taxes for 1379 can be found on Genuki at **www.genuki.org.uk/big/eng/YKS/ Misc/SubsidyRolls/YKS/SubsidyRolls1379Index.html**. Edgar Powell published a transcription of the 1381 poll tax list for Suffolk in 1896 as an appendix to *The Rising in East Anglia in 1381*, and this book is now available in the Internet Archive at **http:// archive.org/details/risingineastangloopoweuoft**. Carolyn Fenwick cautions that some of these old transcriptions are 'so edited and changed from the original as to be virtually useless for historical research'.

Tudor subsidies and muster rolls

Although there were some further taxes in the fifteenth century that were directly assessed on individuals, these were only concerned with the wealthy, and few lists have survived. The next series of public records that provides listings of the names of a substantial proportion of the population are the Tudor subsidies and muster rolls. During the early years of Henry VIII's reign unexpectedly heavy war expenditure had been incurred in France and Scotland, and a new system for raising cash was required. In 1522 a valuation of the whole kingdom was attempted by Cardinal Thomas Wolsey, the king's chief adviser, under the guise of a muster or military survey. This survey laid the groundwork for a whole new series of taxes that were to be levied during the following five years. Disappointingly, few of the returns for the 1522 military survey have survived either in The National Archives or in local records. Five county surveys have been published: *The Certificate of Musters for Buckinghamshire in 1522* (Chibnall, 1973); *The Cornwall Military Survey 1522 ...* (Stoate, 1987); *The Military Survey of Gloucestershire, 1522* (Hoyle, 1993); *The County Community under Henry VIII: the Military Survey, 1522, and Lay Subsidy, 1524–5 for Rutland* (Cornwall, 1980); and *Worcestershire Taxes in the 1520s* (Faraday, 2003). The survey for Exeter, the only surviving portion of the military survey for Devon, was published in *Tudor Exeter* (Rowe, 1977). A transcript of a single hundred in Suffolk was published in *The Military Survey of 1522 for Babergh Hundred* (Pound, 1986), and is also available as a dataset to Ancestry subscribers. The survey for Coventry is included in *Coventry and Its People in the 1520s* (Hulton, 1999).

Fortunately, many of the tax records from the new system that followed the 1522 military survey have survived, and these subsidies are a valuable source of surname information in the years before the introduction of parish registers and in the early decades of the sixteenth century when the survival of parish registers is patchy. The subsidies from 1523 onwards taxed people on the basis of their income from land or annuities, the capital value of their goods, or their wages. The threshold at which people were liable for taxation was in some years set very low, so these subsidies reached right down to the lower echelons of society and included labourers and even some servants. The first of the new subsidies was granted in 1523 and was paid over four years. The tax was levied on every person over the age of 16 at varying rates. Landowners and those with goods with a capital value of £20 or more had to pay the tax at the rate of 1s in the pound. Everyone with goods worth between £2 and £20 paid 6d in the pound. Those with an annual wage of £1 or with goods valued between £1 and £2 was required to pay 4d in the pound. The 1524–25 subsidy for Devon is one of the largest and includes over 28,000 names. The contemporary returns for Suffolk include 17,000 names, Sussex has over 12,000 names and Buckinghamshire over 8,000.

There were further subsidies in 1535–36 and 1540–41, but for both of these the threshold was set very high, and only those with land or goods to the value of £20 or more were liable for the tax. The next important subsidy was granted by Parliament in 1543 in the closing years of the reign of Henry VIII in order to continue the war against Scotland. The lower limit of this subsidy was set at £1 for goods and £1 for land, making a substantial proportion of the population liable for tax. The subsidy was paid over three years in 1543, 1544 and 1545. The Devon returns for 1543 contain around 30,000 names, a slight increase on 1524. Subsidies continued to be granted through to the middle of the seventeenth century with the last subsidy being granted in 1663. From 1563 onwards the threshold at which tax became payable was set much higher, and so the returns are less helpful for investigating the distribution of a surname, though they are useful for investigating the wealthier members of society.

The subsidy rolls have been transcribed and published for many counties, and a list of printed returns is provided in *Tudor Taxation Records* (Hoyle, 1994) or can be found by searching the COPAC or WorldCat catalogues. Records of lay and clerical taxation are held in series E179 at The National Archives. The E179 database also provides details of published transcripts where available and can be searched by place or by date at **www. nationalarchives.gov.uk/e179**. A list of taxation records available online can be found on the Medieval Genealogy website (**www.medievalgenealogy.org.uk/sources/ tax.shtml**). The National Archives has a useful guide to taxation records before 1689 that can be found at **www.nationalarchives.gov.uk/records/research-guides/ taxation-before-1689.htm**.

Before the English Civil War (1642–51) there was no regular standing army in Britain, and able-bodied men aged between 16 and 60 were liable to perform military service in times of need. Muster rolls were compiled at various times for accounting purposes to assess the number of men available for service in the militia. From the 1540s onwards, the militia muster rolls were returned to the secretaries of state and many of these are now held at The National Archives. The deputy lieutenants of the counties retained some muster books, and these are in private collections or in county record offices. At least one sixteenth-century muster roll has been transcribed and published for most English counties. Although the muster rolls only record the details of able-bodied men between the ages of 16 and 60, they are a valuable guide to surname distribution at the county level in the sixteenth century and a useful supplement to the subsidy rolls. The muster rolls also provide a fascinating insight into the weaponry used in medieval warfare as can be seen in the transcription of the 1539 muster roll for Malhamdale in Yorkshire, which is available online at **www.kirkbymalham.info/KMI/malhamdale/muster1539. html**. Gibson and Dell's *Tudor and Stuart Muster Rolls: A Directory of Holdings in the British Isles* (1996) has a comprehensive list of surviving muster rolls, and details of those that have been transcribed and published. A search of the COPAC or WorldCat catalogues will also reveal the availability of printed transcripts. Further information on the militia muster rolls can be found in The National Archives' guide *Militia: Further Research* at **www. nationalarchives.gov.uk/records/research-guides/armed-forces-1522-1914.htm**. The National Archives also has a useful guide entitled *Medieval and Early Modern Soldiers*, which can be found at **www.nationalarchives.gov.uk/records/research-guides/ medieval-early-modern-soldiers.htm**.

West Country Books (**www.westcountrybooks.com**) has sixteenth-century muster rolls available on CD for Cornwall, Devon, Dorset and Somerset, which can either be purchased separately or on a single compilation disc. West Country Books also has a range of sixteenth-century subsidy rolls for Cornwall, Devon, Dorset and Somerset on CD. S&N Genealogy Supplies (**www.genealogysupplies.com**) has muster rolls for Somerset (1569) and Surrey (1544–1684) available on CD, and a subsidy return for Suffolk from 1524. The Parish Chest (**www.parishchest.com**) has a muster roll for Northumberland for 1538, and the Suffolk subsidy returns for 1524 and 1568. These two Suffolk subsidies are also available from Archive CD Books Ireland (**www.archivecdbooks.ie**). Colin Rogers provides a listing of printed sources of pre-1600 subsidy rolls, muster rolls and other name sources in Appendix 3 of *The Surname Detective* (1995).

Online databases

The remaining records for the pre-1600 period do not provide such comprehensive coverage of the population, either at a national or local level, but there are many other records that are useful sources for name references, many of which are now available in online databases that can be searched for early references to your surname of interest. It will be necessary to be very creative with the searches to allow for all possible variant spellings of the name.

Many of the subscription websites such as Ancestry and Findmypast have collections of records that precede the introduction of parish registers. National archives and county record offices have online catalogues that provide details of their holdings, and sometimes offer the opportunity to download digital images either free of charge or for a small fee. The UK National Archives has over 11 million documents in its collections going back to the eleventh century. The Discovery Catalogue (**http://discovery.nationalarchives. gov.uk**) allows the user to search for references to a surname by keyword or by catalogue reference. The searches can be refined by date, making it easy to pick out early references to a surname. The Access to Archives (A2A) website (**www.nationalarchives.gov.uk/a2a**) has details of over 10 million records held in 418 record offices and other repositories in England and Wales. The database has catalogues for about 30 per cent of the archival holdings in England and Wales. The early records often have very detailed descriptions. The online catalogues of local county record offices should also be checked. The ARCHON directory (**www.nationalarchives.gov.uk/archon**) has a complete listing of UK repositories. The National Library of Wales has a large archival holding, and the catalogue can be searched online at **www.llgc.org.uk/index.php?id=240**. Archives Wales (**www.archiveswales. org.uk**) offers an integrated search of the holdings of twenty-one archives in Wales.

British History Online (**www.british-history.ac.uk**) has a large and growing collection of medieval resources, which can be searched by keyword or by record collection. Some of the content, such the *Calendar of State Papers, Domestic* (1547–1704) and the sixty-one volumes of the *Calendar of Close Rolls* (1244–1509), is only available on payment of a small annual subscription. A dedicated website known as State Papers Online (**http://gale. cengage.co.uk/state-papers-online-15091714.aspx**) has a fully searchable database of all the State Papers from 1509 to 1714, but is available only to institutional subscribers. A similar database of State Papers Medieval is currently in preparation. State Papers Online and the premium British History Online content can be accessed on the public computers at The National Archives. The close rolls and state papers relate to the government of the country and the administration of the royal household, and most of the references will relate to notable people, but the volumes cover a wide variety of subject matter and are always worth searching for surname references. Many of the old printed volumes of state papers and close rolls are also available free of charge in the Internet Archive, and some of the close rolls can be found in FamilySearch Books, but extracting the references from the individual books is a much lengthier process than taking them from a single consolidated database. Links to the individual printed volumes of state papers that are available online can be found on the Medieval Genealogy website at **www.medievalgenealogy.org.uk/sources/publicmisc.shtml**. A list of links to the individual volumes of the close rolls can be found at **www.medievalgenealogy.org.uk/sources/rolls.shtml**.

Searchable databases of two important public record sets – the patent rolls and the fine rolls – are now available free online for a limited range of dates. The Calendars of the Patent Rolls from 1216–1452 can be searched at **http://sdrc.lib.uiowa.edu/patentrolls**. The fine rolls from 1216–72 can be searched on the website of the Henry III Fine Rolls Project (**www.finerollshenry3.org.uk**). The Cause Papers Database (**www.hrionline.ac.uk/causepapers**) provides a catalogue to more than 12,000 cases heard between 1300 and 1858 in the Church Courts of the diocese of York. The Soldier in Later Medieval England Project (**www.icmacentre.ac.uk/soldier/database**) has three searchable databases online covering the period from 1369 to 1453. Other projects are also under way. The Gascon Rolls Project (**www.gasconrolls.org**) is in the process of calendaring and digitising the unpublished Gascon Rolls in The National Archives covering the period from 1317 to 1468, and these will eventually be available online in a searchable database. England's Immigrants is a major research project funded by the Arts and Humanities Research Council. The project is in the process of creating a database of around 80,000 immigrants who lived in England between 1330 and 1550. The wesite is now live at **www.englandsimmigrants.com**, though is not scheduled to be completed until 2015.

The Original Record (**www.theoriginalrecord.com**) is a commercial service that offers access to a wide range of medieval records and other more recent records that have been hand-indexed by surname. Documents in Latin have been translated into English. A surname search is free and will reveal all the hits for the surname and the sources where the name is found. Digital scans of the records can be purchased for a fee. Alternatively, one can purchase an e-book with references to a specific surname or pay for a somewhat expensive annual subscription that provides unlimited access to references for up to six surnames. It is a particularly valuable site for early surname references, but many of the sources are out-of-copyright printed books that are now freely accessible in the Internet Archive or have been indexed and made available in other databases. The site is a useful alternative if you want to build up a collection of early references for your surname and don't want to spend a long time searching through books in the Internet Archive yourself. It can also be used to provide leads if you wish to check the sources yourself.

Inquisitions post mortem

Inquisitions post mortem (IPMs) are the most interesting and accessible of all genealogy resources for the medieval period. Inquisitions were introduced in the reign of Henry III, and were a distinctive feature of the feudal system. The earliest IPMs date from 1236 and they survived until 1660 when the system of feudal tenure was abolished upon the restoration of the monarchy under Charles II. Under the feudal system all land was held by the king and was granted to his lords in return for the obligation to perform some service.

Those who held land directly from the king were known as tenants-in-chief. When they died, a Crown official known as an escheator would hold an enquiry before a local jury in order to establish the extent of the land held by the tenant at the time of his death, by what rents or services the land was held, and the name and age of his heir. If the heir was a minor the lands were held in wardship by the Crown until he came of age. The IPMs are a valuable resource for genealogists and local historians. They provide confirmation of familial relationships for the landowning classes, and also provide a wealth of information on the history of individual manors. For the gentry and nobility the IPMs can be used to trace the direct paternal line back for many generations.

When an heir reached the age of majority a separate enquiry known as an *inquisition de aetatis probanda* was held to produce proof of age. A number of parishioners were required to attend and give evidence to the jury. These inquisitions are some of the most delightful documents of all the medieval period as they provide a fascinating snapshot of the people of the parish, with details of their names, ages and interesting snippets of information that are not available elsewhere. The following proof of age for one of my Devon ancestors, John Keynes of Winkleigh, who later became the High Sheriff of Devon, shows the wealth of detail provided:

Proof of age of John son & heir of Thomas de Keynes deceased, taken at Wynkelegh, Saturday after St. Nicholas 47 Edw. III. [Saturday 10 Dec. 1373], before John Matteford (1), escheator.

William Southcote, aged 50, says that said John was aged 21 on Monday after St. Clement last past. Sybil, mother of said William, was godmother to said John, & William was present at the baptism.

Walter Bobbych, aged 43, says the like. Maud, his wife, died & was buried in the churchyard of All Saints, Wynkelegh, on the day of the baptism.

John Michel, aged 45, says the like. He had a serving-maid called Joan atte Were who had then borne a son, who was dead, & she became nurse to John de Keynes.

John Stone, aged 44, says the like. His kinswoman, Julia Moyoun, bore a daughter that day, to whom this deponent was godfather, she was baptized in Wynkelegh church.

William Vautard, aged 40, says the like. His uncle Philip Vautard, was chaplain of Wynkelegh church, & baptized John de Keynes.

John Caperoun, aged 51, says the like. He & Edith Nicol were married in Wynkelegh church in that same week.

Stephen Kyng, aged 47, says the like. John Jolyf, then parish clerk of Wynkelegh, wrote the age of the child in the missal of the church the day he was born.

Thomas Hoye, aged 60, John Lacy, aged 61, Stephen Coterel, aged 43, William Gyfford, aged 47, Roger Aschford, aged 58, agree. On Sunday after St. Nicholas they were with Thomas Keynes, father of said John, when Margery, mother of said John, was purified.[5]

All the IPMs have been fully indexed and most of them have been abstracted and translated into English in two series of printed texts, known as *The Calendars of Inquisitions Post Mortem*, covering the periods 1236–1447 and 1485–1509. These volumes also include the other associated documents such as the proofs of age and assignments of dower, which set out the rights of a widow in her deceased husband's estate. Many of the earlier volumes in this series have now been digitised for the Internet Archive, and links can be found on the Medieval Genealogy website at **www.medievalgenealogy.org.uk/sources/ipm. shtml**. The later volumes, the most recent of which was published in 2009, are available at The National Archives and in some university and large reference libraries. The more recent volumes (from volume 22, 1422) transcribe and index the names of all the deponents and jurors, whereas these were not included in the earlier volumes. In addition, abstracts of IPMs have been collected and published in county volumes, and some of these are now also available in the Internet Archive. For Devon, a set of sixteen volumes of typewritten abstracts is held at the West Country Studies Library in Exeter, and these IPMs are in the process of being indexed for the Devon Wills Project (**http://genuki.cs.ncl.ac.uk/ DEV/DevonWillsProject/TAPS.html**).

When using the printed IPMs, researchers should be aware that with effect from volume 18, covering the years 1399–1405, place-names in the text were translated into their modern equivalents. All the spellings that occur in the manuscripts are listed in the index underneath the modern spelling, but this practice can create difficulties, especially where there are multiple references for a single place-name, as it will not be possible to identify the variant spelling used in each individual IPM. Furthermore, it has been found that some of the modern place-names assigned by the editors are incorrect, though this is more of a problem with the lesser-known place-names and the more obscure manors.[6] A correct identification will usually be possible by searching for references in other contemporary records such as the feet of fines (see opposite).

The Medieval Genealogy website has a guide to IPMs (**www.medievalgenealogy. org.uk/guide/ipm.shtml**) and links to all the volumes that are accessible in the Internet Archive. The National Archives has produced a detailed guide, *Landholders and heirs in inquisitions post mortem 1236–c.1640*, which can be found at **www.nationalarchives. gov.uk/records/research-guides/inqusitions-post-mortem.htm**. 'Mapping the Medieval Countryside: The Fifteenth-Century Inquisitions Post Mortem' is a project at the University of Winchester that aims to make all the existing texts of the IPMs for 1236–1447 and 1485–1509 freely available in a revised and expanded form on the British History Online website. In addition, the more fully calendared volumes from 1399 to 1447 will be enhanced and converted into an interactive open-access geomapped database. In the longer term it is hoped that the project will be able to complete the calendaring of the medieval IPMs for 1447–85 and possibly those for 1509–42. Further information on the project can be found at **www.winchester.ac.uk/academicdepartments/ history/research/inquisitions/Pages/TheInquisitionsPost-MortemProject.aspx**. The historical background is reviewed in *The Fifteenth-Century Inquisitions Post Mortem: A Companion* (Hicks (ed.), 2012).

Feet of fines

The feet of fines are among the most important records for tracing the inheritance of landed property, but can also be a useful source of early references to surnames. The word fine is derived from the Latin word *finis*, meaning 'end'. A fine, or final concord, was a method of recording land conveyances. The final agreement of the transaction between the purchaser (the *querent*), and the seller (the *deforciant*), was normally written out three times on a single sheet of parchment: the first two copies were written side by side at the top of the document and a third copy was written across the bottom. The parchment was then cut into three pieces along wavy lines so that the purchaser and the seller each had a copy of the transaction. The final copy – the foot of the fine – was kept by the king's court as a central record of the conveyance. It was an effective method of protecting against forgery as the three pieces of the parchment would only fit together if they were genuine. The feet of fines run from 1190 to 1833 when the system was abolished, and are mostly arranged in chronological sequences by county. Many of the early feet of fines have been abstracted and published by local record societies, and some of these are now available in the Internet Archive or on British History Online. Chris Phillips is working on a project to provide abstracts of the early feet of fines that have not yet been published, initially for the period 1360–1509. These abstracts are available in a searchable database on his Medieval Genealogy website, where he also provides a complete list of all the published editions arranged by county. Further information can be found at **www.medievalgenealogy.org. uk/fines/index.shtml**. The National Archives has a guide entitled *Land conveyances by feet of fines 1182–1833*, which can be found at **www.nationalarchives.gov.uk/records/ research-guides/land-conveyance-feet-of-fines.htm**.

Manorial records

If you are able to trace a surname back to a specific location then manorial records will be a valuable source of information. They provide details of the everyday lives of our medieval ancestors, and they record the names not just of the lord of the manor but of all his tenants. The Manorial Documents Register (**www.nationalarchives.gov.uk/ mdr**) provides details of the nature and location of manorial records, but is presently only partly computerised. Manor court rolls can date back to the thirteenth century and go right through to the early twentieth century, but the survival of such records is sporadic. There are no documents at all for around a third of manors. Only around one in five manors has a good run of records from the sixteenth or seventeenth centuries, and only one manor in twenty-five has a good run of records prior to the sixteenth century. Most surviving manorial records are now held in county record offices, The National Archives and other repositories such as university libraries, but some are still in private hands. Very few manorial records have been published. *The English Manor c.1200–c.1500* (Bailey, 2002) provides the best introduction to the subject. *Manorial Records* (Harvey, 1999) provides an authoritative overview of the records, and has details of selected texts in print. *The Manor and Manorial Records* (Hone, 1906), though out of date in some respects, provides a helpful overview of the manorial system, and has the advantage of being freely available in the Internet Archive. *My Ancestors were Manorial Tenants* (Park, 2005) is a useful short summary written for genealogists. The online guide *Manors: Further Research* (**www.nationalarchives.gov.uk/records/research-guides/manorial-records.htm**) has details of the holdings at The National Archives.

Feudal aids

The feudal system of land tenure created a wealth of public records, and if the bearers of your surname were lords of the manor, these records will yield an abundance of information. The six printed volumes of *Feudal Aids* (1284–1431) have details of the names of the feudal tenants-in-chief and under-tenants and their manors. The text is in Latin, but the entries are brief and written in a formulaic fashion with a limited vocabulary, and it is usually possible to understand the gist of the content. Here's a typical entry from 1284–86 that confirms that my ancestor Robert Cruwys held the manor of Cruwys Morchard in Devon for one (knight's) fee from the earl of Cornwall:

> Robertus de Crues tenet manerium de MORCEST[RE] pro un. f. de comite Cornubie, et idem comes de rege.

The *Feudal Aids* are now available in the Internet Archive. The Medieval Genealogy website has links to all six printed volumes, and many other online sources relating to land taxes and feudal surveys at **www.medievalgenealogy.org.uk/sources/feudal.shtml**.

The Anglo-American Legal Tradition

The Anglo-American Legal Tradition (**http://aalt.law.uh.edu**) is an extraordinarily ambitious project that is in the process of digitising medieval and early-modern English legal records at The National Archives and making the images freely available online. The project is hosted by the O'Quinn Law Library at the University of Houston Law Center in Texas and is led by Professor Robert Palmer. As of January 2012, over 7 million frames of historical material had been uploaded to the website. The records include pipe rolls, plea rolls, fine rolls, close rolls, feet of fines, chancery proceedings and many other series of public records generated by the State between 1176 and 1800. Transcripts of the documents are not provided though there are some abstracts included in the accompanying wiki. Although it is obviously not possible to do a surname search of digital images, if you do find references to your surname in the published indexes and calendars you will be able to view the original image of the document online. In the long term, the easy access of this material on the Internet should speed up the transcription process and enable many more records to be indexed and put online.

Ireland

Many Irish records were destroyed in the fire in 1922 at the Public Record Office of Ireland in Dublin, but early records relating to Ireland will often be found in English sources. The five printed volumes of the *Calendar of Documents relating to Ireland* (Sweetman (ed.), 1875–86), covering the period 1171–1307 are freely available in the Internet Archive and are a useful source of early references to surnames in Ireland. These volumes bring together all the references to Ireland found in the English public records such as the chancery and exchequer records. One important new database that provides free access to over 20,000 Irish chancery letters from 1244 to 1509 has recently come online, and is an easy-to-use source of early Irish surname references. The database, known as CIRCLE, can be found at **http://chancery. tcd.ie**. The National Archives of Ireland (**www.nationalarchives.ie**) holds some records dating back to the thirteenth century, mainly in the form of transcripts, calendars, abstracts and indexes relating to the original records that were destroyed in the fire.

Scotland

There are two important new online databases that are sources of surname references in the early years of surname formation in Scotland. The Paradox of Medieval Scotland (PoMS) website (**www.poms.ac.uk**) explores social relationships and identities in Scotland in the key period between 1093 and 1286, the period that laid the foundations for modern Scotland. The website has a searchable database that provides biographical information about all known people in Scotland between 1093 and 1286. The complementary Breaking of Britain website (**www.breakingofbritain.ac.uk**) is concerned with the period that 'extends from the failure of Alexander II's short-lived revival of a Scoto-Northumbrian realm in 1216–17 to the formal abolition of cross-border landholding by Robert I in November 1314, following his victory at Bannockburn'. The project will extend the PoMS database to 1314, and will also set up a new database about the people in Northumberland, Westmorland and Cumberland, the three northernmost counties of England, from 1216 to 1307.

The Ragman Rolls, two documents dating from 1291 and 1296, preserve the names of some 2,000 landowners, churchmen and burgesses who signed an oath of loyalty to the

English King Edward I. The list of names can be found on the Rampant Scotland website (**www.rampantscotland.com/ragman**). An 1834 transcription of the Ragman Rolls (in Latin) by the Ballantyne Club can be found in the Internet Archive at **http://archive. org/details/instrumentapublicaoothomuoft**. There are a number of featured articles about the Ragman Rolls on the Breaking of Britain website at **www.breakingofbritain. ac.uk/feature-of-the-month**.

The *Calendar of Documents Relating to Scotland* (Bain (ed.), 4 volumes, 1881–88) is another good source of early surname references in Scotland, and the last three volumes are now online in the Internet Archive.

Reading old handwriting

As so much of the key medieval source material has been transcribed and published it will be possible to collect most of the early surname references from the printed works. There are many other old documents, and particularly wills, which have not yet been transcribed but are a valuable source of genealogical and surname information. There will also be occasions where there will be a need to go back and check the original document, and it will then be necessary to master the art of reading old handwriting. It takes some practice and perseverance, but can be a very rewarding exercise. It is necessary to train the eye to look at each individual letter in turn rather than trying to guess the whole word. It is rather like trying to crack a secret code: once the key words in the text have been identified the letter forms in the more difficult-to-read words can be compared and deciphered. There are a number of useful tutorials on palaeography – the study of old handwriting – available online. The National Archives has a very comprehensive online tutorial (**www. nationalarchives.gov.uk/palaeography**) that also includes quick reference guides to dates and numbers. Cambridge University has an online course on English handwriting from 1500–1700 that can be found at **www.english.cam.ac.uk/ceres/ehoc**. A guide to reading historical Scottish records can be found at **www.scottishhandwriting.com**. The Anglo-Norman Online Hub (**http://paleo.anglo-norman.org**), a website hosted by the universities of Aberystwyth and Swansea, hosts guides to medieval and early modern palaeography. If you require help with transcribing a specific document, the members of Rootsweb's Old English mailing list are usually able to assist. The list has its own companion website (**http://homepages.rootsweb.ancestry.com/~oel**) which has many useful links. The National Archives has a helpful guide to Latin for beginners that can be found at **www.nationalarchives.gov.uk/latin/beginners**. *The Record Interpreter* (Martin, 1910) is a particularly valuable reference book for translating Latin words in printed texts and old documents. The book includes lists of the Latin forms of surnames, given names and British place-names. There are also lists of the most commonly abbreviated Latin words and a glossary of Latin words. *Palaeography for Family and Local Historians* (Marshall, 2010) is an excellent practical guide with examples of all the letters of the alphabet in different hands, and facsimile reproductions of old manuscripts of varying levels of difficulty accompanied by line-by-line transcriptions.

Old-style dates can also be the cause of some confusion. Mike Spathaky has written a helpful introduction to the subject that can be found at **www.cree.name/genuki/ dates.htm**. The Medieval Genealogy website (**www.medievalgenealogy.org.uk/ guide/chron.shtml**) has a page of links to online resources including conversion tools that translate regnal years into modern calendar dates. *A Handbook of Dates* (Cheney and Jones, 2000) is the standard textbook on the subject and includes tables of regnal years, Easter days and lists of saints' days.

Taking it further

It has only been possible to describe the most important name-rich sources for the pre-1600 period that are the easiest to search, provide the widest coverage and are the most accessible, but there is a wealth of further records to be explored. Chris Phillips' Medieval Genealogy website (**www.medievalgenealogy.org.uk**) provides the best introduction to the records, and also includes links to online sources, where available, in the Internet Archive and elsewhere.

County record societies and archaeological societies have transcribed many of the most genealogically useful medieval records, and it is always worthwhile checking their publication lists for titles of interest. The cartularies (manuscript collections) of the religious houses can be a particularly valuable source for early name references and many of these have now been published by the record societies. A complete listing of both monastic and secular cartularies can be found in *Medieval Cartularies of Great Britain and Ireland* (Davis, 2010). A list of record societies and their publications can be found on the Royal Historical Society's website at **www.royalhistoricalsociety.org/textandcalendars.php**. Many of the titles were published in the nineteenth century and in the early years of the twentieth century. These volumes are now out of copyright, and many have been digitised and made available in the Internet Archive. A search for key terms for specific counties will pay dividends and yield many interesting publications. There are also many books in the Internet Archive from the British Record Society, the Scottish Record Society and the Catholic Record Society.

The National Archives has a research guide entitled *Medieval and early modern family history sources*, which can be found at **www.nationalarchives.gov.uk/records/research-guides/medieval-sources-for-family-history.htm**. *Medieval Genealogy* (Chambers, 2005) describes the different classes of medieval records available. *Some Medieval Records for Family Historians* (Franklin, 1994), now sadly out of print, provides a clear and concise introduction to the records that are of most use to family historians. The book includes much interesting background information on medieval society, the manorial system and the lay subsidy rolls. Each chapter is accompanied by an extensive bibliography. *Tracing Your Ancestors from 1066 to 1837* (Oates, 2012) is a short introduction to the subject but, disappointingly in view of its recent publication date, has little information on online sources.

9

DNA AND SURNAMES

What is DNA, this molecule that allows us to travel so far back in the past – this history book we carry around like a gift from a long line of ancestors?

Spencer Wells, *Deep Ancestry: Inside the Genographic Project*
(National Geographic, 2007), pp. 13–14

DNA is an increasingly important component of a surname study. It can be used to verify existing documentary research, but it also takes us back beyond the paper trail and can establish connections between different lines, even if no documentary link can be found. The surname researcher will want to test all the documented lines for the surname to see which ones are related. DNA testing can also be used to explore variant spellings and to establish whether or not these variants have a common root. By analysing the DNA results together with the complementary documentary research, the researcher can investigate whether the surname has a single or multiple origin. DNA testing can also take us back into our deep ancestry and help us to understand the pre-surname history of the male line. DNA testing is normally coordinated within a DNA project run by a volunteer project administrator, although there are also some important surname studies by academics.

How does it work?

All humans share over 99.5 per cent of their DNA in common. It is the few differences in the remaining 0.5 per cent of our DNA that distinguish us from each other. For surname studies we exploit the unique properties of one particular type of DNA – the Y-chromosome, one of the two sex-determining chromosomes. The Y-chromosome contains the gene that determines maleness, and is passed on from father to son, corresponding in most cultures with the transmission of surnames.

The test used in surname projects is known as the Y-chromosome DNA test or Y-DNA test for short. A Y-DNA test can only be taken by a man, as only men inherit a Y-chromosome. Women who wish to explore their surname through DNA testing, therefore, need to recruit a male relative, such as their father, brother, uncle or cousin, to take a test on their behalf. It is not yet possible to sequence the entire Y-chromosome so instead we look at particular locations on the Y-chromosome known as markers. The Y-DNA test looks at a particular type of marker on the Y-chromosome known as a short tandem repeat (STR), which consists of repeating sequences of DNA letters. The number of repeats is counted at each marker to give a numerical value for each marker tested. The Y-chromosome is usually passed on virtually unchanged from father to son, but every now and then a mistake occurs in the copying process. These copying mistakes are known as mutations, and they gradually accumulate over time. In general terms, the more matching markers that two men have in common the more closely related they are. If they have too many mismatching markers then they are unlikely to be related within a genealogical time frame. A DNA test will not give you the name of the common shared ancestor or give you precise dates. Instead, probabilities are used to predict the *range* of generations in which this shared ancestor might have lived. The more markers that are tested the more accurate the predictions.

When Y-DNA testing first began to be used in surname research from 1997 onwards it was only possible to test a very small number of markers. Participants in these early surname studies were tested on 4, 6, 10 or 12 markers, depending on where the testing was done. Since then, the cost of testing has come down and it is now standard practice to test a minimum of 37 markers. Any tests of 12 markers or fewer are considered to be low-resolution tests as they produce too many false-positive matches. At 12 markers some people have matches with hundreds and sometimes thousands of other people with many different surnames, but as more markers are added to the mix the irrelevant matches start to disappear, leaving only the matches that are of genealogical significance. The 37-marker test is now the standard entry-level test, but it is also possible to upgrade as necessary to 67 markers and 111 markers. At 37 markers close relations, such as father and son, uncle and nephew, and first and second cousins, will in most cases match each other on 37 out of 37 markers. This is known as a 37/37 match. In other words, they will have an identical set of numbers on all 37 markers. The further back in time you go the greater the chance of finding a mutation. Two third cousins might, therefore, match on 36 out of 37 markers. Two sixth cousins might match on 35 out of 37 markers. In contrast, if two men only match on 25 out of 37 markers, they will not share a common ancestor within the last 1,000 years or more. However, markers mutate at random, making it difficult to interpret two matching results in isolation. Two men with a documented ancestor in the 1700s sometimes match on all 37 markers, whereas a father and son pair might only match on 36 out of 37 markers.

It is, therefore, very important to combine the results of the DNA testing with the paper records. In the first place DNA testing can be used to verify existing research. If two men with well-documented connecting paper trails have matching DNA results then you have effectively verified the research back to the point where the two men share a common ancestor. If you build up a framework of well-documented family trees and collect DNA test results for the different branches of each tree it is often possible to work out exactly where the mutations have occurred by a process of elimination, and sometimes mutations can occur that are specific to a particular branch of a family tree. However, not all branches will necessarily have living descendants who can test and so there will inevitably be some gaps in the data.

DNA results can also be used within a surname project to establish whether or not two branches are related, even if there is no paper trail to prove a link. A DNA match might connect two trees from two different counties or even two different countries. For example, a colonial American line might match someone with a well-documented English pedigree, or a London tree might match with a tree originating in a specific parish, thus providing a narrower focus for further research.

Every surname will almost certainly have some lines where the link between the Y-chromosome and the surname has been broken because of illegitimacy, adoption or a name change for some other reason. DNA testing can be used to explore the roots of these lines and possibly identify the surname of the biological father of the child. The situation also arises in some surname projects where two people with a well-documented line do not match as expected. This can occur where there has been paternity deception as a result of maternal infidelity or a concealed adoption. The generic term 'non-paternity event' (NPE) is often used to describe all of these scenarios.

The DNA test itself is a simple cheek swab, which can easily be done in the comfort of your own home. The main companies now provide storage facilities so that you don't have to supply additional samples every time you want to order an upgrade. Storage is also vital if the person who is taking the test is the last in his particular line. A relative can be nominated as a beneficiary who can then continue to order additional testing as the science advances and new tests become available.

Deep ancestry

DNA testing can also be used to explore the pre-surname history of the paternal lines within a surname and provide clues to its geographical origin. The Y-STR markers are used to give a prediction of the haplogroup assignment. A haplogroup is a broad population grouping of people who belong on the same branch of the tree of mankind. Haplogroups are identified by letters of the alphabet running from A through to T. By studying the DNA of present populations we have a window into the past and can learn something about our deep ancestry. The regions of the world where these haplogroups are found today with the highest level of diversity, and sometimes the highest density, are generally considered to be the places where these haplogroups originated. Some haplogroups are, for example, associated with Viking ancestry whereas others are thought to be linked to Celtic ancestry. Haplogroups are defined by special markers known as SNPs (pronounced 'snips'), which is short for single-nucleotide polymorphisms. SNPs occur in a cumulative order rather like the rings on a tree and can thus be used to date the origins of the various haplogroups and their subclades. Haplogroups can only be confirmed by specialist SNP testing but, because the Y-DNA databases are now so large, the predictions can usually be made with confidence unless a person has a particularly rare result with no matches in the database. With additional SNP testing the haplogroups can be further refined into sub-branches known as subclades, which are identified by additional letters and numbers to give complicated names such as G2a3b1a or J2a4b1. While the base haplogroups date back many thousands of years, the subclades are of much more recent origin and in some cases date back only 1,000 or 2,000 years. SNP testing can therefore be used as an additional method of sorting results within a DNA project. If two men have different haplogroups you will know immediately that they cannot be related within a genealogical time frame as they will each belong to two different branches of the human family tree that diverged thousands of years ago. Similarly, two men in the same haplogroup but who belong to different subclades of that haplogroup will belong to different sub-branches of the human family tree and will not share a common ancestor in a genealogical time frame.

SNP testing is now increasingly being used within surname projects. The Y-STR markers work well for confirming relationships within the last 500 years or so where there is likely to be extensive documentation for the main trees and against which the DNA results can be calibrated. It is much more difficult to interpret DNA results for trees that are thought to connect 700 or 800 years ago. The results will match on fewer markers and the upper limits of the expected range, within which the two men might share a common ancestor, will fall before the time of the earliest surnames. For the more distant links it is therefore necessary to complement the basic Y-STR testing with SNP testing. The science is advancing very rapidly and new SNPs are being discovered all the time, some of which are of more recent origin, so for some surnames there is a possibility that a branch-specific SNP will eventually be found. For advice on SNP testing it is best to ensure that you get representatives from your surname project into the relevant haplogroup projects. The volunteer haplogroup project administrators will be able to give advice on which advanced tests to order. A list of Y-DNA haplogroup projects is maintained by ISOGG – the International Society of Genetic Genealogy – and can be found in their wiki at **www. isogg.org/wiki/Y-DNA_haplogroup_projects**.

Choosing a testing company

There are a number of companies that offer Y-DNA tests but, at the time of writing, there are just two companies – Family Tree DNA (**www.familytreedna.com**) and Ancestry DNA (**http://dna.ancestry.com**) – that provide the facilities for hosting a DNA project. Early on in a surname study you will want to check to see if there is a pre-existing project for your surname. If a project already exists, you will want to try and collaborate with the project administrator. If not, it is a good idea to set up a skeleton project to 'reserve' your surname, even if you are not yet ready to start collecting DNA results. A project can be started with zero participants. Family Tree DNA is the biggest DNA testing company. It hosts over 7,000 DNA projects and has the world's largest Y-DNA database. Family Tree DNA also has the widest range of DNA tests and offers many specialist tests, such as the advanced SNP tests, which are not available elsewhere. It is, therefore, the company of choice for a DNA surname project at present. Ancestry DNA only offers two basic Y-DNA tests for a limited number of markers, and does not offer any of the advanced tests or even the basic SNP testing that is essential for haplogroup confirmation. The company also provides little in the way of project administration tools. The ISOGG wiki has a chart comparing the facilities of the various companies offering Y-DNA tests, which can be found at **www.isogg.org/wiki/ Y-DNA_testing_comparison_chart**.

Single- and multiple-origin surnames

Researchers often feel a particular affinity for other people who share the same surname, and many surname studies start out with the idea of trying to establish whether or not all the bearers of the surname are related. With a few rare surnames, it is sometimes possible to trace everyone with the surname back to a single founder in the sixteenth or seventeenth century. In rare cases this can happen with a surname that originated with a foundling. David Hey cites the example of the surname Elshaw. All the bearers of this surname can be traced back to one William Elshaw who was admitted to the Foundling Hospital in Ackworth, Yorkshire, as a three-week-old baby.[1] In most cases the surnames that can be linked together into a single tree in this way will share a late-developing variant spelling, and it will be necessary to widen the research to look for alternative spellings in earlier records in order to find the true home of the family name in the Middle Ages. For less frequent surnames, with diligent genealogical research it is usually possible to reconstruct most of the family trees for the surname back to the 1700s or 1600s, but there will always be some loose ends and it will generally not be possible to find documentary proof to link all the trees together into one big family tree. For more common surnames it is self-evident that they will have multiple origins. Every town and village would have had their own smiths, tailors and coopers who gradually adopted their occupation first as a byname and then as a surname. With more frequently occurring occupational and patronymic surnames the researcher might instead be interested in trying to ascertain the number of founders of the surname in medieval times. DNA testing can help to bridge the gap in the documentary records, but is it able to prove a theory that a surname has a single origin?

The Sykes study

The concept that DNA testing could be used to determine whether or not all men with a given surname share a common ancestor was first proposed in a paper published in the *American Journal of Human Genetics* in the year 2000 by Bryan Sykes and Catherine Irven. Sykes, a former professor of genetics at the University of Oxford, is the founder of the DNA testing company Oxford Ancestors, but is best known for his popular science books such as *The Seven Daughters of Eve* and *Blood of the Isles*. Sykes and Irven extracted DNA from forty-eight men with the surname Sykes in West Yorkshire, Lancashire and Cheshire, whose names were selected at random from the electoral register and other published lists. The results were compared with a control group of 139 native English males, and a second control group of twenty-one unrelated male 'neighbours' in the same three counties. It was found that twenty-one of the forty-eight men with the Sykes surname (44 per cent) had identical matching DNA results. None of the men in the two control groups matched this large Sykes group. No other Sykes results occurred at such an elevated level of frequency compared to the control groups. The authors concluded that the results indicated a 'single surname founder for extant Sykes males'. The differing results for the other Sykes men tested were accounted for 'by the historical accumulation of nonpaternity during the past 700 years', which they estimated at a rate of 1.3 per cent per generation. The results were very surprising because Sykes is a common surname and the written records had suggested a multiple origin for the surname.[2]

However, looking at this study with the benefit of hindsight, it is clear that this conclusion was premature. In the ensuing decade, DNA testing has become much more sophisticated. Only four markers were used in this pioneering study, but experience has now shown that a four-marker test is inadequate for confirming or disproving relationships, and even more so when no SNP testing is done to verify the haplogroups. Academic studies in recent years have routinely used 17 markers, complemented by SNP testing for haplogroup confirmation. The volunteer-run DNA studies run by family historians normally use a minimum of 37 markers with SNP testing where appropriate.

Stephen Archer's *British 19th Century Surname Atlas* CD[3] now allows us to generate an instant map showing the distribution of a surname in the 1881 census. The CD shows that there were 14,383 people in Great Britain with the surname Sykes in 1881. The distribution of the surname is shown in Figure 19. As can be seen, there was a particularly strong concentration of the surname in Yorkshire in 1881, but the surname was also prevalent in Lancashire, Cheshire, Lincolnshire, Leicestershire, Northamptonshire and Huntingdonshire. However, the surname was also found in all other English counties apart from Cornwall, and had also spread into South Wales and parts of North Wales. In Scotland there was a hotspot in Peebles, but the surname was also found throughout the southern counties of Scotland. While some of this spread could be accounted for by a gradual diffusion from Yorkshire, such a broad distribution pattern throughout England, Wales and Scotland is more typical of a multiple-origin surname. The World Names Public Profiler online mapping service shows a similarly broad distribution pattern throughout Britain in the present day, though with a high concentration of the surname still found in Yorkshire.

Curiously, the Sykes/Irven study only sampled men who were living in West Yorkshire, Lancashire and Cheshire, the counties that they found had the highest present-day concentrations of the surname. This selective sampling introduced bias into the study. There is no reason to suppose that samples taken from men in these three counties would be at all representative of men from Lincolnshire, Somerset or Kent. Furthermore, the number of men tested was very small in relation to the total population of the surname.

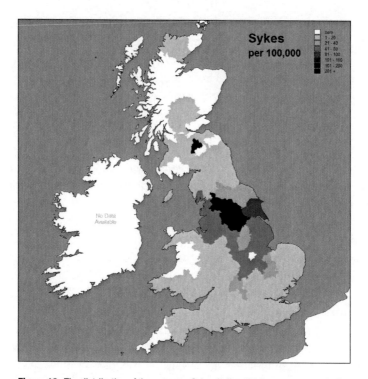

Figure 19. The distribution of the surname Sykes in the 1881 census suggests that the surname has multiple origins, though it has a particularly strong concentration in Yorkshire.

The researchers used a database of 9,885 registered UK voters with the Sykes surname (presumably all males). Their sample of forty-eight men represented just 0.48 per cent of the male Sykes population.

Since the publication of the Sykes/Irven paper, a DNA project for the Sykes surname has been established by the Sikes/Sykes Families Association in the United States. The project has now tested over 100 men with the surname. The focus of their study is very much on the Sykes families in the US, who will not necessarily be representative of the Sykes population in the UK, as only a few men with the surname will have emigrated. The participants in this study were not selected at random but have been targeted specifically by the association to represent particular lineages. The testing was done at a much higher resolution than the Sykes study, and most of their results are based on 25- or 37-marker tests. Although not directly comparable, their results are strikingly different from the early Sykes study. The dominant cluster found by Sykes and Irven is also found in America, but it is only the second largest of a number of large clustered groupings.[4] It is clear that the jury is still out on the Sykes surname and further research is required, but, judging by the preliminary results of the US Sykes study and the distribution of the surname in 1881, the premise that the surname has a single origin seems highly questionable.

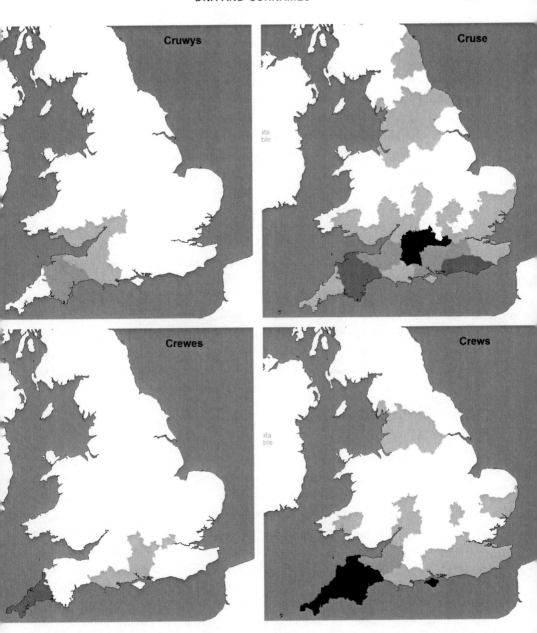

Figure 20. The distribution of the surnames Cruwys, Cruse, Crewes and Crews in the 1881 census. While the surname Cruse has some overlap with the other spellings, it has a much wider distribution and probably has multiple origins.

The Leicester studies

Turi King and colleagues at the University of Leicester adopted a different approach and, rather than focusing on a single surname, explored the link between the Y-chromosome and a range of surnames of varying levels of frequency. By this stage more advanced testing had become available. The researchers were able to test SNPs to confirm the base haplogroups, and the Y-STR testing was done on 17 markers, providing a much higher level of resolution for matching purposes. The research was carried out in two phases. In the first study the researchers selected 150 surnames covering the full frequency spectrum from Smith, the most common surname in Britain, to Rivis/Revis, which has just fifty current name-bearers. The lower limit was set at fifty to avoid accidentally sampling men who were closely related. For each of the 150 chosen surnames two male pairs were tested. Names were selected at random throughout Britain from the electoral register, but participants were asked to complete a questionnaire about their paternal ancestry to exclude close patrilineal relatives and recent name changes. The researchers found that there was a direct correlation between the rarity of the surname and the likelihood of a match. Sixteen of the pairs matched on all 17 markers, and the surnames of all of these pairs, with the exception of the name Major, were low-frequency surnames. A further twenty pairs differed by only a few mutations, and statistical calculations showed that these pairs fell within the lower end of the range of probabilities that could indicate a shared common ancestor since the time of surname formation. In total, the researchers concluded that 24 per cent of the surname pairs in their sample probably shared recent common ancestry.[5]

In a second and much larger study the Leicester researchers analysed forty surnames in detail, again covering the full range of the frequency spectrum. DNA samples were taken from 1,678 men bearing one of the forty chosen surnames or a recognised spelling variant. A minimum of ten men were sampled for each surname with proportionately more men sampled for the more common surnames. The participants were asked to complete a questionnaire in order to exclude patrilineal relatives closer than second cousin, recent name changes and known origin outside the UK. In addition, testing was done on a control group of 110 men with surnames different from each other and from the forty surnames in the study. The DNA results were first divided into haplogroups, and Y-STR testing was then used to identify descent clusters within each haplogroup. The study provided confirmation of the value of DNA testing to prove connections between different variant spellings. For example, the Wadsworths and Wordsworths were grouped together in one descent cluster. Similarly, the Grewcocks, Grocotts and Groococks were all related. For some of the surnames – Attenborough, Haythornthwaite, Herrick, Ketley, Stribling and Swindlehurst – over 70 per cent of the results fell into one large cluster. The highest level of clustering was seen with the surname Attenborough, where 87 per cent of the men belonged in a single descent cluster. For these surnames the results did suggest that the surnames each originated with a single man, with the remaining non-matching results being accounted for by historical levels of non-paternity. All the surnames with a single dominant descent cluster were names that have fewer than

1,000 current name-bearers. Some surnames, such as Buttersfield and Ravenscroft, were dominated by two large clusters. Hey was comprised of three large clusters. At the other end of the scale, the more common surnames of Smith, King, Bray and Stead showed little difference to the control group, which was made up largely of singletons (that is, testees whose Y-DNA signatures were not a close match with any other testee).

In order to aid the interpretation of the results, computer simulations of descent processes were performed. Varying numbers of founders were used. Changes in the size of the population and variance in the numbers of offspring were factored into the calculations. Non-paternity was also included in the simulations, at a rate of 2 per cent per generation. The simulations showed that the chance of survival of a lineage from a single founder after twenty generations was only 9.6 per cent. The authors commented that: 'Generally, the number of founders is a very poor predictor of the likely number of descent clusters observed in simulated data, showing that inferring [a] single foundation, 20 generations ago, from the patterns found in names such as Attenborough is unwise.'[6,7]

An additional problem with the interpretation of these 17-marker Y-DNA results, which the authors themselves recognised, is the possibility that two men match by chance rather than by virtue of sharing the same surname. This is a particular problem with men belonging to the more common haplogroups and who share a more frequently occurring surname. Indeed, the authors found that four pairs in their control group of 110 men had identical matching results despite having different surnames, and these men all belonged to haplogroups R1b and I1, the two most common haplogroups in Britain. The 17-marker test used in the study is a low-resolution test that is effective for identifying descent clusters, but with so few markers there is a wide margin of error when calculating the time when the two men shared a common ancestor. Most surname project administrators will have examples within their projects of men who match with a large variety of different surnames at 25 markers, but most of these matches disappear when the results are compared at 37 markers.

Turi King and Mark Jobling have also written a comprehensive review article entitled 'What's in a name? Y-chromosomes, surnames and the genetic genealogy revolution', which summarises the scientific advances in this area in the last decade.[8]

Irish DNA

Brian McEvoy and Dan Bradley from Trinity College, Dublin, undertook a similar study to examine the link between the Y-chromosome and Irish surnames. DNA samples were collected from 1,125 men with forty-three different surnames. The samples were tested on the same 17 markers that were used in the Leicester studies. The average Irish man has just a 0.2 per cent chance of sharing a DNA signature with another man. This study found that if two men shared the same surname there was an average 8.15 per cent chance of a match, though there was wide variation between surnames. The surnames Ryan, O'Sullivan, O'Neill, Byrne and Kennedy all had one predominant Y-chromosome signature, which the authors interpreted as signifying a single ancestor for these surnames, a conclusion that is in general agreement with expectations from historical accounts. Other surnames, including McCarthy, McGuinness, Donohoe and McEvoy, showed evidence of several male founders, and of these McEvoy had evidence of a dual foundation signature. Kelly and Murphy, the two most common Irish surnames, were marked by a high degree of genetic diversity, implying multiple founders. For the surnames that were considered to have a single origin, such as the two high-frequency surnames Ryan and O'Sullivan, only about 50 per cent of the modern surname-bearers were descended from the original founder. No correlation was found between match probability scores and the current frequency of the surnames. Around 90 per cent of the samples belonged to the haplogroup now known as R1b1a2, which is defined by the SNP marker M269.[9]

The high prevalence of haplogroup R1b1a2 in Ireland can make the interpretation of Irish Y-DNA results difficult, especially when the testing is done at a low resolution. Within the R1b1a2 haplogroup there is one dominant cluster known as the Irish Modal Haplotype (IMH). This DNA signature is shared by 8.2 per cent of Irish men, but is particularly predominant in north-western Ireland where it is found in 21.5 per cent of men. The signature is absent from most of Britain but is found at high frequencies (16.7 per cent) in western and central Scotland, areas that have strong historical links with Ireland. The Irish Modal Haplotype is thought to be associated with descent from the *Uí Néill* – a powerful early medieval Irish dynasty that is reputedly descended from the semi-legendary fifth-century warlord known as Niall of the Nine Hostages. The historical region under *Uí Néill* power coincides with the peak in the frequency of the IMH. The surnames that are linked with the *Uí Néill* genealogies include: (O') Boyle, Bradley, Campbell, Cannon, O'Connor, Devlin, (O')Doherty, O'Donnell, Donnelly, Egan, Flynn, (O')Gallagher, Gormley, Hynes, McCaul, McGovern, (Mc) Kee, McLoughlin, McManus, McMenamin, Molloy, O'Kane, O'Reilly, O'Rourke and Quinn.[10] Family Tree DNA advises that 0.6 per cent of the men in its database have an exact 12-marker match with the Niall signature.[11] These people also continue to have an exceptionally large number of matches with the higher resolution tests. I have one project member with the Niall signature who has almost 500 matches at 37 markers. (Two results are considered to match at 37 markers if they have a minimum of 33 out of 37 markers in common.) His matches have a huge variety of mostly Irish and Scottish surnames, including many of the traditional *Uí Néill* clan names.

Genetic drift

The phenomenon whereby random changes in reproductive success cause dramatic fluctuations in the survival rate of paternal lines is known as genetic drift. This situation can be caused purely by chance. Many family historians will see evidence of this effect in their own surname research. An illegitimate son born in the late eighteenth century can sometimes be the founder of a large dynasty with many living male descendants, whereas a line that can be traced back to the 1600s can be on the verge of extinction with only three or four males left. Other lines will die out completely over time if the last remaining males in the line produce only daughters and no sons – a process that is known in genetic genealogy circles as 'daughtering out'. In contrast, a single emigrant can introduce a surname to a new country such as Australia or America where the surname can flourish and multiply at a much higher rate than in its country of origin. This effect is particularly visible for some surnames that settled in America in the 1600s. Many of these surnames now occur at much higher frequencies in America than in the UK (Table 6). Not only have these surnames multiplied considerably, but where the surname has been researched in great depth in America, it is often found that nearly all the bearers of the surname can be traced back to a single founder or a few key founders. In the case of the Pomeroys, for example, it has been shown that nearly all the many Americans with the surname belong to a well-documented family that can be traced back to an emigrant who settled in Massachusetts in the 1630s.[12] This phenomenon is known as the founder effect. Furthermore, it can sometimes be the case that a surname that flourishes in America or Australia has become extinct in its country of origin.

Consequently, genetic drift can often have a distorting effect in a surname study. If one line has over 1,000 living name-bearers and another line has just two living descendants, a random sample of ten men with the surname is statistically more likely to sample ten men from the large tree and no one from the tree on the verge of extinction, thus creating a false impression of the surname. Clearly, the results of US-only participants in a DNA study should not be used in isolation to form conclusions about the origins of a surname in the UK. Conversely, when studying a surname of UK origin, it is important to collect samples from name-bearers from all countries where the surname is now found in order to ensure that as many lines as possible are tested, as some of these lines will inevitably no longer be found in the UK.

It is, therefore, essential to employ genealogical methods to research the trees for the surname in detail and trace them as far back in time as the surviving records will permit. This process allows the researcher to identify any lines that have been affected by genetic drift or the founder effect, and will also enable the researcher to pinpoint lines where the link between the Y-chromosome and the surname has been broken. This knowledge can then be used to aid the interpretation of the results. With diligent research it will eventually be possible to identify how many different lines there are and to target living descendants of these lines for DNA testing. It will inevitably be the case that some lines will no longer have any living male descendants. If a DNA study is conducted without reference to the genealogical data then the possible effects of genetic drift need to be taken into consideration.

Surname DNA projects

The academic studies can give us a good picture of the overall patterns for a large group of surnames, but because of the limited number of markers used and the possibility that the random sampling has not adequately compensated for the widely differing survival rates of different lines within the surname, it is difficult to extrapolate from these studies when analysing the results of individual surname projects run by family historians. Furthermore, the number of people tested in the academic projects pales into

Table 6. A comparison of the frequency of selected surnames in the 1881 census of Great Britain and the 1880 US census. These surnames now occur at a much higher frequency in the US as a result of the founder effect. In the most extreme example there were over seven times more people with the surname Crews in the US than in Great Britain. The GB census figures are taken from the *British 19th Century Surname Atlas* CD. The 1880 census figures are from Ancestry.com.

Surname	1881 GB census	1880 US census	Difference
Blair	7,778	18,444	X 2.37
Blackstone	225	1,040	X 4.62
Carden	661	1,733	X 2.62
Carpenter	10,250	37,907	X 3.70
Chandler	9,619	18,738	X 1.95
Crews	530	4,034	X 7.61
Davenport	5,676	12,154	X 2.14
Gay	3,991	9,443	X 2.37
Pomeroy	828	3,127	X 3.78
Vick	690	2,559	X 3.71

insignificance when compared to the huge numbers of people who have taken Y-DNA tests with the commercial testing companies. Family Tree DNA, the largest testing company, has an international database of nearly 250,000 Y-DNA test results. There are now over 7,000 DNA projects hosted at Family Tree DNA representing around 40,000 different surnames. These projects are all run by volunteer project administrators who do their research in their own free time and receive no payment for their work. Some are run by a single person. The larger projects will often have a team of administrators working on different aspects of the project. The project administrators bring a variety of different skills, and there is consequently a huge range in terms of the presentation of the projects, the levels of recruitment, the terminology used, the amount of funding available, the analysis of results and the extent and quality of the genealogical research.

Typically, academic projects are funded by grant money, but volunteer project administrators have a much more difficult task on their hands because they not only have to encourage people to join their projects but the participants must in most cases also pay for their own DNA tests. This can introduce bias as the project members are self-selected because of their ability to pay and their interest in finding out more about their genetic heritage. Some projects are run by large family associations that are able to sponsor tests for descendants from a particular line. Other projects find that over time some of their fellow researchers will contribute towards the cost of the tests or pay for targeted tests.

Volunteer-run DNA projects have the advantage of using many more markers than the academic studies. The most recent academic studies have used just 17 markers whereas DNA projects routinely use 37 markers and sometimes as many as 111. The participants are also able to take advantage of the latest advances in SNP testing to get detailed haplogroup subclade assignments.

DNA surname projects have been approached from different angles by scientists and family historians. Some family historians avoid collecting samples on a random basis, and pro-actively target specific lines for testing. The aim is to test at least one and preferably two people from every documented tree. If results do not match as expected and a non-paternity event (NPE) is thought to have occurred, further testing is often undertaken in order to establish where the NPE arose. For older trees going back to the 1600s, tests will often be done on all the different branches in the tree to verify the documentary research and to identify branch-defining mutations. Other family historians, and especially those researching high-frequency surnames, run their projects on a passive basis, waiting for random individuals to come forward for testing. The DNA results are collected and placed in closely matching groups, but the project administrator may do little in the way of original genealogical research, and will simply ensure that project members supply details of their most distant known ancestor on the paternal line. Some family historians' projects are a hybrid of these two extremes.

Many surname studies and DNA projects have a strong geographical bias. The academic studies on surnames have usually only sampled people with the surname living in one country, typically within the British Isles, with the result that the true genetic diversity of the surname is likely to be under-represented, as lineages that are now extinct in the UK but continue to thrive in America or Australia have not been sampled. In contrast, many family historians' DNA projects started in America, often with the objective of using DNA testing to verify the line of an immigrant ancestor or to find out where in Europe their surname originated. These projects have gradually expanded their scope in order to find links across the Atlantic, but most still have large numbers of American participants and relatively few from Europe. In order to reduce the bias, some projects have raised funds to sponsor tests for participants from the British Isles. The Phillips DNA Project (**www.phillipsdnaproject.com**) has been particularly successful in this regard. This project provides a free DNA test to anyone resident in Europe who can provide a five-generation Phillips lineage, and the offer has significantly boosted the UK participation rate. The Larkin DNA project had a particular interest in investigating the surname in Ireland, where the US immigrant ancestors were thought to have originated. The administrator visited Ireland in order to undertake a sampling effort focused on Irish parishes near the Shannon River, and was successful in obtaining thirty-four DNA samples.[13] However, the surname is also found in England, particularly in the north-west and the south-east, and much more sampling will need to be done in England to build up a true picture of the surname. Projects run by administrators in the British Isles or in Australasia tend to have a more even distribution of testees from different countries, and especially where the administrator has already undertaken extensive genealogical research and has built up a wide range of contacts who can be encouraged to participate in the project.

Although some DNA projects have been running for over a decade, most are a work in progress and the project administrators still hope to collect many more results before they are ready to draw any conclusions about the surname as a whole. Even then, most family historians are not in the habit of writing up and publishing their findings, let alone subjecting their research to the academic process of peer review.

All these factors make it difficult for a project administrator to put his or her own results into context in comparison with the results from other projects. The challenges of making inter-project comparisons have been highlighted by James Irvine, who compared the characteristics of twelve Y-DNA projects of varying sizes. He found subtle differences in the advertised sizes of projects, with some projects including mitochondrial DNA and autosomal DNA test results in addition to Y-DNA tests. The number of markers tested varied from project to project, but were largely related to the project start-up date, with early participants tested at 12 markers less likely to upgrade, whereas newer projects benefited from reduced pricing making the 37-marker test a feasible entry-level test. As a measure to assess the progress and representativeness of a project, Irvine established a method for identifying the 'penetration' of the project, or in other words the ratio of DNA tests per head of the population of that surname. He also devised a technique to measure the amount of geographical bias in a surname project to identify which projects had significantly higher ratios of participants from the New World. A particular problem highlighted by this study was the lack of inter-project consistency in the methodology used for grouping project members into closely matching descent clusters. A variety of methods are used to determine the clusters, and even the terminology used to describe the clusters varies. The terms used include groups/subgroups, family groups, lineages, and genetic families. Although there was generally a correlation between the amount of clustering and surname size, the largest cluster was surprisingly found in the Irwin/Irvine project. The Scottish surnames Irwin/Irvine and variants have an estimated world population of 278, 807, yet 66 per cent of the 188 participants who completed tests are placed in a single descent cluster. Although sampling bias undoubtedly plays a part, the size of the Irvine cluster is suggestive of a combination of genetic drift and founder effect. The next largest cluster was seen for the surname Creer from the Isle of Man, which has an estimated world population of 1,759. Twenty-four tests had been completed for this project at that time and 64 per cent of the participants formed a single cluster.[14] The findings of the Creer one-name study and DNA project, the culmination of ten years' research, have now been published in *A Family of Mannin* (Creer, 2011), and the evidence overwhelmingly points to a single origin.[15, 16]

The published findings from other DNA projects are less conclusive. The Pomeroy project was one of the first to adopt DNA testing and has now reached the stage where it has reconstructed all the UK trees in the nineteenth and twentieth centuries. DNA tests have been done on at least one representative from every tree, though in some cases no living male has survived, or the only males available would not volunteer for testing. However, the project has yet to resolve the question of whether or not they are one big family. The early results suggested a multi-founder origin, but the reconstructed trees all cluster in Devon and Cornwall and now that research is under way in the early parish registers, a single origin is looking more plausible as the documentation is now showing that some of the trees trace back to very early illegitimacies.[17, 18, 19]

Early results from the Plant DNA project published in *Nomina* in 2005 suggested that the living population of Plants are descended from a single male ancestor. However, this study used low-resolution DNA tests of mostly 10, 12 and 25 markers, and had a very small sample size of just fourteen males, whereas it is estimated that there are 12,000 living Plants in England and Wales and a further 5,000 in the US.[20] Nevertheless, with the addition of further results, the same pattern has prevailed. By 2010 sixteen of the twenty-eight participants in the project had matching DNA results. These Plants had widely differing genealogies with branches that were quite widely spread from early times. It seems that the main Plant cluster is an abnormally large single family that has enjoyed a high level of reproductive success, but a single large cluster is not necessarily indicative that all living males descend from a single ancestor.[21]

Clearly, it is too early to draw any definitive conclusions based on the currently available DNA evidence as to whether or not any surname has a single origin. The issues are neatly summarised by Redmonds, King and Hey:

> The reality is that non-paternity events and drift have often so clouded the picture that the results of DNA analysis can offer only general support for the supposition that a name has just one founder. With rare names, the genetic evidence can be unequivocal, but in such cases the historical evidence often already seemed firm.[22]

However, the genetic evidence to date from DNA projects for certain high-frequency surnames such as Taylor and Phillips, even allowing for incomplete and geographically biased sampling, has overwhelmingly confirmed that these names have multiple origins, though this was already indicated by the documentary evidence. The picture for other surnames will no doubt become clearer as more people are tested within surname projects and more comparative results become available. The findings of family historians will have much to contribute in this field.

Taking it further

It has only possible to discuss DNA testing in brief in this chapter. The different types of DNA test are discussed in greater detail in *DNA and Social Networking* (Kennett, 2011). This book also provides further guidance on setting up and running a DNA project, and includes a chapter on haplogroups and deep ancestry. *Surnames, DNA and Family History* (Redmonds, King and Hey, 2011) summarises the findings from the academic studies of the last decade. *Trace Your Roots with DNA* (Smolenyak and Turner, 2005), although now out of date in some respects, provides background on the genetics and useful guidance on running a DNA project. Although written from an American perspective, much of the advice is universally applicable. Two books by Chris Pomery, *DNA and Family History* (2004) and *Family History in the Genes* (2007), although again written before the many advances of the last few years, include guidance on running a DNA project and an overview of some of the early surname projects.

ISOGG, the International Society of Genetic Genealogy, has much useful information on its website (**www.isogg.org**) and in its wiki (**www.isogg.org/wiki**). It also has a specialist mailing list for DNA project administrators, where members can seek advice and share their knowledge. Many of the members of the Guild of One-Name Studies are now running DNA projects, and the subject has been the focus of a number of articles in the *Journal of One-Name Studies*, the back issues of which are all freely available online at **www.one-name.org/journal**. The Guild organises occasional DNA seminars in the UK, and also has a DNA adviser who provides help with the setting up of a new DNA project.

10

ONE-NAME STUDIES

Some to the fascination of a name,
Surrender judgment hoodwinked.
William Cowper, *The Task, Book VI*, 'The Winter Walk at Noon'.
The Poems of William Cowper (1835) p.282

The concept of a single-surname study or a one-name study is not a new one. The foundations were laid in the second half of the nineteenth century, which saw the publication in Britain of research into surnames such as Cokayne, Fynmore, Palgrave, and Swinnerton.[1,2,3,4] The early surname researchers tended to be gentlemen genealogists who not only had the leisure time to undertake the research but also had the funds to pay for its publication. As interest in family history research started to grow during the middle half of the twentieth century, some genealogists began to expand their research efforts to focus not just on their own family tree but on the surname as a whole. One very early study was undertaken by Frank Leeson, who extolled the virtues of the one-name study approach in an article published in 1964 in the *Genealogists' Magazine*:

> There is an increasing interest today in the 'total' study of one or more selected surnames, usually in a manner ancillary to other genealogical research undertaken for professional, private or altruistic reasons. All mentions of the selected name or name-sound group are recorded, often, in the first instance, and especially where the name is rare, as a means to widening the knowledge of one pedigree, and later to help others who might be interested in another branch of the same family-group or individual holders of the name. Sometimes a genealogist actively engages in pursuing all family-groups (i.e. distinctive groups of families using the same surname but not in fact related to each other) bearing the same name as a study in heredity and movement, or even for the sheer intellectual pleasure of assembling a three dimensional jigsaw in time, space and relationship.[5]

Another very early one-name study was started by Derek Palgrave in the 1960s, although it had its beginnings about a dozen or so years earlier when his interest was sparked by the discovery of some monuments to the Palgraves in a Norfolk church. Palgrave's early attempts to write to living name-bearers generated few replies, so he started his study by collecting references to the surname from local historical and archaeological publications. He then began to visit local archives and made trips to London to collect references from the civil registration indexes, which at that time were held at Somerset House. The first Palgrave gathering was held in 1973, which eventually led to the formation of the Palgrave Society, a formal one-name group that charges a small annual subscription. The society published its first newsletter, known as the *Palgrave Chronicle*, in 1974. The newsletter continues to be published on a quarterly basis to this day and is now sent out to members of the society around the world. The society has sponsored the publication of a number of short booklets on various aspects of Palgrave history from 1973 onwards, and has also published a substantial 283-page hardback book *The History and Lineage of the Palgraves* (Palgrave and Palgrave-Moore, 1983). Palgrave is a rare locative surname from Norfolk. There were just 211 Palgraves in the 1881 census, and none in the 1880 US census. The current global population is estimated to be around 400.[6]

The Federation of Family History Societies (FFHS) was founded in 1974 and included at its outset representatives from a number of one-name studies, including the Palgrave Society. Derek Palgrave published what is perhaps the first article on the subject of one-name societies in the *Genealogists' Magazine* in 1976.[7] This article was followed by a booklet entitled *Forming a One-Name Group* (1977), which has since been reprinted several times and is now available under the title *One-Name Family History Groups* (2008). The Federation published the first ever Register of One-Name Studies in 1977, which included the details of almost 300 one-name enthusiasts.[8] Derek Palgrave continued to promote the one-name studies cause within the FFHS and chaired the sub-committee that set up the first One-Name Studies Conference, which was held in Leicester in 1978 and attracted sixty-six participants. At that conference a resolution was passed to form a dedicated society for one-name studies, and the new Guild of One-Name Studies was officially launched on 1 September 1979 at a conference hosted by the family history societies of Devon and Cornwall.[9] The late Fred Filby became founder-chairman. Derek Palgrave subsequently held the chair for a number of years, and now serves as the Guild's president.

Meanwhile, on the other side of the Atlantic, J. Douglas Porteous, a professor of geography at the University of Victoria in British Columbia, Canada, had embarked on a pioneering and ambitious study of the surname Mell, the name of his paternal grandfather. Porteous hoped to demonstrate the value of surname studies in geography, their usefulness in providing information on migration and place loyalty, and their potential for locating the possible place of origin of the surname. Sadly his fellow geographers did not take up the baton, and it was to be another twenty years or more before they once again took an interest in surnames. However, Porteous's study, published in 1982, serves as a model example of the methodology used in a one-name study at that time, although he never had any association with the Guild.[10]

In the intervening years the Guild has grown from its modest beginnings into an international organisation that now has over 2,500 members from around the world studying over 8,000 surnames. Almost a quarter of the members who joined the Guild in 1979 are still members today, and the Guild signed up its 6,000th member in February

2012.[11] Inevitably, because of the Guild's UK origins, the majority of the surnames being studied are from the British Isles, but a small and growing number of members are now researching names from Continental Europe, such as Bouteloup (France), Diviani (Switzerland), Lefevre (Belgium/France) and Tomaszewski (Poland). For practical reasons, most of the studies have historically tended to focus on low- or medium-frequency surnames. There are some high-frequency names registered, such as Fisher, Gray, Martin and Phillips, but these are mostly coordinated by a one-name society or run by a collaborative team of researchers. Only one person is allowed to register a surname with the Guild but that person can then field the enquiries to the appropriate person in the research team.

The Guild defines a one-name study in its constitution as: 'research into the genealogy and family history of all persons with the same surname and its variants.' The membership requirements have varied over the years, but the prevailing consensus is that the researcher should strive to study the surname on a global basis. In practice, this does not mean researching the surname in every country of the world. For UK-origin surnames the global focus will mostly be on researching emigrants to North America, Australasia and a few other Commonwealth countries. Members are free to conduct their one-name studies as they see fit, and in reality it is often best to start researching in the country where the surname originated. There are no time constraints on members and no attempt is ever made to check the progress of a study. The only requirement of membership that is rigorously enforced is that members are expected to respond to all enquiries within a 'timely fashion'. The Guild does not by any means have a monopoly on one-name studies. There are probably as many people, if not more, undertaking one-name studies outside the Guild than within it, though some of these are studies that are geographically limited and where research is restricted to a specific region or a single country.

Methodology

The Guild of One-Name Studies has never prescribed the methodology for a one-name study. In the early years the emphasis was on the collection of data, which, in the pre-computer and pre-Internet age, was often an arduous process. In those days, members kept their records in card indexes, names were extracted from telephone directories to measure the distribution of the surname, and it took many months of hard work and multiple trips to London to record all the relevant surname references from the GRO indexes. The Guild's website first went live in 1998 and at that time would-be members were encouraged to collect all references to their surname from civil registration indexes, census indexes, the IGI (International Genealogical Index) and published indexes of wills. They were also expected to 'collect all references' to their registered surname(s) on a worldwide basis. Now, the process of extracting and storing data has been transformed, and work that once took months or years to complete can be done in a matter of days or weeks with a home computer and an Internet connection. Instead, the huge amount of data being made available online presents new challenges, and it is now necessary to prioritise the research and focus on the key datasets rather than aiming to collect all references. Much more emphasis is placed on other aspects of the research process such as reconstructing family trees and analysing the data to look at the distribution of the surname and patterns of migration. Publication is actively encouraged, and many one-name studies now have websites. Although some studies still produce newsletters, other studies have replaced the traditional newsletter with a blog. Some studies have published books on their research, and the arrival of print-on-demand services such as Lulu (**www. lulu.com**) has made publication a less costly undertaking. The Carden one-name study has pioneered the use of print-on-demand publishing, and has produced a range of books on the Carden surname.[12]

Each surname has its own unique history and distribution pattern, and one-namers adopt a variety of different approaches depending upon the time they have available, the size of their study, and their particular interests. Colin Ulph has been running a one-name study of the surname Ulph and variants for over thirty years. Ulph is a low-frequency surname from Norfolk, and there are only around 400 living name-bearers worldwide. There are about 100 people with the surname Aulph, eighty with the name Hulf, and about 700 people with the names Alp, Alpe or Alps. The surname Hulf is only found in England, and Aulph is now only seen in the US and Canada. The study publishes a regular newsletter, and has organised a number of family gatherings. In the last few years a DNA project was added to the study. Colin Ulph describes the way he runs his one-name study and how it has evolved in an article in the *Journal of One-Name Studies*, and it is clear that his research has given him enormous pleasure over the years.[13]

Stuart and Teresa Pask began researching their surname in 1980. The research was initially restricted to their own line, but they gradually expanded their interests to include Pasks worldwide. The study was registered with the Guild in 2003 and includes the variant spellings Paske, Pasque and Parsk. Pask is a low-frequency surname, and it is estimated that there are around 1,800 Pasks and 800 Paskes in the world today. In the UK there are around 1,200 Pasks, and only 150 Paskes. In the US the frequency is reversed: there are now 610 Paskes and 400 Pasks. The Pasks and Paskes originate from four English counties: Lincolnshire, Suffolk, Monmouthshire and Essex. Emigrants have introduced the surname to America, Australia, New Zealand, Canada and South Africa. The surname is only found at low frequency in the US – there were fewer than 100 Pasks and variants in the 1880 US census. Stuart and Teresa Pask have made excellent use of modern-day technology to make their research freely available on the Internet. The Pask one-name study website (**www.pask.org.uk**) includes a large online database with details of over 15,000 people. A blog provides updates on the research, and the study is now complemented by a DNA project. Several books on the Pasks have been self-published on Lulu, and the study also organises occasional family gatherings.[14]

With the advent of the Internet, high-frequency surnames are now a realistic proposition for a one-name study. Paul Howes began researching his surname around five years ago with his cousin Ian Howes. Their research initially focused on Norfolk where their family originated, but gradually expanded into a global study that is now registered with the Guild. There were 10,720 people with the surname Howes and related spellings (Hows, Howse and House) in the 1881 British census, with Howes being the most common spelling. The surname is found throughout southern England. In the US the most prevalent spelling is House. There were 11,985 people with this name in the 1880 census, and just over 3,000 people with the other variant spellings. It is estimated that there are around 50,000 people alive in the world today with one of the four surnames. Of these, about half live in North America, about 40 per cent in the UK and the rest mostly in Commonwealth countries. From the outset the goal was to help other researchers and to share as much information as possible. The study has started by trying to reconstruct all the families in the nineteenth century and will then work backwards in the parish registers. Virtually the entire study is now maintained on the Internet. The Howes family website (**www.howesfamilies.com**) went live in September 2008 with 5,000 people listed in a fully searchable database of reconstructed families. By May 2012 there were over 60,000 people in the database. There were around 23,000 Howes marriages in England and Wales between 1837 and 1950 and the identity of both partners is already known for more than 9,600 of these. Such progress has only been possible with the active collaboration of many other researchers, and has been facilitated by the sharing of information on the Internet. The principal workers on the database live in three different countries – the US, the UK and Spain – a collaboration that would have been inconceivable without the Internet and indeed without a broadband connection.[15]

The Guild is now collaborating with Pharos Teaching and Tutoring (**www. pharostutors.com**) to produce online courses providing instruction in the art of one-name studies. A beginners' course, 'Introduction to one-name studies', was launched in 2009. An advanced course on one-name studies with a focus on analysing the data and publishing the findings was introduced in 2010. Some of the essays that were written as part of the advanced course have since been published in the *Journal of One-Name Studies*, and are excellent examples of the contribution that a one-name study can make to the understanding of a surname. Kim Baldacchino studied the evolution and diffusion of the Devon surname Eastlake from the fourteenth century through to the eighteenth century.[16] Sue Mastel's exemplary study of the Westmorland surname Adamthwaite included surveys of the frequency of the surname over time and an analysis of the early references. She suggests that the surname is derived from a remote farmstead in the Howgill Fells, which still bears the Adamthwaite name today.[17] Douglas McClain Shaw is studying the surname Hembrough, which appears to have a dual origin in Yorkshire and the south-western counties of England. His research made particularly effective use of surname-mapping tools.[18]

The booklet *One-Name Family History Groups* (Palgrave, 2008) contains much useful advice on the methodology of a one-name study and collaborating with other researchers. There is a vast amount of information in the Guild's Members' Room, and particularly in its wiki, on various aspects of one-name studies and the range of international sources that can be used for data collection. The Guild's wiki is currently only available to members, but a booklet, *Seven Pillars of Wisdom: The Art of One-Name Studies* (Guild of One-Name

Studies, 2012), developed from some of the material in the wiki, was published in 2012. The booklet covers many of the practical aspects of running a one-name study, such as setting up a one-name study website, publicising the study, and safeguarding and preserving the research.

The Cruwys/Cruse/Cruise one-name study

My own research into my maiden name Cruwys (pronounced '*cruise*') began in 2002, but I did not initially set out to undertake a one-name study. Indeed I had no idea at the time that such a concept existed. As a child I had visited the parish of Cruwys Morchard in north Devon, which was reputedly where our surname originated. A Cruwys family still live in the manor house to this day, but we did not venture to knock on the door and introduce ourselves. I set out on my research with the initial aim of trying to find out if our family really was from Devon and if it was possible to find a link with the Cruwys Morchard line.

As the research progressed, I found that other family historians would send me details of their own trees just in case they might link up in the future, and genealogy friends sent me references to my surname that they came across in passing. I also found it necessary to reconstruct some of the other family trees for the purposes of elimination, and especially so when trying to sort out all the Johns and Williams. By this stage I was to all intents and purposes doing a one-name study and I registered the surname with the Guild in January 2006. This allowed me to advertise my study to a wider audience and to share the results of my research with other people. The Guild very conveniently provides its members with a free, easy-to-create web page for the study name (**www.one-name.org/profiles/cruwys.html**), which generated more enquiries and brought in more information. The profile page was subsequently complemented with a blog (**http://cruwys.blogspot.co.uk**), which allowed me to document the progress of the study and publish photos and stories on some of the more interesting findings from my research. I have had the advantage of being able to digitise my research from the outset. I started writing up family histories in simple Word files but I soon found it impossible to cope with the increasing amount of interlinked data and decided to input all the trees into a dedicated family history program. This is supplemented with spreadsheets where I store extracted datasets, but I still use Word to store transcriptions of wills and other long documents. I have been fortunate from the outset to benefit from the work of other family historians, some of whom had been researching the surname for twenty years or more. I have slowly incorporated their trees into my database, and have verified records in original sources wherever possible. Each new enquiry brings more information to the study. Some enquirers are able to add little to what I already have but others can sometimes supply the missing jigsaw pieces that enable a whole new branch to be added to an existing tree. Other contacts will set me off on research in an entirely new direction. Most importantly, I find that by maintaining one large database I have a good overall view of the surname and can often spot connections that other people have missed. Also, by maintaining a spreadsheet of all the births, marriages and deaths from the GRO indexes and cross-referencing this with the family trees in my database I am often able to assign a birth, death or marriage by a process of elimination.

Cruwys is an Anglo-Norman name that arrived in Britain some time during the twelfth century. The origin of the name in France has not been confirmed but the most plausible explanation is that the name derives from Creusanisy, now known simply as Anisy, which is just north of Caen in Normandy.[19] An alternative origin, from Cruys-Straëte in the *départemente* of Nord, midway between Dunkirk and Lille in northern France, has been suggested by Reaney.[20] The earliest recorded bearer of the surname is one Ottuel de Crues who is noted in *Domesday Descendants* as follows:

de Crues, Ottuel

Attested Colne charters of c.1160. Held half a fee *de novo* from Oliver de Tracy of Barnstaple in 1166, at Cruwys Morchard, Devon. This was held for one fee by the heirs of Alexander de Crues in 1242 (*Fees*, 748). In 1242 Richard de Crues held one fee of Barnstaple in 'Nytheresse'. (*Fees*, 773).[21]

The manor of Cruwys Morchard in north Devon has been in the continuous possession of the Cruwys family right through to the present day, though the Cruwys family who now live in the manor house are descended from a female line through Harriet Sharland née Cruwys whose son, George, assumed his mother's maiden name by Royal Licence in 1831. The manorial records are still held at the manor house, and the Tracy Deed, the earliest document in the collection, is believed to date from the early 1200s if not earlier.[22]

Cruwys is a low-frequency surname. There were 534 births recorded for the surname in England and Wales in the GRO indexes between 1837 and 2005, 421 marriages and 445 deaths. These figures include a few misspellings such as Crewys, Cruyes and Crwys. There were just 126 people with the surname recorded in the UK electoral register for 2002, and I estimate that there are no more than 300 living name-bearers worldwide today, with most of the other name-bearers being found in Australia, Canada and the USA.

I was eventually able to trace my own line back to a Hannibal Cruse who married Chrystoffe Harrell in 1597 in Winkleigh, Devon. Sadly there are no surviving Winkleigh baptisms prior to 1585 so I have no confirmation of the name of Hannibal's father. All the Cruses in Winkleigh can be assembled into one large tree, and it seems likely that the progenitor of this line is the Thomas Cruse who was buried in Winkleigh in 1596. Thomas appears to have been the son of John Cruwys of Cruwys Morchard who married Anne Keynes of Winkleigh some time in the 1540s. The circumstantial evidence is strong but not fully conclusive.

I found that the Cruwys spelling only began to be used in Devon from the late 1700s onwards, though the spelling was adopted earlier in Cruwys Morchard where it was used consistently from the late 1600s onwards. I encountered a variety of different spellings in the parish registers and other early records. Cruse was now the most usual spelling but other spellings were found including Crewes, Crews, Crewse, Cruise, Cruize and Cruze.

This opened up the possibility that some living people with these spellings might have an ancestor in common with people who adopted the Cruwys spelling. Consequently, the scope of the one-name study was extended to include these variants, though only Cruse and Cruise have been officially registered with the Guild. The addition of the variants complicated the picture because each variant has its own unique distribution pattern (Figure 20, p.157), and what started out as a study of a low-frequency surname has now turned into a much larger study than anticipated. In 1881 the Cruwys heartland can clearly be seen in Devon. Crewes is found almost exclusively in Cornwall, corresponding with the documentary research, which shows that nearly all the people with the surname Crewes descend from Anthony Crewes or Cruwys, a member of the Cruwys Morchard family who moved to Liskeard in Cornwall in the early 1500s.[23] Crews is predominantly found in the south-west. Cruse, in contrast, is widespread throughout the whole of the south of England with hotspots in Devon, Berkshire/Wiltshire and Sussex, and also occurs at low frequencies in the north of England. Cruise is the prevalent spelling in Ireland. In England Cruise is particularly prevalent in Lancashire, probably as a result of migration from Ireland to Liverpool, but is also found in the south-west. Cruse is the most common of the variant spellings in England. There were 868 people with the surname in the 1881 census. I was fortunate that David Cruse, who had been researching his surname for many years, very generously donated his research to me. His research on the Berkshire, Wiltshire, London and Sussex Cruses complemented the work I had already done in Devon. I am now at the stage where virtually every Cruwys can be linked into a tree, but the research into the Cruse surname still has some way to go. All the reconstructed family trees are entered into my family history program, which now contains extensive details on almost 17,000 individuals, though this does also include my research into my other ancestral lines as well. I have 1,020 people in my database with the surname Cruwys, a further 1,037 with the surname Cruse, 352 with the name Crews, and 193 with the surname Scruse (a late variant of the surname Cruse). The Crewes tree from Cornwall is still on paper and has yet to be put into the program.

A DNA project (**www.familytreedna.com/public/CruwysDNA**) was added to the study in 2007 and has brought new insights into the surname. It is also being used to explore a wider range of variant spellings where it is not possible to do the documentary research in depth. As can be seen from the comparative figures from the 1881 British census and the 1880 US census (Table 7), these variants represent a significant challenge, especially in the US. I now maintain a separate database where I record the outline pedigrees of the US Crewses and Cruses in my DNA project, which now contains details of around 1,000 individuals. The DNA project has sixty-nine Y-DNA results from men living in seven different countries. All the Cruwys men, despite the rarity of the surname, fall into two distinct genetic groups, though all the trees, apart from some that are stuck in London, trace back to a few villages in close proximity to each other in north Devon. The only Crewes result to date matches the Cruwys result for my Winkleigh tree, and is consistent with these lines sharing a common ancestor in the 1400s, thus confirming the link to Cruwys Morchard. The surname Cruse has much greater genetic diversity, as was expected

Table 7. The frequency of the surnames Crews, Cruise, Cruse, Cruwys and variants in the 1881 British census and the 1880 US census. The variants have marked differences in their frequency with some variants being exceptionally prolific in the US. Scruse is only found in Britain and Australasia. Screws only occurs in the US.

1881 British census		1880 US census	
Crewes	83	Crewes	41
Crews	530	Crews	4,024
Cruce	23	Cruce	254
Cruice	50	Cruice	107
Cruise	291	Cruise	721
Cruse	868	Cruse	2,126
Cruwys	84	Cruwys	1
Cruys	3	Cruys	7
Cruze	80	Cruze	217
Screws	0	Screws	218
Scruse	48	Scruse	0

given the more widespread distribution. Only one Cruse Y-DNA result so far matches with a Cruwys, and there have been many singleton results suggesting a multiple origin. One Cruise has a distant match with Cruwys and Crewes. The surname Cruise in Ireland is of Anglo-Norman origin, and in medieval records was mostly spelt Cruys. It seems plausible to think that the progenitor of the Irish Cruises was part of the Norman Cruwys family. Nearly all the American men with the surnames Crews and Cruse fall into one large genetic group that has it is origins in seventeenth-century Virginia. It is believed that the surname in the US is derived from the name Crewe. To date, the Americans have no matches with anyone from the UK. It is clear that many more results will be needed before we can gain a full understanding of all the variant spellings, but the DNA project has already successfully linked together many lines where there was no link in the paper trail, and is providing a new focus for the documentary research.

My one-name study has been a fascinating journey of discovery, and an interesting intellectual challenge. I am in contact with many different people from all around the world and it is always a pleasure to be able to help people with their research. It's always very exciting when a new piece of information suddenly allows me to fit together a large section of the jigsaw puzzle, and I enjoy the quiet satisfaction of knowing that I am the world expert on my chosen surname.

APPENDIX A

GENEALOGY WEBSITES

Subscription and pay-per-view

www.1911census.co.uk (£) The 1911 census for England and Wales.

www.ancestry.co.uk and **www.ancestry.com** (£) The market leader with a huge and ever-increasing collection of records. Varying subscription options for access either to UK records or the worldwide record collection.

www.bmdindex.co.uk (£) Births, marriages and deaths (BMD) indexes for England and Wales.

www.bmdregisters.co.uk (£) Nonconformist and non-parochial registers.

www.britishnewspaperarchive.co.uk (£) The British Newspaper Archive (some libraries subscribe to this service and offer free remote access).

www.deceasedonline.com (£) UK burial and cremation records.

www.familyrelatives.com (£) BMD indexes, some parish registers, occupational records and free access to the overseas BMD indexes from 1761–1994.

www.findmypast.co.uk (£) BMDs, censuses, a large parish register collection, passenger lists, military records, education records, etc.

www.thegenealogist.co.uk (£) BMDs, censuses, parish registers, military records, directories, etc.

www.genesreunited.co.uk (£) GenesReunited.

www.theoriginalrecord.com (£) Rare and unusual genealogy records hand-indexed by surname.

www.origins.net (£) British and Irish records including censuses, the National Wills Index (pre-1858) and some specialist collections.

www.parishregister.com (£) Docklands Ancestors – specialist records relating to the Docklands and the East End of London.

www.ukcensusonline.com (£) BMD indexes and censuses.

General websites

http://archive.org The Internet Archive – a rich genealogical source for out-of-copyright books printed prior to 1923.

www.bbc.co.uk/familyhistory A guide to getting started in family history from the BBC.

http://books.familysearch.org FamilySearch Books hosts a collection of more than 40,000 digitised genealogy and family history publications, including much medieval source material.

http://books.google.co.uk Google Books.

www.british-history.ac.uk British History Online.

www.castlegarden.org Immigration records from the United States' first immigration centre.

www.censusfinder.com Links to online census records in North America, the British Isles and Scandinavia.

www.connectedhistories.org A portal for a range of British history sources covering the period 1500–1900.

http://copac.ac.uk COPAC – an integrated catalogue with details of the holdings of over seventy national and specialist libraries in the UK and Ireland.

www.cwgc.org The Commonwealth War Graves Commission website with information on the 1,700,000 men who lost their lives in the two world wars.

www.cyndislist.com Thousands of worldwide genealogy links sorted by category.

www.ellisisland.org Ellis Island passenger records.

http://explore.bl.uk A catalogue of nearly 60 million items in the British Library.

www.familysearch.org The largest collection of free genealogical records.

www.familysearch.org/learn/wiki The FamilySearch wiki.

www.ffhs.org.uk The Federation of Family History Societies has links to the websites of all its member societies both in the British Isles and Australia.

www.freebmd.org.uk Free access to the BMD indexes for England and Wales (not yet fully transcribed).

www.freecen.org.uk Free census transcriptions.

www.freereg.org.uk Free parish register transcriptions.

www.gazettes-online.co.uk Gazettes Online – free access to the *London Gazette*, the *Edinburgh Gazette* and the *Belfast Gazette*, the official newspapers of record for the UK.

http://genealogy.about.com/od/free_genealogy/a/ssdi.htm The US Social Security Death Index (SSDI).

www.genuki.org.uk A free library of genealogical information and links for the UK and Ireland.

www.genuki.org.uk/indexes/OPC.html The Genuki page on the online parish clerk scheme.

www.gro.gov.uk/gro/content/certificates The certificate-ordering service from the General Register Office (England and Wales).

http://hearthtax.org.uk Hearth Tax Online.

www.historicaldirectories.org Historical directories.

www.interment.net An online database of cemetery record transcriptions.

www.medievalgenealogy.org.uk Chris Phillips' Medieval Genealogy website.

www.nationalarchives.gov.uk The UK National Archives.

http://discovery.nationalarchives.gov.uk The catalogue of the UK National Archives with over 20 million descriptions of records covering 1,000 years of history.

www.nationalarchives.gov.uk/A2a Access to Archives (A2A) is a catalogue of the archival holdings of record offices and other repositories in England and Wales.

www.nationalarchives.gov.uk/archon ARCHON – A directory of record repositories in the United Kingdom.

www.oldbaileyonline.org The Proceedings of the Old Bailey (London's Central Criminal Court), 1674–1913.

http://pricegen.com/english_genealogy.html A comprehensive collection of genealogy links.

www.ukbmd.org.uk UKBMD has links to websites offering online transcriptions of UK births, marriages, deaths and censuses for the UK and the Isle of Man. A wide range of other indexes and transcriptions are also available for most counties, including parish records, wills, monumental inscriptions, etc.

www.ukgdl.org.uk A directory of UK genealogy links.

www.worldcat.org WorldCat provides a searchable online catalogue of the holdings of over 10,000 libraries worldwide.

www.worldgenweb.org A directory of worldwide genealogy resources.

Ireland

www.ancestryireland.co.uk (€) The website of the Ulster Historical Foundation has BMDs, census records, directories, memorial inscriptions, etc. Some indexes can be searched free of charge.

www.askaboutireland.ie Historical information about Ireland. The site includes a searchable database to Griffith's Valuation Indexes with links to the original text and digital maps.

www.census.nationalarchives.ie The 1901 and 1911 censuses.

www.dublinheritage.ie Online databases for Dublin, including parish registers and electoral registers.

www.emeraldancestors.com (€) Births, marriages, deaths and census records for Northern Ireland.

www.failteromhat.com/griffiths.php Griffith's Valuation Indexes.

www.findmypast.ie (€) Irish records from Findmypast.

http://freepages.genealogy.rootsweb.ancestry.com/~registryofdeeds An index of names that appear in wills, land transactions and other documents held at the Registry of Deeds in Dublin.

www.from-ireland.net Dr Jane Lyons' Irish genealogy and family history website with lots of transcriptions and indexes.

www.groireland.ie The General Register Office for Ireland.

www.igp-web.com The Ireland Genealogy Project.

www.irishgenealogy.ie Irish church records.

www.irish-genealogy-toolkit.com Irish Genealogy Toolkit.

www.irishhistoryonline.ie A bibliography of Irish history.

www.irishmanuscripts.ie Irish Manuscripts Commission.

www.irishnewspaperarchive.com (€) The Irish Newspaper Archive.

www.irishorigins.com (€) Irish Origins.

www.libraryireland.com Library Ireland – free Irish books and directories.

www.nationalarchives.ie The Irish National Archives.

www.nidirect.gov.uk/general-register-office-for-northern-ireland The General Register Office for Northern Ireland.

www.nli.ie National Library of Ireland.

www.proni.gov.uk The Public Record Office of Northern Ireland.

www.rootsireland.ie (€) A large collection of records from the Irish Family History Foundation.

Scotland

www.gro-scotland.gov.uk General Register Office for Scotland.

www.nas.gov.uk National Archives of Scotland.

www.nls.uk The National Library of Scotland.

www.nrscoltand.gov.uk National Records of Scotland.

www.rps.ac.uk Records of the Parliament of Scotland: a searchable database covering the years 1235 to 1707.

www.scan.org.uk/catalogue Scottish Archive Network Catalogue.

www.scotlandsinformation.com Scottish archives, libraries and museums.

www.scotlandspeople.gov.uk (£) BMDs, censuses, parish registers, wills, etc. for Scotland.

Wales

www.ancientwalesstudies.org Ancient Wales studies.

www.archiveswales.org.uk Archives Wales – a catalogue to the holdings of twenty-one archives in Wales.

www.llgc.org.uk National Library of Wales.

http://cadair.aber.ac.uk/dspace/handle/2160/4026 The Bartrum Project – Welsh Genealogies AD 300–1400.

DNA Websites

www.cyndislist.com/surnames/dna A user-submitted list of surname DNA projects from Cyndi's List.

http://dna.ancestry.com Ancestry DNA.

www.dna-testing-adviser.com Richard Hill's independent guide to DNA testing.

www.familytreedna.com FamilyTree DNA.

www.kerchner.com/dna-info.htm Charles Kerchner's genetic genealogy resources page.

www.isogg.org ISOGG – the International Society of Genetic Genealogy.

www.isogg.org/wiki The ISOGG wiki.

www.jogg.info The *Journal of Genetic Genealogy.*

www.worldfamilies.net Educational resources for project administrators and project listings by haplogroup, surname, size and geographical area.

www.ysearch.org A public Y-DNA database sponsored by Family Tree DNA.

APPENDIX B

SURNAME WEBSITES

General

www.surnamestudies.org.uk Surname Studies website – a continuation of the former Modern British Surnames website created by the late Philip Dance and now sponsored by the Guild of One-Name Studies.
www.americanlastnames.us American Last Names.
www.americansurnames.us American Surnames.
www.britishsurnames.co.uk British Surnames.
www.sog.org.uk/library/surnames_and_families.shtml Searching for surnames at the Society of Genealogists.
www.surnamedb.com The Internet Surname Database.
http://surnames.behindthename.com Behind the Name: the etymology and history of surnames.
www.s-gabriel.org/names/english.shtml Medieval Names Archive.

Regional and specialist websites

www.cornishsurnames.com Graham Owen's Cornish Surnames website.
http://freepages.history.rootsweb.ancestry.com/~kernow/index.htm Jim Thompson's website on Cornish surnames and their meanings.
http://genuki.cs.ncl.ac.uk/DEV/DevonSurnames/index.html Studies on Devon Surnames by Matt Hooper
http://avonvalleycollection.bravehost.com/search.html The Gypsy Surname Index of Great Britain, compiled by Jan James.

Continental Europe

http://home.scarlet.be/marcel.vervloet/page9.htm A Dutch website with alphabetical listings of surnames from Belgium and northern France and their etymologies largely taken from the *Woordenboek van de familienamen in België en Noord-Frankrijk*.

http://jeantosti.com/noms/a.htm *D'où vient votre nom?* An online French surname dictionary.

www.geneanet.org/nom-de-famille *D'où vient mon nom?* An online French surname database from Geneanet.

www.italyworldclub.com/genealogy/surnames Etymology and origin of Italian surnames.

Surname interests

http://boards.ancestry.co.uk Ancestry message boards.

http://boards.rootsweb.com RootsWeb message boards.

http://lists.rootsweb.ancestry.com/index RootsWeb mailing lists.

http://rsl.rootsweb.ancestry.com The RootsWeb Surname List.

www.genealogywise.com GenealogyWise – a social network for genealogists.

www.one-name.org The Guild of One-Name Studies.

www.onlinenames.net.au Graham Jaunay's online name listings.

www.rootschat.com Rootschat: a genealogy forum with boards for listing surname interests.

www.scgsgenealogy.com/SurnameWall.htm The Southern California Genealogical Society's Virtual Surname Wall.

http://surnamesite.com/surnames.htm The Surname Registry from the Surname Site.

www.ukgid.com The UK Genealogy Interests Directory.

www.uk-surnames.com A surname listing site for research interests in the UK.

APPENDIX C

LAY SUBSIDY ROLLS

*The lay subsidy rolls are held at The National Archives and are included in series E179. The E179 database (**www.nationalarchives.gov.uk/e179**) contains detailed descriptions of every document in the series. The following is a list of all the thirteenth- and fourteenth-century subsidy rolls that are in print or available online.*

England

Bedfordshire
Gaydon, A.T. (ed.), *Miscellanea: The Taxation of 1297* (Bedfordshire Historical Record Society vol. 39, 1959).

Hervey, S.H.A. (ed.), *Two Bedfordshire Subsidy Lists: 1309 and 1332*, Suffolk Green Books (*sic*), no 18. Paul & Mathew, 1925. Ancestry (£): **http://search.ancestry.co.uk/search/db.aspx?dbid=5843**. Included in Ancestry's 'Bedfordshire, England, Extracted Parish Records' and listed as 'Suffolk Green Books, Subsidy Lists, 1309–1332'.

Jenkinson, H., 'An early Bedfordshire Taxation' (1237) in F.A. Page-Turner (ed.), *Miscellanea* (Bedfordshire Historical Record Society, vol. 2, 1914).

Bristol
Fuller, E.A., 'The Tallage of 6 Edward II (Dec. 16, 1312) and the Bristol Rebellion' in C.S. Taylor (ed.), *Transactions of the Bristol and Gloucestershire Archaeological Society for 1894–5*, vol. 19, 1894–95, pp.171–278 (detailed local rolls). Internet Archive: **http://archive.org/details/transactionsbris19bris**.

Buckinghamshire
Chibnall, A.C. (ed.), *Early Taxation Returns* (1327 and 1332 subsidies) (Buckinghamshire Record Society, 1966).

Cumberland
Steel, J.P. (ed.), *Cumberland Lay Subsidy: Being the Account of a Fifteenth and Tenth collected 6th Edward III* [1332] (Titus Wilson, 1912). Internet Archive: **http://archive.org/**

details/cu31924030265536; British History: **www.british-history.ac.uk/source.
aspx?pubid=385**.

Derbyshire

Cox, J.C., 'Derbyshire in 1327: being a lay subsidy roll' in *Journal of the Derbyshire
Archaeological and Natural History Society*, vol. 30, 1908, pp.23–96.

Devon

Erskine, A.M. (ed.), *The Devonshire Lay Subsidy of 1332*, new series, vol. 14 (Devon and
Cornwall Record Society, 1969).

Dorset

Rumble, A.R. (ed.), *The Dorset Lay Subsidy Roll of 1327* (Dorset Record Society, 1980).
Mills, A.D. (ed.), *The Dorset Lay Subsidy Roll of 1332* (Dorset Record Society, 1971).

Essex

Ward, J.C. (ed.), *The Medieval Essex Community: The Lay Subsidy of 1327* (Essex Record
Office, Essex Historical Documents 1, 1983).

Gloucestershire

Franklin, P. (ed.), *The Taxpayers of Mediaeval Gloucestershire. An Analysis of the 1327 Lay Subsidy
Roll with a New Edition of its Text* (Sutton Publishing, 1993).

Hertfordshire

Brooker, J. and Flood, S. (eds), *Lay Subsidy Rolls for Hertfordshire, 1307–8 & 1334*, vol. XIV
(Hertfordshire Record Society, 1999).

Huntingdonshire

Raftis, J.A., and Hogan, M.P. (eds), *Early Huntingdonshire Lay Subsidy Rolls* (Pontifical
Institute of Mediaeval Studies, 1976).

Kent

Hanley, H.A. and Chalklin, C.W. (eds), 'The Kent lay subsidy roll of 1334/5' in DuBoulay,
F.R.H. (ed.), *Documents Illustrative of Medieval Kentish Society* (Kent Records 18, 1964).
Kent Archaeology: **www.kentarchaeology.org.uk/Research/Pub/KRV/18/3/
058-172.htm**.

Lancashire

Vincent, J.A.C. (ed.), *Lancashire Lay Subsidies: Volume I Henry III to Edward I* (1216–1307)
(Lancashire and Cheshire Record Society, vol. 27, 1893). Internet Archive: **http://
archive.org/details/lancashirelaysu000ffigoog**.

Rylands, J.P. (ed.), 'The Exchequer lay subsidy roll of Robert de Shireburn and John de Radcliffe, taxers and collectors in the county of Lancaster AD 1332' in *Miscellany Relating to Lancashire and Cheshire*, vol. II, Lancashire and Cheshire Record Society 31, 1896.

The Record Society, *The Book of the Abbot of Combermere, 1289–1529; The Exchequer Book of the Abbot of Combermere, 1289–1529; The Exchequer Lay Subsidy Roll for Lancashire, 1332* (1896) (Kessinger Legacy Reprints, Kessinger Publishing, 2010).

Leicestershire

Fletcher, W.G.D. (ed.), 'The earliest Leicestershire lay subsidy roll, 1327' in *Associated Architectural Societies Reports. Transactions of the Leicestershire Architectural and Archaeological Society*, 1888–89, vol. XIX, pp.209–312; vol. XX, pp.131–78.

Lincolnshire

Lincolnshire Lay Subsidy, 1332. Postles, D.: **www.historicalresources.myzen.co.uk/ LINC/lincers.html**.

O'Brien, K.M., 'An index to the 1332 Lay Subsidy Rolls for Lincolnshire': **www.s-gabriel.org/names/mari/LincLSR**.

London

Ekwall, E., *Returns from Lay Subsidies raised in the City of London in 1292 and 1319 …* : British History Online: **www.british-history.ac.uk/source.aspx?pubid=11**.

Curtis, M., 'The London Lay Subsidy of 1332' in Unwin, G. (ed.), *Finance and Trade under Edward III: The London Lay Subsidy of 1332* (1918), pp.35–92. British History Online: **www.british-history.ac.uk/source.aspx?pubid=177**.

Northumberland

Bradshaw, F., 'The Lay Subsidy Roll of 1296: Northumberland at the end of the Thirteenth Century', *Archaeologia Aeliana*, 3rd series, vol. 13 (Andrew Reid, 1916).

Fraser, C.M. (ed.), *The Northumberland Lay Subsidy Roll of 1296* (Society of Antiquaries of Newcastle upon Tyne, Record Series 1, 1968).

Rutland

Rutland Lay Subsidy 1296–97. Postles, D.: **www.historicalresources.myzen.co.uk/ RUTLS/ruthome.html**.

Shropshire

Fletcher, W.G.D. (ed.), 'The Shropshire lay subsidy of 1327', part 1, in *Transactions of the Shropshire Archaeological and Natural History Society*, 3rd series, vol.VI, 1906.

Fletcher, W.G.D. (ed.), 'The Shropshire lay subsidy of 1327', part 2, in *Transactions of the Shropshire Archaeological and Natural History Society*, 3rd series, vol.VII, 1907, pp.351–78. Internet Archive: **http://archive.org/details/transactionsofsh1907shro**.

Somerset

Dickinson, F.H. (ed.), 'Exchequer Lay Subsidies, which is a tax roll for Somerset of the First Year of Edward 3rd [1327]', in *Kirkby's Quest for Somerset*, etc. Somerset Record Society, vol. 3, 1889, pp.79–284. Internet Archive: **http://archive.org/details/kirbysquestforso0odickgoog**.

Staffordshire

Wrottesley, G. (ed.), 'The Exchequer lay subsidy of A.D. 1327' in William Salt Archaeological Society (ed.), *Collections for a History of Staffordshire* 1886, vol. VII, part I, pp.193–255. British History Online: **www.british-history.ac.uk/source.aspx?pubid=464** Internet Archive: **http://archive.org/details/staffcollections07stafuoft**.

Suffolk

Powell, E. (ed.), *A Suffolk Hundred in 1283: The Assessment of the Hundred of Blackbourne for a Tax of One Thirtieth, and a Return showing the Land Tenure there* (Cambridge University Press, 1910). Internet Archive: **http://archive.org/details/cu31924030265528**.

Powell, E. (ed.), *Suffolk in 1327 being a Subsidy Return* (Suffolk Green Books, no. IX, vol. II, George Booth, 1906). Ancestry: **http://search.ancestry.co.uk/search/db.aspx?dbid=5936**. (Included in the Ancestry collection of 'Suffolk, England, Extracted Parish Records' and listed as 'Suffolk: Subsidy Returns, 1327'.) Also available from S&N Genealogy Supplies (**www.genealogysupplies.com**).

Surrey

Surrey Record Society, *Surrey Taxation Returns: Fifteenths and Tenths. Part A: The 1332 Assessment* (Surrey Record Society Publications, no. XVIII, 1922). Internet Archive: **http://archive.org/details/surreytaxationre00surruoft**.

Sussex

Hudson, W. (ed.), *The Three Earliest Subsidies for the County of Sussex in the Years 1296, 1327, 1332* (Sussex Record Society, vol. 10, 1910). British History Online: **www.british-history.ac.uk/source.aspx?pubid=513**.

Warwickshire

Carter, W.F. (ed.), *The Lay Subsidy Roll for Warwickshire of 6 Edward III (1332)* (Dugdale Society, vol. 6, 1926).

Westmorland

Farrer, W. and Curwen, J.F. (eds), *Records relating to the Barony of Kendale*, vols 1 and 2, 1923–24. The 1332 subsidy returns are published separately on the individual parish pages.

Wiltshire

Crowley, D. (ed.), *The Wiltshire Tax List of 1332* (Wiltshire Record Society, vol. 45, 1989).

Worcestershire

Willis Bund, J. and Amphlett, J., *Lay Subsidy Roll for the County of Worcestershire circ. 1280* (Worcestershire Historical Society, 1893). Internet Archive: **http://archive.org/details/laysubsidyrollf00exchgoog**.

Eld, F.J. (ed.), *Lay Subsidy Roll for the County of Worcester I Edward III* [1327] (Worcestershire Historical Society, 1895). Internet Archive: **http://archive.org/details/worcestersubedward00greauoft**.

Amphlett, J. (ed.), *Lay Subsidy Roll, A.D. 1332–3 and Nonarum Inquisitiones, 1340, for the County of Worcester* (Worcestershire Historical Society, 1899). Internet Archive: **http://archive.org/details/laysubsidyrollad00greauoft**.

Yorkshire

Brown, W. (ed.), *Yorkshire Lay Subsidy being a Ninth collected in 25 Edward I (1297)* (Yorkshire Archaeological Society, Record Series, vol. 16, 1894). Internet Archive: **http://archive.org/details/recordseries16yorkuoft**.

Brown, W. (ed.), *Yorkshire Lay Subsidy, being a Fifteenth, collected 30 Edward I (1301)* (Yorkshire Archaeological Society, Record Series, vol. 21, 1897). British History: **www.british-history.ac.uk/source.aspx?pubid=398**. Also available on CD from the Parish Chest (**www.parishchest.com**) and Anguline Research Archives (**http://anguline.co.uk**).

Parker, J. (ed.), 'Lay Subsidy Rolls, 1 Edward III [1327]: North Riding & the City of York' in *Miscellanea Volume II* (Yorkshire Archaeological Society, Record Series, vol. 74, 1929).

Stansfield, J. (ed.), 'Two subsidy rolls of Skyrack, *temp.* Edward. III' [1327–77] in *Miscellanea I* (Thoresby Society, vol. 2, 1891).

Wales

Note: The lay subsidy for Wales was levied in 21 Edward I (20 November 1292–19 November 1293). The printed texts are variously dated 1292 or 1293. Some of the authors have chosen the earlier date and others the later date, but they are all referring to the same subsidy.

Jones, F. (ed.), 'The subsidy of 1292' in *Bulletin of the Board of Celtic Studies*, vol. 13, May 1950, pp.210–30. This article discusses the subsidy of 1292–93, but the main part of the text is taken from E179 242/48 and has a very large number of names; pp.215–25 has lists of taxers and jurors in various parts of South Wales and a few parts of neighbouring English counties; pp.225–30 has lists of taxpayers in the lordships of Abergavenny (Monmouthshire) and Cilgerran (Pembrokeshire) from E179/242/56.

Anglesey

A transcription of E179/242/49 relating to Aberffraw is printed in Seebohm, F., *The Tribal System in Wales*, 2nd edn (Longmans, Green & Co, 1904), Appendix A f, pp.37–43: Internet Archive: **http://archive.org/details/tribalsystemin2d00seebuoft**.

This assessment includes both a list of individuals and details of the goods on which they were assessed, but unfortunately Seebohm did not expand the Latin abbreviations, making it difficult to read. Seebohm dates the assessment to 1320–40, but The National Archives have shown that the script and content date from an earlier period and have catalogued the document as part of the subsidy granted to Edward I in 1290 that was collected in 1292–93.

Caernarfonshire

Jones-Pierce, T., 'A Lleyn lay subsidy account' and *idem*, 'Two early Caernarvonshire accounts. Nefyn lay subsidy, 1293…' in *Bulletin of the Board of Celtic Studies*, vol. 5, 1930, pp.54–71, and pp.142–8. A transcript of E179/242/50A and E179/242/50B.

Merionethshire

Williams-Jones, K. (ed.), *The Merioneth Lay Subsidy Roll, 1292–93* (University of Wales, 1976).

Monmouthshire

Hopkins, A., 'The lay subsidy of 1292: Monmouth and the Three Castles' in *Studia Celtica*, vol. 30, 1996, pp.189–96. This is a transcription of E179/242/59, which was an assessment of individuals in the honour of Monmouth and Three Castles (the lordships or manors of Grosmont, Whitecastle and Skenfrith). The list includes a huge variety of names with some surnames, and others in the form of *de, filio/filia, ap*, etc.

A transcript of a list of taxpayers in the lordship of Abergavenny was included in Francis Jones (1950), *Bulletin of the Board of Celtic Studies* (see above).

Montgomeryshire

A transcript of all the lay subsidy rolls for Montgomeryshire is contained in the Leonard Owen Manuscripts held at The National Library of Wales: MS 18163, pp.1–164 and pp.169–244. It is described in the catalogue of the NLW as: 'Extracts, unbound in folder, made by John Hobson Matthews from Monmouthshire Lay Subsidy lists in the Public Record Office [now The National Archives].'

Morgan, R., 'A Powys lay subsidy roll', *Montgomeryshire Collections*, vol. 71, 1983, pp.91–112. A transcript of E179/242/54.

Pembrokeshire

The 1292–93 lay subsidy relating to the lordship of Cilgerran in north Pembrokeshire, being part of TNA E179 242/56, was published in Owen, H., *A Calendar of the Public Records Relating to Pembrokeshire*, vol. 2 (Honourable Society of Cymmrodorion, 1914).

A full transcription of E179 242/56 appears in Francis Jones (1950), *Bulletin of the Board of Celtic Studies* (see opposite).

Radnorshire

Faraday, M.A. (ed.), 'The Assessment for the Fifteenth of 1293 on Radnor and other Marcher lordships', published in two parts in *The Transactions of the Radnorshire Society*, vol. 43, 1973, pp.79–85, and 1974, vol. 44, pp.62–8. A transcript of TNA E179/242/57 and part of E179/242/48.

APPENDIX D

ORGANISATIONS AND JOURNALS

American Name Society

www.wtsn.binghamton.edu/ANS

The American Name Society was founded in 1951 to 'promote onomastics, the study of names and naming practices, both in the United States and abroad'. The society publishes a peer-reviewed quarterly journal *Names: A Journal of Onomastics*.

British Association for Local History

www.balh.co.uk

An organisation set up to 'encourage and assist the study of local history as an academic discipline and as a rewarding leisure pursuit for both individuals and groups'. The society publishes a quarterly journal, *The Local Historian*.

Foundation for Medieval Genealogy

http://fmg.ac

The FMG is open to anyone with an interest in medieval genealogy (pre-1500). The society's journal *Foundations*, now published annually, is available for a very modest fee to online users or as a printed copy to subscribers. The society has a number of useful open access resources available on its website.

Guild of One-Name Studies

www.one–name.org

An international organisation for family historians who are conducting a one-name study or who have a general interest in surnames. *The Journal of One-Name Studies* (*JOONS*) is published quarterly. Digital copies of previous issues are available at **www.one–name. org/journal** with recent issues restricted to members only.

International Council of Onomastic Sciences

www.icosweb.net

A scholarly international organisation for those who have a special interest in all types of names. ICOS publishes the peer-reviewed journal *Onoma*, and holds a conference every three years.

Local Population Studies Society

www.localpopulationstudies.org.uk

A UK society for individuals with an interest in all aspects of local population history. The society publishes a bi-annual journal, *Local Population Studies*, and organises two conferences each year. Back issues of the first eighty issues of the journal from 1968 through to 2008 are available free of charge on the society's website.

Local History Online

www.local–history.co.uk

The website of *Local History Magazine*, a national local history journal that has been published since 1984. The website has useful listings of local history societies, as well as details of local history courses and events.

Society for Name Studies in Great Britain and Ireland

www.snsbi.org.uk

The society promotes the study of both place-names and surnames. It publishes the annual journal *Nomina* and holds an annual conference.

APPENDIX E

LINGUISTIC RESOURCES

Dictionaries

The *Oxford English Dictionary* (OED) (**www.oed.com**) is the accepted authority on the evolution of the English language over the last millennium. It traces the meaning, history and pronunciation of over 600,000 words from the English-speaking world and includes over 3 million quotations documenting the earliest printed references to each word. It is no longer available in a printed edition but it is published online. Most local libraries have purchased a subscription and it can be accessed at home with your library card. The OED website has two free essays by Peter McClure that will be of particular interest to surname researchers:

- Surnames as sources in the OED: w**ww.oed.com/public/surnamesassources**
- English personal [given] names in the OED: **www.oed.com/public/personalnamesinoed**

www.bosworthtoller.com The digital edition of the *Bosworth-Toller Anglo-Saxon Dictionary*.

www.doe.utoronto.ca ($) *The Dictionary of Old English* provides coverage of the vocabulary of the English language from the year 600 to 1150. To date only entries for the letters A to G have been published. The database is only available online in the UK from a few subscribing universities.

http://quod.lib.umich.edu/m/med The electronic *Middle English Dictionary* covering the period 1100–1500.

http://home.comcast.net/~modean52/index.htm The Old English Made Easy website has a dictionary page with both 'Old to Modern' and 'Modern to Old' English dictionaries.

www.mun.ca/Ansaxdat/vocab/wordlist.html A Modern English to Old English vocabulary.

www.anglo-norman.net The Anglo-Norman Online Hub provides free access to the electronic edition of the Anglo-Norman Dictionary.

Dialect dictionaries

The seminal work in the field is *The English Dialect Dictionary* edited by Joseph Wright, and grandiosely subtitled *being the complete vocabulary of all dialect words still in use, or known to have been in use during the last two hundred years; founded on the publications of the English Dialect Society and on a large amount of material never before printed.* The work was published on behalf of the English Dialect Society by Henry Frowde in six volumes between 1898 and 1905. Digital copies of the six volumes are now available in the Internet Archive:

Volume I   A–C: **http://archive.org/details/englishdialectdio1wrig**
Volume II   D–G: **http://archive.org/details/englishdialectdio2wrig**
Volume III   H–L: **http://archive.org/details/englishdialectdio1wrig**
Volume IV   M–Q: **http://archive.org/details/englishdialectdio4wrig**
Volume V   R–S: **http://archive.org/details/englishdialectdio5wrig**
Volume VI   T–Z: **http://archive.org/details/englishdialectdio6wrig**

A project is under way at Innsbruck University, Austria, to create a fully searchable electronic version of the dictionary. At the time of writing the database is in beta-testing. Further details can be found at **www.uibk.ac.at/anglistik/projects/speed**.

Barry, M.V., Halliday, W.J., Orton, H., Tilling, P.M. and Wakelin, M.F., *The Survey of English Dialects* (Routledge, 1999 (reprint)). (Originally published in separate volumes.)

Numerous specialist dialect dictionaries for individual counties have been published and can be found in local libraries. A number of out-of-copyright local dialect books are freely available in the Internet Archive (**http://archive.org**).

Oxford Reference Online

Oxford Reference Online (**www.oxfordreference.com**) is an electronic database provided by Oxford University Press that can be accessed at home with a library card from a subscribing library. It is available from most libraries in the UK. The database includes numerous bilingual dictionaries, and English dictionaries from various English-speaking countries around the world, as well as many other useful reference books.

Ireland

www.dil.ie The *Electronic Dictionary of the Irish Language* (eDIL)
A digital edition of the complete contents of the Royal Irish Academy's *Dictionary of the Irish Language* based mainly on Old and Middle Irish materials.

http://celt.ucc.ie *The Corpus of Electronic Texts* (CELT)
An electronic database of over 1,000 Irish literary and historical texts, some of which date back to the thirteenth century. There are almost 15 million words in the database providing a rich resource for Irish and Gaelic words.

Scotland

www.dsl.ac.uk The Dictionary of the Scots Language.

Websites

www.bbc.co.uk/voices Voice recordings from the BBC.

www.bl.uk/learning/langlit/sounds The British Library's 'Sounds Familiar' website with recordings of accents and dialects from around the UK.

www.cornishdialect.oldcornwall.org The dialect of Cornwall.

www.bbc.co.uk/devon/voices2005/features/devon_dialect.shtml Devon dialects.

www.norfolkdialect.com The Friends of the Norfolk Dialect website.

APPENDIX F

PLACE-NAME RESOURCES

Books

The *Survey of English Place-Names* is a scholarly series of publications produced by the English Place-Name Society, which aims to examine the origins and development of all the country's place-names. The published work is arranged by historic counties. The first volume, on Buckinghamshire, was issued in 1923. There are now over eighty volumes in the series, and further volumes are still in preparation. A full list of the titles in the series, and of the forthcoming volumes, can be found at **www.nottingham.ac.uk/ ins/placenamesociety**. The individual volumes are quite expensive and for the family historian it will be more economical to consult the appropriate titles of interest at the nearest large reference library. A project to digitise the *Survey of English Place-Names* and make the material available online for a wider audience started in November 2011 and is scheduled to be completed by August 2013.

Gelling, M., 'Place-names' in Hey, David, ed., *The Oxford Companion to Family and Local History*, 2nd edn (Oxford University Press, 2008). An informative review of the history of place-name research and the current state of the art.

Hope, R.C., *A Glossary of Dialectical Place Nomenclature to which is appended a list of family surnames pronounced differently from what the spelling suggests* (Simpkin, Marshall and Co., 1883): **http://archive.org/details/aglossarydialecoohopegoog**.

McKay, P. and Anderson, A.M., *A Dictionary of Ulster Place-Names*, 2nd edn (Cló Ollscoil na Banríona, 2007).

Mills, A.D., *A Dictionary of British Place-Names*, revised edition (Oxford University Press, 2011). Also available as an electronic database via Oxford Reference Online with a local library card from subscribing libraries.

Mills, A.D., *A Dictionary of London Place-Names*, 2nd edition (Oxford University Press, 2010). Also available as an electronic database via Oxford Reference Online with a local library card from subscribing libraries.

Nicolaisen, W.F.H., *Scottish Place-Names*, 3rd edn (John Donald, 2011).

Olausson, L. and Sangster, C., *Oxford BBC Guide to Pronunciation: The Essential Handbook of the Spoken Word* (Oxford University Press, 2006). A guide to the pronunciation of 15,000 difficult words and names. This publication supersedes the *BBC Pronouncing Dictionary of British Names* that was first published in 1971.

Owen, H.W. and Morgan, R., *Dictionary of the Place-Names of Wales* (Gomer Press, 2007).

Watts, V., Insley, J. and Gelling, M., *The Cambridge Dictionary of English Place-Names: Based on the Collections of the English Place-Name Society* (Cambridge University Press, paperback edition, 2011).

General online resources

www.britishlistedbuildings.co.uk British Listed Buildings.

www.digital-documents.co.uk/archi/placename.htm Archaeology UK's place-name finder.

www.gazetteer.co.uk A gazetteer of 50,000 British place-names provided by the Association of British Counties.

www.genuki.org.uk/big/Gazetteer The Genuki gazetteer covers England, Ireland, Wales, Scotland and the Isle of Man.

www.geonames.org A worldwide database containing 8 million place-names that are geo-referenced and linked to Google Maps.

www.getty.edu/research/tools/vocabularies/tgn The Getty thesaurus of geographic names online.

www.ordnancesurvey.co.uk/oswebsite/freefun/didyouknow Ordnance Survey gazetteer with entries for over 250,000 place-names.

www.ordnancesurvey.co.uk/oswebsite/freefun/didyouknow/placenames The Ordnance Survey's guide to the history and hidden meanings of British place-names with downloadable guides to Welsh, Gaelic, Scandinavian and Scottish place-names.

www.visionofbritain.org.uk/descriptions A historical gazetteer from the Vision of Britain through Time Website. The gazetteer incorporates the full text of three nineteenth-century descriptive gazetteers, and has a total of over 90,000 entries. It is particularly useful for translating old place-name spellings into their present-day equivalents.

www.wikipedia.org Wikipedia is often a good starting point for information on place-names, though articles lacking sources should be used with caution. The French-language Wikipedia is useful for identifying French place-names.

England

www.english-heritage.org.uk/nmr The National Monuments Record, the public archive of English Heritage.

http://keithbriggs.info/English_placename_element_distribution.html Keith Briggs' maps of English place-name element distribution.

www.nationalarchives.gov.uk/mdr The Manorial Documents Register (MDR) from The National Archives. The MDR is currently only partially computerised but provides a useful resource for those counties already in the database.

www.nottingham.ac.uk/ins The Institute for Name Studies is the focus for research and teaching in the field of name studies at the University of Nottingham. It also houses the English Place-Name Society and the *Survey of English Place-Names*. The website provides a useful key to English place-names (**http://kepn.nottingham.ac.uk**), which has details of over 14,000 place-names and their meanings, and provides links showing the placement on a local map. The Vocabulary of English Place-Names, an online database of place-name elements, is currently in preparation.

County resources

www.cornwall.gov.uk/default.aspx?page=22518 Gazetteer of Cornish manors.

http://genuki.cs.ncl.ac.uk/DEV/Gazetteer/index.html The Genuki Devon gazetteer has listings for over 12,000 places including farms, houses, inns, manors, etc.

http://genuki.cs.ncl.ac.uk/DEV/DevonManors A guide to the manors of Devon compiled by Ian Mortimer.

www.essex.ac.uk/history/esah/essexplacenames Essex place-names.

Scotland

www.electricscotland.com/history/gazetteer/index.htm *The Ordnance Gazetteer of Scotland* edited by Francis H. Groome (1892–96).

www.gaelicplacenames.org/database.php Gaelic Place-Names of Scotland database.

www.historic-scotland.gov.uk/historicandlistedbuildings.htm Historic and listed buildings in Scotland.

www.rcahms.gov.uk The Royal Commission on the Ancient and Historical Monuments of Scotland has information on over 300,000 places in Scotland.

www.scotlandsplaces.gov.uk A gazetteer of Scottish places past and present compiled from the holdings of the Royal Commission on the Ancient and Historical Monuments of Scotland, The National Archives of Scotland and the National Library of Scotland.

www.spns.org.uk The Scottish Place-Name Society. The society has a very extensive bibliography of general works on the subject of place-names, and recommendations on specific titles for Scottish place-names.

Wales

www.cymdeithasenwaulleoeddcymru.org The Welsh Place-Name Society.

www.data-wales.co.uk/accent.htm The pronunciation of Welsh place-names.

www.e-gymraeg.co.uk/enwaulleoedd/amr The Welsh Place-Name Database. A database of the historical forms of 330,000 place-names in Wales gathered by Professor Melville Richards (1910–73).

www.e-gymraeg.co.uk/enwaucymru Enwau Cymru database. A resource for checking corresponding English and Welsh forms of place-names.

http://placenames.bangor.ac.uk/English The Place-Name Research Centre at the University of Wales, Bangor.

www.rcahmw.gov.uk Royal Commission on the Ancient and Historical Monuments of Wales.

Ireland

www.buildingsofireland.ie Buildings of Ireland, the National Inventory of Architectural Heritage.

www.doeni.gov.uk/niea/buildings_database.htm Northern Ireland Buildings Database.

www.irishtimes.com/ancestor/placenames/index.cfm An online search facility for the 65,000 entries in the *1851 General Alphabetical Index to the Townlands and Towns, parishes and Baronies of Ireland.*

www.irish-place-names.com The Irish Place-Names database.

www.logainm.ie The Placenames Database of Ireland.

www.osi.ie Ordnance Survey Ireland

www.placenamesni.org The Northern Ireland Place-Name Project.

http://publish.ucc.ie/doi/locus Fr Edmund Hogan's *Onomasticon Goedelicum* (Dublin, 1910). An index to the Gaelic names of places and tribes.

www.seanruad.com IreAtlas The Irish townland database.

www.ulsterplacenames.org The Ulster Place-Name Society.

POPULATION STATISTICS

Worldwide

https://www.cia.gov/library/publications/the-world-factbook The CIA World Factbook.
www.prb.org The Population Reference Bureau.

The British Isles

www.histpop.org The Online Historical Population Reports Website. Population reports for Britain and Ireland from 1801 to 1937 including the annual reports on births, marriages and deaths from the Registrar-General and the statistical reports from the censuses.
http://homepage.ntlworld.com/hitch/gendocs/pop.html The GenDocs website has some useful summary tables showing the population of Great Britain and Ireland at various times between 1570 and 1931, taken from a 1941 edition of *Whitaker's Almanac*.
www.hpss.geog.cam.ac.uk/research/projects/occupations/englandwales1379-1911 The population geography of England and Wales *c.* 1379–1911. There are links to some interesting maps featuring various aspects of the population geography of England and Wales. This web page is part of a project looking at the occupational structure of Britain from 1379–1911.
www.statistics.gov.uk/hub/population/index.html UK Office for National Statistics.
www.visionofbritain.org.uk The Vision of Britain through Time website includes a large library of local statistics for administrative units.
www.york.ac.uk/depts/maths/histstat/king.htm Gregory King's tables with estimates of the population of England in 1688 by class and occupation.

Ireland
www.cso.ie Central Statistics Office Ireland.
http://ncg.nuim.ie/redir.php?action=projects/famine/explore The National Centre for Geocomputation Online Atlas Portal provides online access to The Irish

Famine Population Data Atlas 1841–2002 and The Atlas of Irish Famine Data 1841–51.
www.nisra.gov.uk Northern Ireland Statistics and Research Agency (NISRA).

Scotland

http://edina.ac.uk/stat-acc-scot The Statistical Accounts of Scotland 1791–1845.
Two statistical accounts of Scotland were published covering the 1790s and 1830s. The
information was largely provided by the parish ministers. As well as information on
population statistics, the reports provide a fascinating record of life in Scotland during
the agricultural and industrial revolutions. The scanned images can be browsed free of
charge, but a subscription is required to access additional features such as the ability to
search by keyword. Subscriptions start from £10 for two months' access.

United States

www.census.gov US Census Bureau.
www.census.gov/population/www/censusdata/hiscendata.html Selected
historical decennial census population and housing counts from the US census.
http://quickfacts.census.gov/qfd State and county quick facts.
http://mapserver.lib.virginia.edu An historical census browser from the University
of Virginia Library.
http://en.wikipedia.org/wiki/List_of_U.S._states_by_historical_population
A table summarising the population statistics of US states derived from census data.

Books

Hey, D., 'Population levels and trends' in Hey, D. (ed.), *The Oxford Companion to Family and Local History*, 2nd edition (Oxford University Press, 2008). A comprehensive overview of population trends in the British Isles and a survey of the literature.

Laslett, P. and Wall, R., *Household and Family in Past Time* (Cambridge Group for the History of Population and Social Structure, Cambridge University Press, first published 1972, digitally reprinted 2008).

Wrigley, E.A. and Schofield, R.S., *The Population History of England 1541–1871* (Cambridge Studies in Population, Economy and Society in Past Time, Cambridge University Press, 1981, 1989).

Wrigley, E.A., Davies, R.S., Oeppen, J.E. and Schofield, R.S., *English Population History from Family Reconstitution 1580–1837* (Cambridge Studies in Population, Economy and Society in Past Time, Cambridge University Press, first published 1997, digitally reprinted 2005).

In addition, the Surname Studies website has an extensive list of books on the subject of
population statistics: **www.surnamestudies.org.uk/statistics/guide.htm**.

NOTES

Definitions

1. *Oxford English Dictionary*, 2nd edn (1989); online version March 2012: **www.oed.com**.

Introduction

1. *Oxford English Dictionary*, 2nd edn (1989); online version March 2012: **www.oed.com**. The actual number of words in the English language is not known. For a discussion see: **http://oxforddictionaries.com/words/how-many-words-are-there-in-the-english-language**. For the 2001 electoral register unique spellings (e.g. Clark and Clarke) were counted as separate surnames. The figure is taken from Mateos, P., Longley, P. and Cheshire, J., 'Family names as indicators of Britain's changing regional geography', UCL Working Papers Series, Paper 149, 1 May 2009. Available from **www.bartlett.ucl.ac.uk/casa/publications/working-paper-149**.

1 The History of Surnames

1. Magnier, M., 'Identity issues in Mongolia', *Los Angeles Times*, 23 October 2004. **http://articles.latimes.com/2004/oct/23/world/fg-names23**.
2. Skoch, I.R., 'Wanderlust: Iceland, where everyone's related to Björk', *Global Post*, 26 October 2011. **www.globalpost.com/dispatch/news/offbeat/111011/wanderlust-iceland-where-everyone-related-bjork**.
3. Llewellen, M., 'Chinese family names' in Hanks, P. (ed.), *Dictionary of American Family Names* (Oxford University Press, 2003).
4. Liu, Y., Chen, L., Yuan, Y. and Chen, J., 'A study of surnames in China through isonymy' in *American Journal of Physical Anthropology*. Article first published online on 28 March 2012. Available from **http://onlinelibrary.wiley.com/doi/10.1002/ajpa.22055/abstract**.
5. 'China has 4,100 meaningful names' in *People's Daily Online*, 13 January 2006. Available from **http://english.people.com.cn/200601/13/eng20060113_235293.html**.
6. 'China renews top 100 surnames, Li still the biggest' in *People's Daily Online*, 11 January 2006. Available from **http://english.people.com.cn/200601/11/eng20060111_234647.html**.
7. LaFraniere, S., 'Name not on our list? Change it, China says' in *New York Times*, 20 April 2009. Available from **www.nytimes.com/2009/04/21/world/asia/21china.htm**.

8. Liu, Y., Chen, L., Yuan, Y and Chen, J., 'A study of surnames in China through isonymy' in *American Journal of Physical Anthropology*. Article first published online: 28 March 2012. Available from **http://onlinelibrary.wiley.com/doi/10.1002/ajpa.22055/abstract**.

9. 'Chinese family names' on the Asia home website: **www.asia-home.com/china/surname/lang/en.php**.

10. Grossman, S., 'China to stop giving orphans surnames like "State," "Party"' in *Time.com*, 14 February 2012. Available from **http://newsfeed.time.com/2012/02/14/china-to-stop-giving-orphans-surnames-like-state-party**.

11. Salway, B., 'What's in a name? A survey of Roman onomastic practice from *c.* 700 B.C. to A.D. 700' in *The Journal of Roman Studies*, 1994, vol. 84, pp.124–45.

12. Holt, J.C., *What's in a Name? Family Nomenclature and the Norman Conquest (The Stenton Lecture 1981)* (University of Reading, 1982). Available from **www.reading.ac.uk/history/research/hist-stentonlectures.aspx**.

13. Camp, A.J., *My Ancestors Came With the Conqueror: those who did and some of those who probably did not* (Society of Genealogists, 1990).

14. *Ibid.*

15. McKinley, R., *A History of British Surnames* (Longman, 1990), p.28.

16. Holt, J.C., Op. cit., p.20.

17. McKinley, R., Op. cit., p.29.

18. *Ibid.* pp.31–2.

19. Redmonds, G., Hey, D. and King, T., *Surnames, DNA, and Family History* (Oxford University Press, 2011), pp.3–4.

20. McConnachie, A., 'A history of immigration to Britain', special report in *Sovereignty*, November 2002. Available from **www.sovereignty.org.uk/features/articles/immig.html#22**.

21. Hey, D., *Family Names and Family History* (Hambledon and London, 2000), pp.94–7.

22. 'Early Jewish settlement in Britain'. Available from **www.movinghere.org.uk/galleries/histories/jewish/origins/origins.htm**.

23. Verstegan, R., *A Restitution of Decayed Intelligence. In Antiquities: Concerning the most noble and renowned English Nation* (1628), p.295. Available from **http://books.google.co.uk/books?id=vCxQAQAAIAAJ&source=gbs_navlinks_s**.

24. Percentages calculated from Table 1 in the Introduction to McKinley, R., Op. cit., p.23.

25. Millard, A., 'Letter to the editor' in *Journal of One-Name Studies*, vol. 11, no. 3, 2012, p.7.

26. Matheson, R.E., *Varieties and synonymes of surnames and Christian names in Ireland: for the guidance of registration officers and the public in searching the indexes of births, deaths, and marriages*, 2nd edn (His Majesty's Stationery Office, 1901), p.20. Available from **http://archive.org/details/varietiessynonymoomath**.

27. McKinley, R., Op. cit., pp.44–5.

28. *Sixth Detailed Annual Report of the Registrar-General of Births, Deaths and Marriages, Scotland* (Registrar-General's edition) (Her Majesty's Stationery Office, printed by Murray and Gibb, 1864), p.lv. Available from **www.histpop.org**.

29. Donaldson, G., 'Foreword' in Cory, K.B., *Tracing Your Scottish Ancestry*, 3rd edn (Polygon, 2004), p.xi.

30. General Register Office for Scotland, *Surnames in Scotland over the last 140 years*. Occasional paper no. 9, published on 18 February 2003. Available from **www.gro-scotland.gov.uk/statistics/theme/vital-events/births/popular-names/archive/surnames-in-scotland-over-the-last-140-years.html**.

31. McElduff, F., Mateos, P., Wade, A. and Borja, M.C., 'What's in a name? The frequency and geographic distributions of UK surnames', in *Significance*, December 2008, pp.189–92. Available from **www.ucl.ac.uk/paediatric-epidemiology/pdfs/Signficance_Surnames_Paper.pdf**.

2 The Classification of Surnames

1. Camden, W., *Remaines Concerning Britain* ... (1605, seventh impression edited by John Philipot, 1674), pp.140–1.
2. Lower, M.A., *English Surnames: An Essay on Family Nomenclature, Historical, Etymological and Curious* ... (John Russell Smith, 1842). A second enlarged edition was published in 1843. The third edition, published in 1849, was further expanded and divided into two volumes. In the later editions some changes were made in the nomenclature of the categories and a few additional categories were added, though the basic structure was little changed.
3. Lordan, C.L., *Of Certain English Surnames and their occasional odd Phases when seen in Groups* (Houston and Sons, 1874, 1879).
4. Bardsley, C.W., *English Surnames: their Sources and Significations*, 2nd edn (Chatto & Windus, 1873), p.8.
5. Bardsley, C.W., *A Dictionary of English and Welsh Surnames with special American Instances* (Henry Frowde, 1901), p.2.
6. *Ibid.*, p.5
7. McKinley, R., *The Surnames of Sussex* (Leopard's Head Press, 1988), p.2.
8. Cheshire, J.A., Mateos, M., Longley, P.A., *Family Names as Indicators of Britain's Regional Geography*, CASA working paper 149. Published online 1 May 2009. Available from **www.bartlett.ucl.ac.uk/casa/publications/working-paper-149**.
9. Reaney, P.H. and Wilson, R.M., *A Dictionary of English Surnames*, 3rd edn (Oxford University Press, reprinted 2005).
10. McKinley, R., *A History of British Surnames* (Longman, 1990), p.55.
11. Hey, D., *Family Names and Family History* (Hambledon, 2000), p.4.
12. Reaney, P.H., *The Origin of English Surnames* (Routledge and Kegan Paul, 1967), p.43.
13. McKinley, R., *British Surnames*, Op. cit., p.56.
14. Jones, R., Thinking through the manorial affix: people and place in later medieval England', in Sylvester, R. and Turner, S. (eds), *People and Place in Medieval England* (Oxbow, 2012), pp.255–71 (in press).
15. McKinley, R., *British Surnames*, Op. cit., pp.72–89.
16. MacLysaght, E., *The Surnames of Ireland*, 6th edn (Irish Academic Press, 2007), p.ix.
17. McKinley, R., *British Surnames*, Op. cit., p.98.
18. Reaney and Wilson, *Dictionary of English Surnames*, Op. cit.
19. McKinley, R., *British Surnames*, Op. cit., pp.92–3.
20. *Ibid.*, pp.126–7.
21. 'Scottish surnames and variants' on ScotlandsPeople website. Available from **www.scotlandspeople.gov.uk/content/help/index.aspx?560**.
22. Rowlands, J. and Rowlands, S., *The Surnames of Wales* (Genealogical Publishing, 1996).
23. McKinley, R., *British Surnames*, Op. cit., p.172.
24. Reaney and Wilson, *Dictionary of English Surnames*, Op. cit.
25. *Ibid.*, p.xli.
26. McClure, P., 'Surnames as sources in the OED' in *Oxford English Dictionary*: **www.oed.com/public/surnamesassources**.
27. 'The London lay subsidy of 1332: Account of subsidy collectors' in *Finance and Trade under Edward III: The London Lay Subsidy of 1332*, 1918, pp.61–92. Available from **www.british-history.ac.uk/report.aspx?compid=33007**.
28. Definition of baxter from *Middle English Dictionary*. Available from: **http://quod.lib.umich.edu/m/med/med_ent_search.html**. Reaney and Wilson, Op. cit,. suggest that Baxter is derived from the Old English word *baecestre*, but the northern distribution, and hence later formation of the surname, implies a Middle English origin.

29. McLysaght, *Surnames of Ireland*, Op. cit.
30. Reaney and Wilson, *Dictionary of English Surnames*, Op. cit.
31. Hanks, P. and Hodges, F., *A Dictionary of Surnames* (Oxford University Press, 1988).
32. *Ibid.*
33. Camden, W., *Remaines concerning Britain* (1605, 7th impression; 1674), p.186.
34. Reaney, *Origin*, Op. cit., pp.170–1.
35. *Sixteenth Annual Report of the Registrar-General of Births, Deaths, and Marriages in England* (Registrar-General's edition) (Her Majesty's Stationery Office, 1856), p.xvii.
36. Reaney and Wilson, *Dictionary of English Surnames*, Op. cit., p.xliii.
37. *Ibid.*
38. Erskine, A.M. (ed.), *The Devonshire Lay Subsidy of 1332* (Devon and Cornwall Record Society, 1969).
39. McLysaght, *Surnames of Ireland*, Op. cit.
40. Rogers, C.D., *The Surname Detective* (Manchester University Press, 1995), p.204.
41. Hanks and Hodges, *Dictionary*, Op. cit.
42. Camden, W., *Remaines concerning Britain* (1605, 7th impression, 1674), p.174.
43. Lower, M.A., *English Surnames*, Op. cit., vol. I.
44. Reaney, *Origin*, Op. cit., pp.57–8.
45. Reaney and Wilson, *Dictionary of English Surnames*, Op. cit., p.xvi.
46. Hanks and Hodges, *Dictionary*, Op. cit., p.7.
47. Rogers, C.D., *Surname Detective*, Op. cit., p.211.

3 Variants and Deviants

1. Dixon, B.H., *Surnames* (John Wilson and Son, 1857), p.xxiii.
2. Redmonds, G., *Surnames and Genealogy: A New Approach* (Federation of Family History Societies, 2002), p.125.
3. Brown, M., 'Some Devon Surname Aliases': **http://genuki.cs.ncl.ac.uk/DEV/DevonMisc/Aliases.html**.
4. Hooper, M.D., 'Aliases – a discriminant function': **http://genuki.cs.ncl.ac.uk/DEV/DevonMisc/AliasesDiscriminant.html**.
5. Tweedie, N., 'How Queen's English has grown more like ours' in the *Daily Telegraph*, 4 December 2006. Available at **www.telegraph.co.uk/news/uknews/1535934/How-Queens-English-has-grown-more-like-ours.html**.
6. Redmonds, *Surnames*, pp.130–1.
7. *Ibid.*, pp.205–7.
8. 'Raymond Luxury Yacht', *Monty Python's Flying Circus*. Available on YouTube: **www.youtube.com/watch?v=tyQvjKqXAoY**.
9. Ferguson, R., *Surnames as a Science* (Routledge, 1883), p.119.
10. Hanks, P. and Hodges, F., *A Dictionary of Surnames* (Oxford University Press, 1988).
11. Kneebone, R., personal communication.
12. Mathieson, H., 'Dangerfield one-name study profile page' on the Guild of One-Name Studies website: **www.one-name.org/profiles/dangerfield.html**.
13. Palgrave, D., 'Many surname variants are really misspelt deviants', *Journal of One-Name Studies*, January–March 2004, vol. 8, no. 5, pp.6–9. Available at **www.one-name.org/journal/pdfs/variants.pdf**.
14. 'Variants and Deviants', Guild of One-Name Studies website: **www.one-name.org/onsvarnt.html**.
15. Palgrave, D., 'Surname variants', Op. cit., pp.6–9.
16. Mokotoff, G., 'Soundexing and Genealogy': **www.avotaynu.com/soundex.htm**.

17. About NameX: **www.origins.net/namex/aboutnamex.html**.

18. Phillimore, W.P.W., *Memorials of the Family of Fynmore* … (published by the author, 1886).

19. This account is based on personal communications from Polly Rubery and Linda Hansen combined with information extracted from Polly's website at **www.rowberry.org**. The DNA project results can be seen at **www.familytreedna.com/public/Rowberry**. George Ruberry's service papers are at The National Archives (reference WO 97/116/17). Information on the Gomery one-name study can be found at **www.one-name.org/profiles/gomery. html**.

20. Titford, J., *Searching for Surnames* (Countryside Books, 2002), p.84.

21. Mitchelmore M., 'Surname variants: there's much more to Mitchelmore', *Journal of One-Name Studies*, October–December 2011, pp.20–1. Additional information supplied by Michael Mitchelmore, personal communication. A full list of the variant spellings can be found at **www. mitchelmore.info/history/spelling.htm**.

4 Surname Mapping

1. Camden, W., *Remaines Concerning Britain* … (7th impression, 1605), p.142.

2. Oliver, G., 'On the origin of proper names', *Gentleman's Magazine*, 1830, vol. 100, part I, pp.298–300. Available at **http://books.google.co.uk/books?id=3ioVp2JRpPwC&pg=PA298**.

3. Lower, M.A., *English Surnames: An Essay on Family Nomenclature, Historical, Etymological and Curious* … *Volume II*, 1849, pp.29–32.

4. Leeson, F., 'The study of single surnames and their distribution' in *Genealogists' Magazine*, December 1964, vol. 14, pp.405–12. Reprinted in the *Journal of One-Name Studies*, 1989, vol. 3, no. 6, pp.174–81 and available at **www.one-name.org/journal/pdfs/vol3-6.pdf**.

5. Kaplan, B.A. and Lasker, G.W., 'The present distribution of some English surnames derived from place names' in *Human Biology*, 1983, 55 (2), p.243.

6. Lasker, G., 'The frequencies of surnames in England and Wales' in *Human Biology*, May 1983, vol. 55, no. 2, pp.331–40.

7. Mascie-Taylor, C.G.N. and Lasker, G.W., 'Geographic distribution of surnames in Britain: the Smiths and Joneses' in *Journal of Biosocial Science*, 1984, 16, pp.301–8.

8. Mascie-Taylor, C.G.N. and Lasker, G.W., 'Geographical distribution of common surnames in England and Wales', *Annals of Human Biology*, 1985, Sep–Oct; 12(5) pp.397–401.

9. Cheshire, J., Longley, P. and Singleton, A., 'The surname regions of Great Britain', *Journal of Maps*, 2010 pp.401–9. Available from **www.tandfonline.com/TJOM**.

10. Rogers, C., *The Surname Detective* (Manchester University Press, 1995), p.224.

11. Schürer, K., 'Surnames and the search for regions', *Local Population Studies*, no. 72 (Spring, 2004), pp.50–76. Available at **www.localpopulationstudies.org.uk/PDF/LPS72/LPS72.pdf**. Also available at **www.casa.ucl.ac.uk/surnames/papers.htm**.

12. Cheshire, J.A., Mateos, P. and Longley, P.A., *Family Names as Indicators of Britain's Regional Geography*, CASA working paper 149. Published online 1 May 2009. Available from **www.bartlett.ucl.ac.uk/casa/publications/working-paper-149**.

13. Cheshire, Longley and Singleton, 'Surname regions', Op. cit., pp.401–9.

14. Longley, P.A., Cheshire, J.A., Mateos, P., 'Creating a regional geography of Britain through the spatial analysis of surnames' in *Geoforum* 2011, 42, pp.506–16.

15. Cheshire, J., Mateos, P. and Longley, P., 'Delineating Europe's cultural regions: population structure and surname clustering', in *Human Biology*, October 2011, vol. 83, no. 5, pp.573–98. Available from **http://pablomateos.blogweb.casa.ucl.ac.uk/files/2011/10/Cheshire-Mateos-Longley_2011_Human-Biology.pdf**.

16. Field, K. and Beale, L., 'Geo-genealogy of Irish Surnames', *Journal of Maps*, 2010, pp.651–56. 10.4113/jom.2010.1128. Available at **www.tandfonline.com/TJOM**.

17. GenMap can be purchased from Archer Software (**www.archersoftware.co.uk**).

18. Family Atlas can be purchased direct from RootsMagic in America (**www.rootsmagic.com/family-atlas**) or from S&N Genealogy in the UK (**www.genealogysupplies.com**).

5 Surname Frequency

1. *Sixteenth Annual Report of the Registrar-General of Births, Deaths, and Marriages in England* (Registrar-General's edition), Her Majesty's Stationery Office (published by Longman, Brown, Green, and Longmans, 1856). Available from **www.histpop.org**.

2. Lasker, G., 'The frequencies of surnames in England and Wales' in *Human Biology*, May 1983, vol. 55, no. 2, pp.331–40.

3. Camp, A., 'The frequency of common surnames' in *Genealogists' Magazine*, September 1997, vol. 25, pp.452–5.

4. *Sixth Detailed Annual Report of the Registrar-General of Births, Deaths and Marriages, Scotland* (Registrar-General's Edition), Her Majesty's Stationery Office, (printed by Murray and Gibb, 1864). Available from **www.histpop.org**.

5. General Register Office for Scotland, *Surnames in Scotland over the last 140 years*, occasional paper no. 9, published on 18 February 2003. Available from **www.gro-scotland.gov.uk/statistics/theme/vital-events/births/popular-names/archive/surnames-in-scotland-over-the-last-140-years.html**.

6. Matheson, R.E., *Special report on surnames in Ireland, with notes as to numerical strength, derivation, ethnology, and distribution; based on information extracted from the indexes of the General Register Office. Appendix to the twenty-ninth detailed annual report of the Registrar-General of Marriages, Births, and Deaths in Ireland*, Her Majesty's Stationery Office, 1894. Available from **http://archive.org/details/cu31924029805540**.

7. Schürer, K., 'Surnames and the search for regions' in *Local Population Studies*, no. 72, (Spring 2004), pp.50–76. Available from **www.localpopulationstudies.org.uk/PDF/LPS72/LPS72.pdf**. Also available at **www.casa.ucl.ac.uk/surnames/papers.htm**.

8. Stephen Archer's *British 19th Century Surname Atlas* CD can be purchased from **www.archersoftware.co.uk**.

9. Mateos, P., Longley, P. and Cheshire, J., *Family names as indicators of Britain's changing regional geography*, UCL Working Papers Series, Paper 149, 1 May 2009. Available at **www.bartlett.ucl.ac.uk/casa/publications/working-paper-149**.

10. Cheshire, J., Longley, P. and Singleton, A., 'The surname regions of Great Britain', *Journal of Maps*, 2010, pp.401–9. Available at **www.tandfonline.com/TJOM**.

11. McElduff, F., Mateos, P., Wade, A. and Borja, M.C., 'What's in a name? The frequency and geographic distributions of UK surnames', *Significance*, December 2008, pp.189–92. Available at **www.ucl.ac.uk/paediatric-epidemiology/pdfs/Signficance_Surnames_Paper.pdf**.

12. Irvine, J., 'Towards improvements in Y-DNA surname project administration', *Journal of Genetic Genealogy*, vol. 6, no. 1, Fall 2010. Available from **www.jogg.info/62/index.html**.

13. IBM Initiate Master Data Service Release Notes. Available at **http://tinyurl.com/IBMMasterData**.

14. World Names Public Profiler Frequently Asked Questions: **http://worldnames.publicprofiler.org/FAQ.aspx**.

15. 'Ten of the most common surnames in the world', The World Geography website, 12 April 2012. Available at **www.theworldgeography.com/2012/02/10-of-most-common-surnames-in-world.html**.

6 Has it Been Done Before?

1. Draper, S. and Hanks, P., 'The "Family Names of the United Kingdom" (FaNUK) Project', *Journal of One-Name Studies*, July–September 2011, vol. 10, issue 11, pp.22–3. Available at **www. one-name.org/members/journal/vol10-11.pdf#page=25**.

7 Laying the Foundations: the Key Datasets

1. Table 4.19: 'Housing and consumer durables', *General Household Survey 2007 Report*, Office for National Statistics, 22 January 2009. Available at **www.ons.gov.uk/ons/rel/ghs/general-household-survey/2007-report/index.html**.
2. 'Blow to UK liquidity as ex-directory figure hits 58%', report from GB Group, 1 February 2011. Available at **www.gb.co.uk/gbgroup/gb-news/2011/blow-to-uk-liquidity-as-ex-directory-figure-hits-58**.
3. Pomery, C., 'The advantages of a dual DNA/documentary approach to reconstruct the family trees of a surname', *Journal of Genetic Genealogy*, Fall 2009, vol. 5, no. 2. Available at **www.jogg. info/52/index.html**.
4. Pomery, C., 'Defining a methodology to reconstruct the family trees of a surname within a DNA/documentary dual approach project', *Journal of Genetic Genealogy*, Fall 2010, vol. 6, no. 1. Available at **www.jogg.info/62/index.html**.

8 Surname Origins: Pre-1600 Resources

1. Hey, D., *Family Names and Family History* (Hambledon and London, 2000), p.52.
2. *Berkeley Castle guidebook* (English Life Publications, 1990). The guidebook includes an outline of the Berkeley family tree commencing with Roger de Berkeley (d.1093).
3. Reaney, P.H. and Wilson, R.M., *A Dictionary of English Surnames* (3rd edn, Oxford University Press, reprinted 2005), pp.xxv–xxviii.
4. Reaney, P.H., *The Origin of English Surnames* (Routledge & Kegan Paul, 1967), pp.97–116.
5. 'Chancery inquisition post mortem Edward III', File 235 (60), Writ dated at Westminster 1 Dec. 47 Edw. III. (1373). Abstract from a collection at the West Country Studies Library, Exeter, Devon.
6. Padel, O., 'Place-names and calendaring practices' in Hicks, M. (ed.), *The Fifteenth-Century Inquisitions Post Mortem* (Boydell, 2012), pp.223–37.

9 DNA and Surnames

1. Hey, D., 'Locating the Home of a Family Name', Appendix in Reaney, P.H., Wilson, R.M., *Oxford Dictionary of English Surnames* (Oxford University Press, 2005), p.518.
2. Sykes, B. and Irven, C., 'Surnames and the Y-chromosome' in *American Journal of Human Genetics*, 2000, April; 66(4): pp.1417–19. Available from **www.ncbi.nlm.nih.gov/pmc/articles/ PMC1288207**.
3. Stephen Archer's *British 19th Century Surname Atlas* CD can be purchased from **www.archersoftware.co.uk**.
4. The website of the Sikes/Sykes Families Association: **http://sikes-sykesfamilies.rootsweb. com**.
5. King, T.E., Ballereau, S.J., Schürer, K. and Jobling, M.A., 'Genetic signatures of coancestry within surnames', *Current Biology*, 2006; 16: pp.384–8.

6. King, T.E. and Jobling, M.A., 'Founders, drift and infidelity: the relationship between Y-chromosome diversity and patrilineal surnames', *Molecular Biology and Evolution* 2009; 26: pp.1093–102.

7. Redmonds, G., King, T. and Hey, D., *Surnames, DNA and Family History* (Oxford University Press, 2011), pp.173–93.

8. King, T.E. and Jobling, M.A., 'What's in a name? Y-chromosomes, surnames and the genetic genealogy revolution', *Trends in Genetics*, August 2009, vol. 25, issue 8, pp.351–60.

9. McEvoy, B. and Bradley, D.G., 'Y-chromosomes and the extent of patrilineal ancestry in Irish surnames', *Human Genetics*, 2006; 119(1–2): pp.212–19. Available at **www.ncbi.nlm.nih.gov/pubmed/16408222**.

10. Moore, L.T., McEvoy, B., Cape, E., Simms, K., Bradley, D.G., 'A Y-chromosome signature of hegemony in Gaelic Ireland', *American Journal of Human Genetics*, 2006; 78(2): pp.334–8. Available at **www.ncbi.nlm.nih.gov/pubmed/16358217**.

11. 'Matching Niall Nóigiallach – Niall of the Nine Hostages', Family Tree DNA website: **www.familytreedna.com/landing/matching-niall.aspx**.

12. Pomery, C., 'Divided by the pond. Why genetic drift means US results can't pinpoint the origin of a British surname', *Eastman's Online Genealogy Newsletter*, Plus Edition, 23 September 2009.

13. Larkin, B.T., 'Larkin DNA Project – Ancestral Parish Sampling on the Shannon River' in *Journal of Genetic Genealogy*, Fall 2010, vol. 6, no. 1.

14. Irvine, J., 'Towards improvements in Y-DNA surname project administration', *Journal of Genetic Genealogy*, Fall/Autumn 2010, vol. 6, no. 1. Available at **www.jogg.info/62/index.html**.

15. Creer, J., *A Family of Mannin* (self-published, 2011). Available at **www.lulu.com**.

16. A full report on the Creer DNA project is available on the Creer DNA project website at **www.ballacreer.com/Creer%20DNA%20Study2.htm**.

17. Pomery, C., 'The advantages of a dual DNA/documentary approach to reconstruct the family trees of a surname' in *Journal of Genetic Genealogy*, Fall 2009, vol. 5, no. 2. Available at **www.jogg.info/52/index.html**.

18. Pomery, C., 'Defining a methodology to reconstruct the family trees of a surname within a DNA/documentary dual approach project' in *Journal of Genetic Genealogy*, Fall 2010, vol. 6, no. 1. Available at **www.jogg.info/62/index.html**.

19. Pomery, C., *Pomeroy Family Association Annual report 2011*. Available at **www.pomeroyfamilyhistory.com/downloads**.

20. Plant, J.S., 'Modern methods and a controversial surname' in *Nomina* 2005, vol. 28, pp.115–33. Available at **http://cogprints.org/5985**.

21. Plant, J.S., 'Understanding the royal name Plantagenet. How DNA helps', an expanded version of an article that was originally published in the *Journal of One-Name Studies*, July 2010, vol. 10, issue 8, pp.14–15. Available at **www.plant-fhg.org.uk/plant_and_plantagenet.pdf**.

22. Redmonds, G., King, T. and Hey, D., *Surnames, DNA and Family History* (Oxford University Press, 2011), p.185.

10 One-Name Studies

1. Cokayne, A.E., *Cockayne memoranda: Collections towards a historical record of the family of Cockayne* (privately printed, 1869).

2. Palmer, C.J. and Tucker, S., *Palgrave Family Memorials* (Miller & Leavins, 1878).

3. Phillimore, W.P.W., *Memorials of the Family of Fynmore* (published by the author, 1886).

4. Bridgeman, Rev. C. and Swynnerton, Rev. C., 'A history of the family of Swynnerton of Swynnerton …', in *Collections for a History of Staffordshire*, William Salt Archaeological Society 1886, vol. 7, part II, pp.1–189.

5. Leeson, F., 'The study of single surnames and their distribution', *Genealogists' Magazine*, December 1964, vol. 14, pp.405–12. Reprinted in the *Journal of One-Name Studies*, 1989, vol. 3, no. 6, pp.174–81: **www.one-name.org/journal/pdfs/vol3-6.pdf**.

6. Further information on the Palgrave one-name study can be found on the Palgrave profile page on the Guild of One-Name Studies website at **www.one-name.org/profiles/palgrave. html** and on the Palgrave Society's website at **www.ffhs.org.uk/members/palgrave.htm**.

7. Palgrave, D., 'One-name societies', *Genealogists' Magazine*, 1976, vol. 18, no. 6, pp.296–8.

8. Filby, F.N., 'Looking back ten years and beyond' in *Journal of One-Name Studies*, Spring 1989, vol. 3, no. 5, pp.162–70. Available at **www.one-name.org/journal/pdfs/vol3-6.pdf**.

9. Palgrave, D.A., 'History and development of the Guild from its early days', *Journal of One-Name Studies*, October–December 2004, vol. 8, issue 8, pp.19–21. Available at **www.one-name.org/ journal/pdfs/vol8-8.pdf#page=19**.

10. Porteous, J.D., 'Surname geography: a study of the Mell family name *c.* 1538–1980' in *Transactions of the Institute of British Geographers*, New Series, vol. 7, no. 4 (1982), pp.395–418.

11. Kemball, C., 'The Guild moves on' in *Journal of One-Name Studies*, April–June 2012, vol. 11, issue 2, p.17.

12. Carden, A., 'The delights of Lulu' in *Journal of One-Name Studies*, April–June 2007, vol. 9, issue 6, pp.6–8. Available at **www.one-name.org/journal/pdfs/vol9-6.pdf#page=6**.

13. Ulph, C., 'How I run the Ulph one-name study', *Journal of One-Name Studies*, July–September 2011, vol. 10, issue 11, pp.25–8. Available at **www.one-name.org/members/journal/ vol10-11.pdf#page=25**.

14. Pask, T., personal communication.

15. Howes, P., 'Howes that?' in *Family Tree* magazine, February 2012, pp.59–62. The details in the article have been supplemented with additional information provided by Paul Howes.

16. Baldacchino, K., 'Out of Devon: The Eastlake surname comes of age' in *Journal of One-Name Studies*, January–March 2012, vol. 11, issue 1, pp.18–20.

17. Mastel, S., 'Adamthwaite ... Adam's clearing in the Eden Valley' in *Journal of One-Name Studies*, April–June 2012, vol. 11, issue 2, pp.6–8.

18. Shaw, D.M., 'Hembrough: a locative surname and its places' in *Journal of One-Name Studies*, April–June 2012, vol. 11, issue 2, pp.14–16.

19. Barber, H., *British Family Names – Their Origin and Meaning* ... (2nd edn, E. Stock, 1903), p.124.

20. Reaney, P.H. and Wilson, R.M., *A Dictionary of English Surnames* (Routledge, 1991), p.119.

21. Keats-Rohan, K.S.B., *Domesday Descendants: A Prosopography of Persons Occurring in English Documents: 1066–1166, Vol. II: Pipe Rolls to Cartae Baronum* (Boydell Press, 2002), p.423.

22. Kennett, D., 'The Tracy Deed', Genuki South Molton: **http://genuki.cs.ncl.ac.uk/DEV/ SouthMolton/TracyDeed.html**.

23. Johns, T., *Crewes of South Cornwall and their Ancestors in Liskeard, Cornwall and Cruwys Morchard, Devon* (privately printed, 2001).

BIBLIOGRAPHY

The subject of surnames has generated a vast quantity of literature in the last few hundred years and it is not practical or necessary to list all the titles here. For those who wish to pursue the subject in depth an extensive bibliography of surname literature is provided on the Surname Studies website at **www.surnamestudies.org.uk/bibliography/index.html** *where works are categorised by both location and topic, and indexed by author.*

Adolph, A., *Tracing Your Scottish Family History* (Collins, 2008).

Amsden, P.C., *A Guide to Making Contact with Relatives* (Federation of Family History Societies, 1999). Available as a free download in the Members' Room on the website of the Guild of One-Name Studies.

Anonymous, *The Norman People and their existing Descendants in the British Dominions and the United States of America* (Henry S. King & Co., 1874). **http://archive.org/details/normanpeopletheioobyulond**

Arthur, W., *An Etymological Dictionary of Family and Christian Names. With an Essay on their Derivation and Import* (Sheldon, Blakeman & Co., 1857). **http://archive.org/details/etymologicaldictooarthuoft**

Anderson, W., *Genealogy and Surnames: with some Heraldic and Biographical Notices* (William Ritchie, 1865). **http://archive.org/details/genealogyandsurooandegoog**

Ash, R., *Potty, Fartwell & Knob: Extraordinary but True Names of British People*, revised edition (Headline, 2008). An amusing collection of funny, bizarre and sometimes rude names!

Ayto, J., *Encyclopedia of Surnames* (A & C Black, 2007).

Bailey, M., *The English Manor c. 1200–c. 1500* (Manchester University Press, 2002).

Bailey, K., *Economy and Society in Medieval Buckinghamshire: The Hundred Rolls 1254–1280 Including a Listing of First Names and Surnames*, Buckinghamshire Papers no. 7 (Buckinghamshire Archaeological Society, 2006).

Bain, J., *Calendar of Documents Relating to Scotland* (four volumes covering: 1108–1272, 1272–1307, 1307–57, and 1357–1509 (with addenda 1221–1435). HM General Register House, 1881–88. A supplementary fifth volume of additions and corrections for 1108–1516, edited by G.G. Simpson and J.D. Galbraith, was published in 1986). **http://archive.org/search.php?query=Calendar%20documents%20Scotland**

Bannister, J., *A Glossary of Cornish Names, Ancient and Modern, Local, Family, Personal, &c.: 20,000 Celtic and Other Names, Now or formerly in Use in Cornwall* (Williams & Norgate, 1871). **http://archive.org/details/cu31924029805441**

Barber, Rev. H., *British Family Names – Their Origin and Meaning with Lists of Scandinavian, Frisian, Anglo-Saxon and Norman Names*, 2nd edn (E. Stock, 1903). **http://archive. org/details/britishfamilyna00barbgoog**

Bardsley, C.W., *English Surnames: Their Sources and Significations*, 2nd edn (Chatto & Windus, 1875). **http://archive.org/details/englishsurnamestoobardiala**

———, *A Dictionary of English and Welsh Surnames with special American Instances* (Henry Frowde, 1901). **http://archive.org/details/adictionaryeng1oogoog**

———, *Romance of the London Directory* (Hand and Heart Publishing, 1879). **http:// archive.org/details/romanceoflondondoobardrich**

Barker, S., Spoerlein, S., Vetter, T. and Viereck, W., *An Atlas of English Surnames*, University of Bamberg Studies in Linguistics (Peter Lang, 2007).

Baring-Gould, S., *Family names and their Story* (Seeley & Co., 1910, 1913). **http://archive. org/details/familynamestheiroobariuoft**

Barrow, G.B., *The Genealogist's Guide: an Index to Printed British Pedigrees and Family Histories, 1950–1975* (Research Publishing Company, 1977).

Beattie, A.M., *Shetland Surnames*, 2nd edn (Shetland Family History Society, 2010).

Bell, R., *The Book of Ulster Surnames*, revised edn (Blackstaff Press, 1997).

Bevan, A., *Tracing your Ancestors in The National Archives*, 7th edn (The National Archives, 2007).

Bigwood, R., *Tracing Scottish Ancestors* (Collins Pocket Reference Series) (Collins, 1999).

Black, G.F., *The Surnames of Scotland: Their Origin, Meaning and History* (Birlinn, 2007. First published in 1946).

Bowditch, N.I., *Suffolk Surnames* (John Wilson and Son, 1857, reprinted 1858). Interesting and unusual surnames found in nineteenth-century Suffolk, Massachusetts. **http:// archive.org/details/surnamessuffolkoobowdrich**

Bridgeman, Rev. C. and Swynnerton, C., 'A history of the family of Swynnerton of Swynnerton, and of the younger branches of the same Family settled at Eccleshall, Hilton, and Butterton' in *Collections for a History of Staffordshire*, William Salt Archaeological Society 1886, vol. 7, part II, pp. 1–189. **http://archive.org/details/ staffcollectionso7stafuoft**

Camden, W., *Remaines Concerning Britain: Their Languages, Names, Surnames, Allusions, Anagramms, Armories, Moneys, Impresses, Apparel, Artillerie, Wife Speeches, Proverbs, Poesies, Epitaphs* (1605, Seventh impression edited by John Philipot, 1674). **http://archive. org/details/remainesconcernioocamd**

Camp, A.J., *My Ancestors Came With the Conqueror: those who did and some of those who probably did not* (Society of Genealogists, 1990).

Chambers, P., *Medieval Genealogy* (The History Press, 2005).

Chapman, C.R., *Pre-1841 Censuses and Population Listings in the British Isles*, 5th edn (Lochin Publishing, 2002). **www.lochinpublishing.org.uk**

Charnock, R.S., *Ludus Patronymicus; or, the Etymology of Curious Surnames* (Trübner & Co., 1868). **http://archive.org/details/luduspatronymicuoocharrich**

———, *Patronymica Cornu-Britannica; or, The Etymology of Cornish Surnames* (Longmans, Green, Reader and Dyer, 1870). **http://archive.org/details/ patronymicacornoichargoog**

Cheney, C.R., *A Handbook of Dates for Students of British History*, new edition revised by Michael Jones (Cambridge University Press, 2000).

Chibnall, A.C. (ed.), *The Certificate of Musters for Buckinghamshire in 1522*, Buckinghamshire Record Society, vol. 17, 1973.

Cokayne, A.E., *Cokayne memoranda: Collections towards a historical record of the family of Cockayne* (privately printed, 1869). **http://archive.org/details/cockaynememorandoicoka**

Cornwall, J.C.K., *The County Community under Henry VIII: the Military Survey, 1522, and Lay Subsidy, 1524–5 for Rutland* (Rutland Record Society, 1980).

Cory, K.B., *Tracing Your Scottish Ancestry*, 3rd edn, revised and updated by L. Hodgson (Polygon, 2004).

Davis, G.R.C., *Medieval Cartularies of Great Britain and Ireland*, revised by C. Breay, J. Harrison, D.M. Smith (British Library, 2010).

Davis, G., *Research your Surname and Your Family Tree* (How To Books, 2010).

Dauzat, A., *Dictionnaire Étymologique des Noms de Famille et Prénoms de France* (Larousse, 1951).

Deacon, B., *The Cornish Family* (Cornwall Editions, 2004). Includes much useful content on the origins and evolution of Cornish surnames.

Dixon, B.H., *Surnames* (John Wilson and Son, 1855, reprinted 1857). **http://archive.org/ details/surnamesoodixo**

Dorward, D., *Scottish Surnames* (Mercat Press, 2002 (first published in 1978 by William Blackwood, Edinburgh)).

Dunkling, L., *Dictionary of Surnames* (Harper Collins, 1998).

———, *Guinness Book of Names*, 7th edition (Guinness Publishing, 1995 (first published 1974)). An entertaining look at all aspects of naming with lots of lists.

Durie, B., *Scottish Genealogy*, 3rd edn (The History Press, 2012).

Ewen, C.L., *A History of Surnames of the British Isles: A Concise Account of their Origin, Evolution, Etymology and Legal Status* (Kegan Paul, Trench, Trubner & Co., 1931).

———, *A Guide to the Origin of British Surnames* (John Gifford, 1938).

Faraday, M.A., *Worcestershire Taxes in the 1520s: The Military Survey and Forced Loans of 1522–3 and the Lay Subsidy of 1524–7* (Worcestershire Historical Society, 2003).

Fenwick, C.C. (ed.), *The Poll Taxes of 1377, 1379 and 1381. Part 1: Bedfordshire to Leicestershire* (Oxford University Press/British Academy, 1998).

——— (ed.), *The Poll Taxes of 1377, 1379 and 1381. Part 2: Lincolnshire to Westmoreland* (Oxford University Press/British Academy, 2001).

——— (ed.), *The Poll Taxes of 1377, 1379 and 1381. Part 3: Wiltshire to Yorkshire* (Oxford University Press/British Academy, 2005).

Ferguson, R., *English Surnames: and their Place in the Teutonic Family* (G. Routledge & Co., 1858). **http://archive.org/details/englishsurnameso1ferggoog**

——, *The Teutonic Name System of France, Germany and England* (1864). **http://archive. org/details/teutonicnamesystooferg**

——, *Surnames as a Science* (Routledge, 1883). **http://archive.org/details/ surnamesassciencooferguoft**

Finlayson, J., *Surnames and Sirenames: The Origin and History of Certain Family and Historical Names* (Simpkin Marshall, 1863). **http://archive.org/details/cu31924029805383**. Includes 'an historical account of the names Buggey and Bugg'.

Fordant, L., *Tous les Noms de Famille de France et leur Localisation en 1900* (Archives & Culture, Paris, 1999).

Franklin, P., *Some Medieval Records for Family Historians* (Federation of Family History Societies, 1994).

Freeman, J., *Discovering Surnames: Their Origins and Meanings*, 3rd edn (Shire Publications, 2001 (first published 1968)).

Freedman, T., *Wordsworth Dictionary of Surnames* (Wordsworth Editions, 1997).

Gibson, J. and Dell, A., *The Protestation Returns 1641–42 and other contemporary Listings: Collection in Aid of Distressed Protestants in Ireland; Subsidies; Poll tax; Assessment or Grant; Vow and Covenant; Solemn League and Covenant* (Federation of Family History Societies, 2004 update).

Gibson, J., *The Hearth Tax, other later Stuart Tax Lists and the Association Oath Rolls*, 2nd edn (Federation of Family History Societies, 1996).

Gibson, J.S.W. and Dell, A., *Tudor and Stuart Muster Rolls: A Directory of Holdings in the British Isles* (Federation of Family History Societies, 1996).

Grehan, I. and Dolan, P., *The Dictionary of Irish Family Names* (Roberts Rinehart Publishers, 1997). The origins and distribution of over 550 Irish family names.

Grenham, J., 'Grenham's Irish Surnames' (CD) (Eneclann, 2002). Available from Archive CD Books Ireland. **www.archivecdbooks.ie**

——, *Tracing Your Irish Ancestors*, 4th edn (Gill & Macmillan, 2012).

Guild of One-Name Studies, *Seven Pillars of Wisdom: The Art of One-Name Studies* (2012). **www.one-name.org**

Guppy, H.B., *Homes of Family Names in Great Britain* (Harrison and Sons, 1890). **http:// archive.org/details/homesoffamilynamoogupprich**

Hanks, P. and Hodges, F., *A Dictionary of Surnames* (Oxford University Press, 1988).

——, *The Oxford Names Companion* (Oxford University Press, 2002). A compilation volume containing *The Oxford Dictionary of Surnames*, *A Dictionary of First Names* by Hanks and Hodges, and *A Dictionary of British Place-Names* by A.D. Mills and A. Room.

Hanks, P. (ed.), *Dictionary of American Family Names* (Oxford University Press, 2003). Three volumes covering 70,000 surnames. Also available as a digital dataset from subscribing libraries.

Harrison, H., *Surnames of the United Kingdom: A Concise Etymological Dictionary. Volume I: A–L* (The Eaton Press, 1912).

———, *Surnames of the United Kingdom: A Concise Etymological Dictionary. Volume II M–W* (The Eaton Press, 1918). **http://archive.org/details/cu31924092512635** (Vol II only)

Harvey, P.D.A., *Manorial Records,* Archives and the User Series, no. 5 (British Records Association, revised edition, 1999).

Herber, M., *Ancestral Trails*, 2nd edn (The History Press, 2005).

Hervey, J. (ed.), *The Hundred Rolls and Extracts Therefrom made by authority, 2nd Edward I, with a translation by the late Lord John Hervey. County of Suffolk* (Suffolk Institute of Archaeology and Natural History, 1902).

Hey, D., *Family Names and Family History* (Hambledon and London, 2000).

——— (ed.), *Oxford Companion to Family and Local History*, 2nd edn (Oxford University Press, 2008).

Hicks, M., *The Fifteenth Century Inquisitions Post Mortem: A Companion* (Boydell and Brewer, 2012).

Holt, J.C., *What's in a Name? Family Nomenclature and the Norman Conquest* (The Stenton Lecture 1981) (University of Reading, 1982). **www.reading.ac.uk/history/ research/hist-stentonlectures.aspx**

Hone, N.J., *The Manor and Manorial Records* (Methuen, 1906). **http://archive.org/ details/manormanorialrecoohoneiala**

Hooke, D. and Postles, D. (eds), *Names, Time and Place: Essays in memory of Richard McKinley* (Leopard's Head Press, 2003). **www.oxbowbooks.com**

Hope, R.C., *A Glossary of Dialectical Place Nomenclature to which is appended a list of Family Surnames pronounced differently from what the Spelling suggests* (Simpkin, Marshall and Co., 1883). **http://archive.org/details/aglossarydialecoohopegoog**

Hoyle, R.W., *The Military Survey of Gloucestershire, 1522* (The Bristol & Gloucestershire Archaeological Society, 1993).

Hoyle, R., *Tudor Taxation Records: A Guide for Users* (PRO Publications, 1994).

Hulton, M., *Coventry and Its People in the 1520s*, vol. XXXVIII (Dugdale Society, 1999).

Humphery-Smith, C., *The Phillimore Atlas and Index of Parish Registers*, 3rd edn (Phillimore, 2002).

Ingraham, E.D., *Singular Surnames* (John Campbell and Son, 1873). A thirty-page booklet with a collection of amusing surname references. **http://archive.org/details/ singularsurnamesooingr**

Keats-Rohan, K.S.B. and Thornton, D.E. (eds), *Domesday Names: An Index of Latin Personal and Place Names in Domesday Book* (Boydell Press, 1997).

Keats-Rohan, K.S.B., *Domesday People: A Prosopography of Persons Occurring in English Documents: 1066–1166, Vol. I: Domesday Book* (Boydell Press, 1999).

———, *Domesday Descendants: A Prosopography of Persons Occurring in English Documents: 1066–1166, Vol. II: Pipe Rolls to Cartae Baronum* (Boydell Press, 2002).

Kennett, D., *DNA and Social Networking: A Guide to Genealogy in the Twenty-First Century* (The History Press, 2011).

Kent Hundred Rolls Project, *Kent Hundred Rolls* [1274–75] (Kent Archaeological Society, 2007). **www.kentarchaeology.ac/khrp/hrproject.pdf**

Kneen, J.J., *The Personal Names of the Isle of Man* (published under the auspices of Tynwald by the Manx Museum and Ancient Monuments Trustees, 1937. Reprinted in 1981 by Scolar Press).

Lamb, G., *Orkney Surnames* (Paul Harris Publishing, 1981).

Lasker, G.W. and Mascie-Taylor, C.G.N., *Atlas of British Surnames* (Published for the Guild of One-Name Studies. Wayne University Press, 1990).

Lasker, G.W., *Surnames and Genetic Structure* (Cambridge University Press, 2008 (first published 1985)).

Loyd, L.C., *The Origins of some Anglo-Norman Families*, vol. 103 (Harleian Society, 1951. Reprinted by the Genealogical Publishing Co., 1999).

Long, H.A., *Personal and Family Names: A Popular Monograph on the Origin and History of the Nomenclature of the Present and Former Times* (Hamilton, Adams & Co., 1883). **http:// archive.org/details/personalfamilynaoolong**

Lordan, C.L., *Of Certain English Surnames and Their Occasional Odd Phases When Seen in Groups* (Houston and Sons, 1874, 1879). **http://archive.org/details/ ofcertainenglishoolordiala**

Lower, M.A., *English Surnames: Essays on Family Nomenclature, Historical, Etymological, and Humorous*, 1st edn (John Russell Smith, 1842). **http://archive.org/details/ fleuronenglishoolowegoog**

———, *English Surnames: An Essay on Family Nomenclature, Historical, Etymological, and Humorous; with Several Illustrative Appendices. Volume I*, 3rd edn (John Russell Smith, 1849). **http://archive.org/details/englishsurnamesoilowe**

———, *English Surnames: An essay on Family Nomenclature, Historical, Etymological, and Humorous; with Several Illustrative Appendices. Volume II*, 3rd edn (John Russell Smith, 1849). **http://archive.org/details/englishsurnameso2lowe**

———, *Patronymica Britannica: A Dictionary of the Family Names of the United Kingdom* (John Russell Smith, 1860). **http://archive.org/details/patronymicabritaoolowe**

Mac Giolla-Domhnaigh, P., *Some Anglicised Surnames in Ireland* (Reprinted in 1974 as *Some Ulster Surnames*). **www.libraryireland.com/AnglicisedSurnames/Contents.php**

MacLysaght, E., *Irish Families: their Names, Arms and Origins* (Irish Academic Press, Revised and enlarged 4th edn, 1985. (First published 1957)).

———, *More Irish Families: a new revised and enlarged edition of More Irish families, incorporating Supplement to Irish Families with an essay on Irish chieftainrie* (Irish Academic Press, 1982. (First published 1960)).

———, *The Surnames of Ireland*, 6th edition (Irish Academic Press, 1985).

Marshall, G.W., *The Genealogist's Guide*, 4th edn (Billing and Sons, 1903). **http://archive. org/details/cu31924029579699**

Marshall, H., *Palaeography for Family and Local Historians*, 2nd edn (Phillimore, 2010).

Martin, C.T., *The Record Interpreter*, 2nd edn (Stevens and Sons, 1910). **http://archive. org/details/recordinterpreteoomartuoft**

Matheson, R.E., *Special report on surnames in Ireland, with notes as to numerical strength, derivation, ethnology, and distribution; based on information extracted from the indexes of the General Register Office. Appendix to the twenty-ninth detailed annual report of the Registrar-General of Marriages, Births, and Deaths in Ireland* (Her Majesty's Stationery Office, 1894). **http://archive.org/details/cu31924029805540**

———, *Varieties and synonymes of surnames and Christian names in Ireland: for the guidance of registration officers and the public in searching the indexes of births, deaths, and marriages*, 2nd edn (His Majesty's Stationery Office, 1901). **http://archive.org/details/varietiessynonymoomath**

McKinley, R.A., *Norfolk Surnames in the Sixteenth Century* (Leicester University Press, 1965).

———, *Norfolk and Suffolk Surnames in the Middle Ages. English Surnames Series Volume II* (Leopard's Head Press, 1975).

———, *The Surnames of Oxfordshire. English Surnames Series Volume III* (Leopard's Head Press, 1977).

———, *The Surnames of Lancashire. English Surnames Series Volume IV* (Leopard's Head Press, 1981).

———, *The Surnames of Sussex. English Surnames Series Volume V* (Leopard's Head Press, 1988).

———, *A History of British Surnames* (Longman, 1990).

McLaughlin, E., *Surnames and their Origins* (1997). **www.genfair.co.uk**

Mitchell, B., *The Surnames of Derry* (Genealogy Centre of Derry, 1992). **http://books. familysearch.org**

———, *The Surnames of North West Ireland: Concise Histories of the Major Surnames of Gaelic and Planter Origin* (Genealogical Publishing Co. Inc., 2009).

Moisy, H., *Noms de Famille Normands* (Librairie A. Franck, 1875 (in French)). **http:// archive.org/details/nomsdefamillenooomoisgoog**

Morgan, T.J. and Morgan, P., *Welsh Surnames* (University of Wales Press, 1985).

Morlet, M-T., *Dictionnaire Étymologique des Noms de Famille* (Librairie Académique Perrin, 1991 and 1997 (in French)).

Moore, A.W., *Manx Names or The Surnames and Place-Names of the Isle of Man* (Elliot Stock, 1906). **http://archive.org/details/manxnamesorsurnoomoorgoog**

National Archives of Scotland, *Tracing Your Scottish Ancestors: The Official Guide* (Birlinn, 2011).

Oates, J., *Tracing Your Ancestors from 1066 to 1837* (Pen and Sword Books, 2012).

O Flannghaile, T., *Celtic Surnames* (1896). **www.libraryireland.com/articles/ CelticSurnames/index.php**

Ó Murchadha, D., *Family Names of County Cork* (Glendale Press, 1985).

Palgrave, D. and Palgrave-Moore, P., *The History and Lineage of the Palgraves* (Palgrave Society, 1983). **www.ffhs.org.uk/members/palgrave.htm**

Palgrave, D., *One-Name Family History Groups* (Halsted Trust, 2008 (first published in 1977 as *Forming a One-Name Group*)). Available from the Family History Partnership. **www.thefamilyhistorypartnership.com/prod129.htm**

Palmer, C.J. and Tucker, S., *Palgrave Family Memorials* (Miller & Leavins, 1878). **http://archive.org/details/palgravefamilym00palmgoog**

Park, P.B., *My Ancestors were Manorial Tenants* (Society of Genealogists, 2005).

Picard, M., *On the Problematic Surnames in the Dictionary of American Family Names: A Genealogically Based Reanalysis of the Unidentified and Uncertain Origins* (VDM Verlag, 2010).

Phillimore, W.P.W., *Memorials of the Family of Fynmore, with Notes on the Origin of Fynmore, Finnimore, Phillimore, Fillmore, Filmer, etc.* (published by the author, 1886). **http://archive.org/details/memorialsoffamiloophil**

———, *A Supplement to how to write the History of a Family* (published by the author, 1896). Available from **http://archive.org/details/howtowritehistooophilgoog**

Pomery, C., *DNA and Family History: How Genetic Testing Can Advance Your Genealogical Research* (The National Archives, 2004).

———, *Family History in the Genes: Trace Your DNA and Grow Your Family Tree* (The National Archives, 2007).

Postles, D., *The Surnames of Devon. English Surnames Series Volume VI* (Leopard's Head Press, 1995).

———, *The Surnames of Leicestershire and Rutland. English Surnames Series Volume VII* (Leopard's Head Press, 1998).

——— (ed.), *Naming, Society and Regional Identity: papers presented at a symposium held at the Department of English Local History, University of Leicester* (Leopard's Head Press, 2002). **www.oxbowbooks.com**

———, *The North through its Names: A Phenomenology of Medieval and Early-Modern Northern England*, English Surname Series vol. VIII (Oxbow Books, 2007).

Pound, J. (ed.), *The Military Survey of 1522 for Babergh Hundred* (Suffolk Records Society/Boydell Press, 1986).

Quilliam, L., *Surnames of the Manks* (Cashtal Books, 1989).

Reaney, P.H., and Wilson, R.M., *A Dictionary of English Surnames*, 3rd edn (Oxford University Press, reprinted 2005).

Reaney, P.H., The *Origin of English Surnames* (Routledge & Kegan Paul, 1967).

Record Commission, *Rotuli Hundredorum*, two vols (1812, 1818). These volumes are also available on CD or as a download from TannerRitchie Publishing (**www.tannerritchie.com**).

Redmonds, G., *Yorkshire West Riding, English Surnames Series* vol. I (Phillimore, 1973).

———, *Yorkshire Surnames: Bradford and District* (GR Books, 1990).

———, *Yorkshire Surnames Series: Huddersfield and District* (GR Books, 1992).

———, *Surnames and Genealogy: A New Approach* (New England Historic Genealogical Society, 1997; Federation of Family History Societies, 2002).

————, *Yorkshire Surnames: Halifax and District* (GR Books, 2002).

————, *Names and History: People, Places and Things* (Hambledon, 2004).

Redmonds, G., Hey, D. and King, T., *Surnames, DNA, and Family History* (Oxford University Press, 2011).

Richards, B., *Cornish Family Names* (The History Press, 2009).

Rogers, C.D., *The Surname Detective: Investigating Surname Distribution in England, 1086–Present Day* (Manchester University Press, 1995. Digital reprint, 2007).

Rowe, M., *Tudor Exeter: Tax Assessments 1489–1595 including the Military Survey 1522* (Devon and Cornwall Record Society, 1977).

Rowlands, J. and Rowlands, S., *The Surnames of Wales: For Family Historians and Others* (Genealogical Publishing, 1996). A second edition is currently in preparation.

———— and ————, *Welsh Family History: A Guide to Research*, 2nd edn (Genealogical Publishing Co., 2009).

———— and ————, *Second Stages in Researching Welsh Ancestry* (Genealogical Publishing Co., 2010).

Savin, A., *DNA for Family Historians* (privately printed, 2000–03). **www.savin.org/dna/dna-book.html**

Searle, W.G., *Onomasticon Anglo-Saxonicum: A List of Anglo-Saxon Proper Names from the Time of Beda to that of King John* (Cambridge University Press, 1897). **http://archive.org/details/onomasticonan00sear**

Seary, E.R. and Kirwin, W., *Family Names of the Island of Newfoundland*, revised edition (McGill-Queen's University Press, 1998).

Smith, E.C., *New Dictionary of American Family Names*, Gramercy (1988, first published in 1956 as *Dictionary of American Family Names*). Information on the nationality, origin and meaning of around 25,000 surnames.

Smolenyak, M. and Turner, A., *Trace Your Roots with DNA: Using Genetic Tests to Explore Your Family Tree* (Rodale Books, 2005).

Stoate, T.L., *The Cornwall Military Survey 1522 with the Loan Books and a Tinners' Muster c.1535* (privately printed, 1987). Available on CD from West Country Books: **www.westcountrybooks.com**.

Stone, E. and Hyde, P., *Oxfordshire Hundred Rolls of 1279: Bampton and Witney Borough*, vol. 46 (Oxfordshire Record Society, 1969).

Sturges, C.M. and Haggett, B.C., *Inheritance of English Surnames* (Hawgood Computing, 1987).

Sweetman, H.S. (ed.), *Calendar of Documents relating to Ireland* … Five volumes covering: 1171–1251, 1252–84, 1285–92, 1293–1301 and 1302–07 (HM Treasury, 1875–86). **http://archive.org/search.php?query=Calendar%20documents%20Ireland**

Thomson, T.R., *Catalogue of British Family Histories*, 3rd edn (Research Publishing Company in conjunction with the Society of Genealogists, 1980).

Titford, J., *Searching for Surnames* (Countryside Books, 2002).

————, *Penguin Dictionary of British Surnames* (Penguin, 2009). A new edition of the dictionary originally compiled by Basil Cottle in 1967.

Tooth, E., *The Distinctive Surnames of Staffordshire* (4 vols). *Volume I: Surnames Derived from Local Placenames and Landscape Features; Volume 2: Surnames Derived from Occupations, Trades, Position and Rank; Volume 3: Nicknames; Volume 4: Personal and Pet Names* (Churnet Valley Books, 2000–10).

Trevor, J. (ed.), *The Warwickshire Hundred Rolls of 1279–80: Stoneleigh and Kineton Hundreds* (Oxford University Press for the British Academy, 1992).

Verstegan, R., *A Restitution of Decayed Intelligence* …, pp.277–312 (John Bull, 1628 (first published 1605)). **http://books.google.co.uk/books?id=vCxQAQAAIAAJ&source=gbs_navlinks_s**

Webb, C., *Genealogical Research in Victorian London*, 8th edn (West Surrey Family History Society, 2000).

———, *Genealogical Research in late Victorian and Edwardian London*, 5th edn (West Surrey Family History Society, 2004).

Weekley, E., *Romance of Names* (John Murray, 1914). **http://archive.org/details/romanceofnames00weekiala**

———, *Surnames*, 2nd edn (John Murray, 1917). **http://archive.org/details/surnames00weekuoft**

White, G.P., *A Handbook of Cornish Surnames*, 3rd edn (Truran, 1999 (first published 1972)).

Whitmore, J.B., *A Genealogical Guide* (Harleian Society, 1947–53).

Woulfe, P., *Irish Names and Surnames* (M.H. Gill, 1922). **http://archive.org/details/irishnamessurnam00woul** and **www.libraryireland.com/names/contents.php**

Wrottesley, G. (ed.), 'The Staffordshire Hundred Rolls, temp. Henry III and Edward I. From the originals in the Public Record Office' in *Collections for a History of Staffordshire*, vol. 5, part 1 (William Salt Archæological Society, 1884). **http://archive.org/details/collectionsfora03socigoog**.

INDEX

Page numbers in bold indicate tables or figures.